T0211955

Communications
in Computer and Information Science   1401

More information about this series at http://www.springer.com/series/7899

Ajantha Dahanayake · Oscar Pastor ·
Bernhard Thalheim (Eds.)

Modelling to Program

Second International Workshop, M2P 2020
Lappeenranta, Finland, March 10–12, 2020
Revised Selected Papers

 Springer

Editors
Ajantha Dahanayake 🆔
Lappeenranta-Lahti University
of Technology
Lappeenranta, Finland

Oscar Pastor 🆔
Universidad Politécnica de Valencia
Valencia, Spain

Bernhard Thalheim 🆔
Christian-Albrechts-University Kiel
Kiel, Germany

ISSN 1865-0929 ISSN 1865-0937 (electronic)
Communications in Computer and Information Science
ISBN 978-3-030-72695-9 ISBN 978-3-030-72696-6 (eBook)
https://doi.org/10.1007/978-3-030-72696-6

This Springer imprint is published by the registered company Springer Nature Switzerland AG
The registered company address is: Gewerbestrasse 11, 6330 Cham, Switzerland

Preface

Programming has become a technique for everybody, especially for non-computer scientists. Programs have become an essential part of modern infrastructure. Programming is nowadays a socio-material practice fundamental to the disciplines of science and engineering. Programs of the future must be understandable by all parties involved, must be accurate and precise enough for the task they support, and must support reasoning and controlled realisation and evolution at all levels of abstraction.

The workshop discusses novel approaches to programming based on modelling approaches such as model-driven development (MDE, MDA, MDD) and conceptual-model programming and their future developments. In future, application engineers and scientists are going to develop and to use models instead of programming in the old style. A model may combine several facets at the same time and may thus have a structure where some facets support specific purposes and functions.

A model is a well-formed, adequate, and dependable instrument that represents origins and that functions in utilisation scenarios. Its criteria of well-formedness, adequacy, and dependability must be commonly accepted by its CoP within some context and correspond to the functions that a model fulfils in utilisation scenarios. The model should be well formed according to some well-formedness criterion. As an instrument or more specifically an artefact a model comes with a background that is often given only in an implicit and hidden form and not explicitly explained.

The list of workshop topics includes

- notions of models that can be understood and used as programs,
- models-at-runtime,
- advanced conceptual modelling,
- conceptual-model programming,
- modelling foundation,
- transformation of models to programs,
- model suites/ensembles for programmers,
- modelling as the first step to programming and its revisions,
- advanced model-driven programming and software modernisation,
- modelling in applications.

M2P 2020 is the second workshop. The first one was organised at ADBIS 2019 in Bled. The papers were published in the CCIS series by Springer (ADBIS2019, CCIS 1064).

We thank the Lappeenranta-Lahti University of Technology, Finland for hosting the M2P workshop in March 2020.

Last but not least, thanks to the reviewers, who contributed fruitful comments to improve the papers.

February 2021   Ajantha Dahanayake
                                                                      Oscar Pastor
                                                                   Bernhard Thalheim

Organisation

Program Committee Members

Ajantha Dahanayake (Co-chair)	Lappeenranta-Lahti University of Technology, Finland
Igor Fiodorov	Plekhanov Russian University of Economics (PRUE), Moscow, Russia
Albert Fleischmann	InterAktiv Unternehmungsberatung, Germany
Elyar Gasanov	Moscow State University, Russia
Giovanni Giachetti	Universidad Tecnológica de Chile INACAP, Chile
Hannu Jaakkola	Tampere University, Finland
Tomas Jonsson	Genicore AB, Sweden
Meriem Kherbouche	Eötvös Loránd University, Hungary
András J. Molnár	SZTAKI, Hungary
Bálint Molnár	Eötvös Loránd University, Hungary
Boris Novikov	National Research University Higher School of Economics, Russia
José Ignacio Panach Navarrete	Universitat de València, Spain
Óscar Pastor (Co-chair)	Universitat Politècnica de València, Spain
Andreas Prinz	University of Agder, Norway
Elena Ravve	ORT Braude College of Engineering, Israel
Maksim Shishaev	Murmansk Arctic State University, Russia
Nikolay Skvortsov	FRC CSC Russian Academy of Sciences, Russia
Monique Snoeck	KU Leuven, Belgium
Alexander Sotnikov	Joint Supercomputer Center of the Russian Academy of Sciences, Russia
Srinath Srinivasa	International Institute of Information Technology, Bangalore, India
Sergey Stupnikov	Institute of Informatics Problems, Russian Academy of Sciences, Russia
Bernhard Thalheim (Co-chair)	Christian Albrechts University Kiel, Germany
Tatjana Welzer	University of Maribor, Slovenia
Manal Yahya	Lappeenranta-Lahti University of Technology, Finland

Additional Reviewers

Holger Giese	Hasso Plattner Institute at the University of Potsdam, Germany
Ana León	Universitat Politècnica de València, Spain
Heinrich C. Mayr	Alpen-Adria- Universität Klagenfurt, Austria

José Reyes   Universitat Politècnica de València, Spain
Klaus-Dieter Schewe   Zhejiang University, UIUC Institute, China
Veda Storey   GSU, USA
Marina Tropmann-Frick   Hamburg University of Applied Sciences, Germany

Contents

Introduction to M2P

From Models_For_Programming to Modelling_To_Program and Towards Models_As_A_Program

Bernhard Thalheim[✉]

Department of Computer Science, University Kiel, Kiel, Germany
bernhard.thalheim@email.uni-kiel.de

Abstract. The history of programming languages can be separated into four or five generations. Most languages are nowadays at the level of the third or fourth generation. The fifth generation programme failed mainly due to the infrastructure that has been available at that time. We are going to revive this fifth generation programming efforts by deployment of models as a source code for compilation to programs. Currently models are used as a blueprint or as some inspiration for programmers. At present, we are able to develop an approach of modelling to program. In future, we might have models as programs. This programme will then result in true fifth generation programming.

This Ansatz requires models at a higher quality level. Models at this level will become executable if they are precise and accurate. This paper summarises and discusses the vision that models will become programs in future. Models are used for programming as a communication mediator. Modelling as an art will be an integrative part of program development. Mastering modelling as technology will result in modelling as programming. In future, models will become itself programs. We present some of the main issues for research.

Keywords: Models for programming · Modelling to program · Modelling as programming · Models as programs · True fifth generation programming

1 The Vision: Next Generation Programming

Modelling can be considered as the fourth dimension of Computer Science and Computer Engineering beside structuring, evolution, and collaboration. Models are widely applied and used in everyday life and are widely deployed in our area. Typical scenarios are: prescription and system construction, communication and negotiation, description and conceptualisation, documentation, explanation and discovery for applications, knowledge discovery and experience propagation, and explanation and discovery for systems. Programming is currently

I want to express my special thanks to all participants of the M2P workshops at Bled (2019) and Lappeenranta (2020). Thanks to Tomas Jonsson for proofreading this paper.

© Springer Nature Switzerland AG 2021
A. Dahanayake et al. (Eds.): M2P 2020, CCIS 1401, pp. 3–44, 2021.
https://doi.org/10.1007/978-3-030-72696-6_1

based on intentional development models. Models are often explicitly specified. Sometimes they are implicit. We concentrate in this chapter on the first scenario, i.e. models as a means for construction. Generation zero of model usage is the starting point. The current state-of-the-art can be characterised as a movement from *Modelling-for-Programming (M4P)* where models are used as yet-another-development document for programming or throw-away-inspiration for the coding towards *Modelling_to_Program (M2P)* which is essentially a revival or reactivation or renaissance of modelling as an art. The main activity for M2P is model-based development. They are useful for developing the program in its essentials. But there are other ways to code without models.

We may distinguish three generations for this agenda for the system construction scenario after revival, reactivation, and enlivenment of models instead of only using models beside blueprint and inspiration:

First generation: **Modelling to Program** (M2P). Models can also be used as a source code for program generation. The result of such generation process may be enhanced by program refinement approaches. The model must be of a higher quality compared to current approaches. It must be as precise and accurate as appropriate for the programmer's task without loss of its explanation power. It must become adaptable to new circumstances. Maintenance of programs can be supported by maintenance of models. The first generation is thus based on *model-based development* and reasoning.

Second generation: **Modelling as Programming** (MaP). Modelling becomes an activity as programming nowadays. Some models can directly be used as an essential part of sources for programs, esp. executable programs. They are neatly integratable with other source codes. Modelling languages have reached a maturity that allows to consider a model at the same level of precision and accuracy as programs. Models are validated and verified and as such the basis for program validation and verification. Models will become adaptable and changeable. Computer Engineering incorporates modelling.

Third generation: **Models as a Program** (MaaP). Models can be directly used as a source code for or instead of programs. If a separation of concern approach is used for model development then the source for programs consists of a *model suite* with well associated sub-models. Compilers will translate the model or the model suite to executable programs. Maintenance of programs is handled at the model level. Models can be directly translated as programs, i.e. programming can be performed almost entirely through modelling. Third generation modelling is then *true fifth generation programming* which essentially frees the program developer from writing third or fourth generation programs. Everybody – also programming laymen and non-programmers – who can specify models will become a programmer.

The current-state-of-the-art is going to be analysed in the next section. The following sections discuss then our vision for the second and third generation. Figure 1 visualises the vision towards models as programs with the current situation, towards modelling to program and modelling as programming, and finally models as a program.

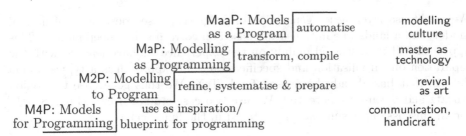

Fig. 1. From current state-of-art to next generation programming as model-based thinking

The final stage of model-based reasoning for system construction will be the usage of models as a program. We shall then partially replace programming by models. The transformation of the model suite to a program (MaaP) will also be based on a compiler. Programming will be mainly modelling. In this case, we may consider modelling as true fifth generation programming.

The Storyline of This Vision Paper

This paper presents the vision for first, second and third generation modelling as an outline for a series of workshops. Visions are visions. We thus need to sketch the path towards a new way of programming that is called true fifth generation programming (5PL) in Sect. 5. This paper aims at introducing the entire M2P, MaP, and MaaP programme. We abstain from long citation lists in the next sections. Subsection 3.2 summarises the large body of knowledge that is already available.

The current Ansatz in Computer Science is to utilize models as an blueprint for programming or at least as inspiration. Models can be thrown away after programs have been developed. The software crisis, the data crisis, and the infrastructure crises show that the model_for_programming approach must be revised. Section 2 discusses well-known approaches to model-based development, its issues, and its problems. Typical specific approaches are model-driven development, conceptual-model programming, model-driven web engineering, and models@runtime. We realise that model-based development is still often essentially model-backed development. For this reason, Section 3 revisits the current state-of-art. The body of knowledge already supports to step towards modelling to programming. There are tools available. These tools may be combined with heritage programming (often called legacy programming what highlights the negative side only). Since a model typically focuses on some aspects on certain abstraction level, we have to use a collection of well-associated models, i.e. a model suite. Model suites also enable us in layered model-based development.

Section 4 discusses features, approaches, and ideas for modelling to program and furthermore for modelling as programming. These modelling approaches can be supported by literate modelling that uses model suites. Section 5 discusses then some of the deliverables we envision for true fifth generation programming.

We might use layering for generation of programs, based on a suite of normal models and a landscape initialisation based on corresponding deep models. This approach will be discussed mainly on the experience we have learned with the separation on initialisation and specification. This approach is a typical onion Ansatz that has already been used for LaTeX. We thus generalise this onion Ansatz and discuss its potential. We use two case studies from [53,69,78,104]. for the discussion. A summary is sketched in the final Sect. 6.

2   Current Approaches to Model-Based Development

Models are used as instruments in many reasoning and especially engineering scenarios. The reasoning and development process is then model-determined. Depending on the function that a model plays in a programmer's scenario we distinguish three general roles for models: (1) models are instruments for program construction that integrate existing so far constructions and corresponding reasoning techniques; (2) models are the target of reasoning; (3) models as a unique subject of reasoning and its preliminaries. These roles have to be supported by sophisticated reasoning mechanisms such as logical calculi. Modelling uses beside the classical deductive reasoning also other reasoning approaches such as Programming and reasoning must be supported by a mechanism, e.g. logical calculi with abduction or induction.

2.1   M4P: Models for Programming

Model-based reasoning is an essential feature of all mental models such as perception models which are representing some (augmented) reality and domain-situation models which are representing a commonly agreed understanding of a community of practice. Model-based reasoning supports modelling based on data similar to inverse modelling. It comprehends the background of each model considered. It allows to consider the corresponding limitations and the obstinacy of models, esp. modelling languages. As a reasoning procedure, it is enhanced by well-formed calculi for reasoning. Model-based reasoning is compatible with all kinds of development procedures (water, spiral, agile, extreme). It also allows to handle uncertainties and incompleteness of any kind.

The model-for-programming approach uses models as some kind of blueprint and as a description mediator between the necessities in the application area and the program realisation.

Model-based development and engineering is a specific form of engineering where the model or model suite is used as a *mediator* between ideas from the application domain and the codification of these ideas within a system environment. It has been considered for a long time as a *'greenfield'* development technique that starts with requirements acquisition, elicitation, and formulation, that continues with system specification, and terminates with system coding. Models are used as mediating instruments that allow to separate the description phase from the prescription phase. Engineering is, however, nowadays often starting with legacy systems that must be modernised, extended, tuned, improved, etc. This kind of *'brownfield'* development may be based on models for the legacy systems and on macro-models representing migration strategies that guide the system renovation and modernisation. The heritage model (or legacy models) is used as an origin for a sub-model of the target system.

The four supporting means for model-based engineering are the modelling know-how, the experience gained in modelling practices, the modelling theory, and finally the modelling economics. The last two means, however, need a deeper investigation. Specific forms of model-based reasoning for system construction are, for instance,

- *model-driven architectures and development* based on a specific phase-oriented modelling mould,
- *conceptual-model programming* oriented on executable conceptual models,
- *models@runtime* that applies models and abstractions to the runtime environment,
- *universal applications* based on generic and refinable models and with generators for derivation of the specific application,
- *domain-specific modelling* based on domain-specific languages,
- *framework-driven modelling* (e.g. GERA or MontiCore),
- *pattern-based development* based on refinable pattern,
- *roundtrip engineering* supported by tools that maintain the coexistence of code and model,
- *model programming* where the model is already the code and lower levels of code are simply generated and compiled behind the scenes,
- *inverse modelling* that uses parameter and context instantiation for model refinement,
- *reference modelling* that is based on well-developed and adaptable reference models, and
- *model forensics* which starts with model detection through analysis of the code, i.e. the model origin is the code.

These approaches develop models by stepwise refinement of the root or initial model, by selection and integration of model variations, and by mutation and recombination of the model. Models are typically model suites.

The mediator function of models is illustrated for 'greenfield' system construction in Fig. 2. System construction is a specific kind of modelling scenario that integrates description and prescription. It might also be combined with the conceptualisation scenario. B. Mahr pointed out that origins also come with their theories. We may add also the deep model behind the origin.

During a *relevance stage* (or cycle), we first reason about the ways of operating in an application. This step may also include field testing of current artifacts within the given environment. Next we select, reason about, and revise those properties $\Phi(O)$ that are of relevance for system construction. The next phase is based on classical requirements engineering. We identify requirements (or business needs). These requirements become objectives $\Psi(M)$ which must be satisfied by the model. These objectives are biased by the community of practice (CoP).

8   B. Thalheim

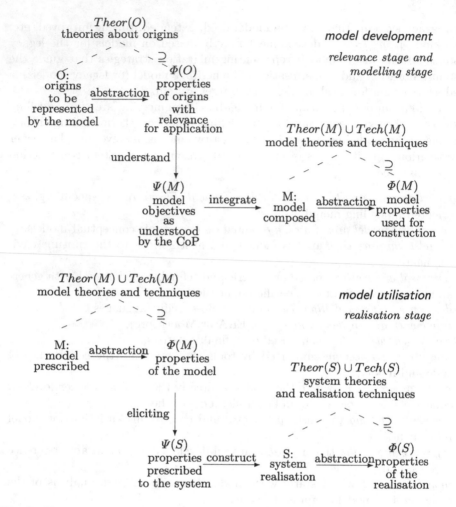

Fig. 2. Straightforward model-based system development starting with description models which are transformed to prescription models for system realisation (modified from [101])

The *modelling stage* starts with the objectives as they are understood in the community of practice. Modellers compile and integrate these objectives in a model (or model suite). The 'ways of modelling" is characterised

- by the *modelling acts* with its specifics,
- the *theories and techniques that underpin modelling acts*,
- the *modellers* involved into with their obligations, permissions, and restrictions, with their roles and rights, and with their play;
- the *aspects* that are under consideration for the current modelling acts;
- the *objectives* that are guiding the way of modelling;
- the *resources* that bias the modelling act.

The *realisation stage* uses prescription properties as a guideline for construction the system. Model-based engineering is oriented on automatic compilation of the entire system or at least of parts of it. If the system is partially constructed and thus must be extended then the compilation must provide hooks in the compiled code. These hooks allow to extend the system without revising the rest of the compiled code.

Validation compares the properties of origins $\Phi(O)$ with the properties of the model $\Phi(M)$. *Verification* compares the properties of model $\Phi(M)$ with the properties of the system $\Phi(S)$. *Model assessment* compares the model objectives $\Psi(M)$ with the properties of the model $\Phi(M)$. *System assessment* compares the system objectives $\Psi(S)$ with the properties of the system $\Phi(S)$.

2.2 Model-Driven Development

In general, model-driven development is nothing else than a very specific form of the model development and usage process. We use only the last three in a specific form. The first two levels are assumed to be given.

Essentially, model-driven development (MDD) does not start with a computation-independent model. The process starts with modelling initialisation. The CIM is already based on a number of domain-situation models and some insight into the application situation or a model of the application situation. These models are the origins of the models under development and are then consolidated or toughened. The CIM describes the system environment, the business context, and the business requirements in a form that is used by the practitioners in the application domain. This model becomes refined to the PIM by services, interfaces, supporting means, and components that the system must provide to the business, independent of the platform selected for the system realisation. The chosen platform forms the infrastructure for the system realisation. The PIM is then refined to a platform-specific model PSM. In general, a number of models are developed, i.e. a model suite as shown in Fig. 3.

The main concept behind this approach is the *independence* of the models on the platform respectively on the algorithmics setting. This independence allows to separate the phases. A system is then specified independently of the software execution platform and independently of the chosen set of algorithms. The transformation is typically a two directional. Model-driven architectures are based on three tenets: direct and proper representation of concepts and terminology in the application domain, automation for generation of routine components instead of human interaction, and open standards promoting reuse and proper tool deployment.

Model driven development assumes that the models at each phase can be transformed to each other. This rigid requirement cannot be used in many construction scenarios. For instance, database model development is based on forgetful mappings. The conceptual model contains conceptual information that is irrelevant for the "logical" or "physical" models and thus neglected during development.

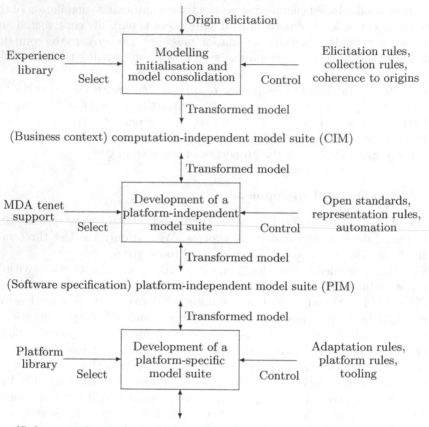

Fig. 3. The three phases in model-driven development for construction scenarios

2.3 Conceptual-Model Programming

Conceptual-model programming uses a compiler approach to programming. The model will be the source code for the compiler or transformer. The result of compilation should be then code which might be used for another compilation. The compiler assures that the model might already be used as (the final) code. The execution of the code corresponds to the conceptual specification.

Advanced conceptual-model programming is based on three theses:

- Conceptual-modelling languages must provide compiler facilities that allows to directly execute models.
- Conceptual-modelling languages must support co-design of database structure, of user interfaces, and of database access and user interaction.

– "The model-compiled code is beyond the purview of conceptual-model programming programmers—both for initially creating the application system
being developed and for enhancing or evolving the application system." [33].

As a consequence, application-system development becomes entirely model-
driven. Conceptual-model programming constitutes model-complete software
development.

This approach requires that models are of high quality.

– *Models are complete and holistic.* The conceptual model supports all necessary
co-design elements such as structuring, behaviour, and user support. The
model itself can be a model suite.
– *Models are conceptual but precise.* All model elements must be precisely
defined through proper element definition. At the same time, these elements
have to be properly associated to the concept space that is used for conceptualisation of the model. Parsimony and economy of model elements guide
the notation.

Provided that the model has high quality then evolution of an application can
be directly represented through evolution of the model. It, thus, asserts that
conceptual-model programming is essentially programming. The model is the
kernel of code that can be easily adapted to the specific platform requirements.

2.4 Model-Driven Web Engineering

Model-driven development and engineering can be based on generic models.
These models ease the selection of the normal model in dependence on a
computation-independent model suite. They are also early serving as an additional entry at the modelling initialisation phase (Fig. 3) and at the landscape
(Fig. 4) determination. The problem space, focus, scope, and codified concepts
will be set through the utilisation of such generic models. Additionally, generic
models will be used at the extrinsic (source) reflection layer (Fig. 4). Generic
models and reference models can be refined by the data and other information
on hand.

Website development and web information system development is a typical
example of model-based reasoning on the basis of generic models and of refinable
specifications. Website construction benefits from the usage of previous models and programs, esp. generic ones. These generic models compile experience
gained in similar web engineering projects. This experience elicitation, evaluation, appreciation, and acquisition is a specific *rigor stage* (or cycle). Generic
models stem from models that have been already used. The generalisation procedure that led to the generic model allows to derive the specific refinement mechanisms for mapping the generic model to the old specific one. Generic models
come then with a *refinable specification* and with a *refinement calculus*.

Model-based reasoning and website model-based development is based on
the specification language SiteLang (see below). Website development is page-
oriented where pages are essentially media objects with their structuring, their

functionality (especially navigation, import/export, search), their runtime adaptation features to actors or users, their databases support, and their specific navigation-oriented flow of work. Websites can be categorised, e.g. business websites for a business with customer collaboration according to the used business culture. This categorisation is the basis for generic model suites of the website. The normal model can be then derived from the generic model and the computation-independent model.

2.5   Models@Runtime

Most model-driven development and most-driven architecture are concerned with the development process. Models@Runtime take a different turn towards support of software after it has been installed. Beside model-based evolution support, models are additionally developed on top of the code. The code will then be the origin. The model suite reflects essential properties of a system. This approach aims at development of proper performance models that characterise the software and its behaviour.

The Model@Runtime approach extends the applicability of models and abstractions to the runtime environment. This approach provides means for handling complexity of software and its evolution if effective technologies exist for code analysis and change in a given environment. Models are used for reasoning about runtime behaviour, for appropriate adaptation of systems at runtime, and for capturing runtime phenomena in systems such as time, memory, energy, location, platform, and personalisation concerns. Models provide meta-information, for instance, in order to automate runtime decision-making, safe adaptation of runtime behaviour, and optimal evolution or modernisation of systems. Modern systems are increasingly complex. This complexity is a challenge that needs to be managed especially in the case of evolving hybrid infrastructures consisting of a manifold of heterogeneous services, resources, and devices.

Typical tasks are the following ones: (a) creating or updating the models suite that represents a system according to evolution of the system or to changes in system's environments; (b) developing appropriate adaptation strategies; analysing and maintaining model suites while parts of the corresponding systems are changing; (c) propagating changes in the model suite back to the system; (d) adaption of emerging systems and their model suites in ways that cannot be anticipated at model development and system programming time; (e) enabling features supporting continuous design, deployment, and quality of service analysis for performance optimisation; (f) optimisation and tuning; (g) reducing uncertainty that arise due to environment changes, due to system integration and migration, due to changes of quality concerns, and due to changes and extensions of the system user communities and evolving viewpoints.

We envision that the modelling-as-programming approach allows to solve some of these challenges. Models@Runtime are an example of model-based reasoning despite the classical system construction scenario. Models are used for exploration, for exploration, for discovery of obstacles, for observation, and improvement of current solution, i.e. the scenarios targeted on system modernisation beside model-based development. It integrates also model checking.

2.6 Lessons Learned with Model-Based Development

Model-driven development highly depends on the quality of models. Although model-driven development will be supported by compilers in the future, it is currently mainly using an interpreter approach. Models must be doubly well-formed according to well-formedness criteria for the model itself and well-formed for proper transformation in the interpreter approach. For instance, database schemata have to be normalised. BPMN diagrams must be well-formed in order to be uniquely interpretable. Otherwise, the interpreter approach will not result in models that have a unique meaning. Model-based development has at least four different but interleaved facets: (i) model-driven development with stepwise adaptation of the model (suite), (ii) model-driven programming as conceptual-model programming, (iii) model-based development with generic or reference models as the starting point, and (v) model-based assessment and improvement of programs. The interpreter approach can be sufficient in the case of high-quality models. The classical approach to database modelling that uses a normalisation after translation, however, shows that compiler approaches are better fitted to model-based reasoning and development and to Modelling as Programming. If a model suite is going to be used as the basis for model-based development then the models in the model suite must be tightly associated. Tracers and controllers for associations among sub-models and coherence within a model suite are an essential prerequisite for proper model-based development. Often model suites are only loosely coupled. A compiler has to support sophisticated integration and harmonisation in the last compiler phase what is also a theoretical challenge.

3 Revisiting the State-of-Art

3.1 Currently: Model-Backed Development

Model-based development, model-based design, and model-based architecture use a world of models. So far, we did not reach the stage that models are systematically and skilled used for generation of programs. Programming is rather based on blueprint models or inspiration models. These models will not be changed whenever the program is under change. They are then throwaway origins in the programming process. Development is therefore model-backed. The potential for model-based development is, however, obvious. Software engineering is now paying far more attention to the needs, cultures, habits, and activities of business users. Users have their own understanding of the application that must be harmonised with the perception of developers.

Model-based development is currently revitalised [1], e.g. in the MontiCore project (see, for instance, [47]). The revival led to a new stage in generative software engineering for domain-specific languages which reflect the worlds of business users. In general however, modelling is still not considered to be a mandatory activity for programmers. It is still considered to be some kind of luxury.

We further observe that model-backed development has already been applied directly with the beginning of programming. Programmers have had their models. These models have, however, been implicit and have been stated rather seldom. Changes in the software did not use the models behind. They rather led to additional hidden models. These implicit models became hidden legacy since documentation of software has been and is still a big issue and is often completely neglected. The explicit model-backed development became important with the advent of the internet software and the turn towards user-oriented software.

3.2 The Body of Knowledge

Our approach to model-based reasoning is based on [20,73,81]. Figure 2 follows the reconsideration in [101] of the work by B. Mahr [74] Other variants of model-based development are conceptual-model programming and model driven architectures [33,85], universal applications with generators for derivation of the specific application [82], pattern-based [6], and many other project like the CodeToGo project. SPICE and CMM added to this approach quality issues and matured co-design methodology [10,38,51,91,100]. Model-driven development, engineering and architecture (MDD, MDE, MDA) taught some valuable lessons reported about model-driven approaches, e.g. [29,39] and the list in [114]. Model-driven development can be extended by literate programming [64], database programming [93], programming with GitHub [56], 'holon' programming [31], refinement [13], multi-language approaches [35], and schemata of cognitive semantics [70]. Projects like the Axiom project [25], the mathematical problem solver [87], and RADD (Rapid application and database development) [7,97,99] show how MaP can be accomplished.

An essential method for model-based programming is based on refinement styles. A typical refinement style is practised in the abstract state machine approach [12,15]. A program is specified in a rather abstract block-oriented form based on changeable functions. These function can be refined to more detailed ones without context dependence to already specified ones.

Our vision approach can also be based on interpreters instead of compilers or compiler-compilers. Typical examples are [23,24] using MetaCASE [58,59], Come-In-And-Play-Out [45] based on algorithmics [19,44], and model-driven web engineering approaches (beside [92], for instance, Hera [48], HDM [41], MIDAS [113], Netsilon [80], OOHDM [94], OOWS [84] RMM [50], UWE [65], WAE2 [21], Webile [89] WebML [18], WebSA [77], W2000 [8], and WSDM [110]). The interpreter approach is useful in the case of relatively simple modelling languages.

The interpreter approach to partially (and fragmentary) program generation can be applied as long as languages are strictly layered and there is no dependence among the layers. Optimisation is not considered. First interpreter approach to database structuring followed this approach for the entity-relationship model (based on rigid normalisation of the source schema before interpreting with attribute, entity, relationship layers whereas the last one allows very simple cardinality constraints). Constraint enforcement is a difficult problem which requires compilation, denormalisation, and specific supporting means.

The compiler approach [86,116] allows to generate proper programs. The rule-based approach to database schema transformation in [67] extends [34]. It uses the theories of extended entity-relation modelling languages [99] and the insight into techniques such as web information systems [92] and BPMN semantification [14,16]. We use advanced programming techniques and theories like attribute grammars [28], graph grammars [32,99], database programming through VisualSQL [52], performance improvement [108], and normalisation techniques like those for storyboards in [78].

The fifth generation computer project [2,3,36,79,111,112] inspired our approach to modelling as programming. We base our changes on advices by H. Aiso [4] who chaired the architecture sub-committee in the Japanese fifth generation computer project.

3.3   Experience Propagation Through Reference Models

Computer Engineering developed a rich body of successful applications that form a body of experience. This experience can also be used in a completely different development style instead of 'greenfield' or 'brownfield' development. Already by investigating so-called 'legacy' systems, we have had to realise that solutions incorporate tacit knowledge of programmers. We should therefore call these older solutions better *heritage* since they allow us to inherit the skills of generations of programmers despite changing hardware and software. Heritage systems provide a rich body of already available solutions.

A typical direction of heritage system development are reference models. Reference models [9,37,75,96,107] are generalisations of existing successful system solutions. The experience gained in such applications can be generalised to classes of similar solutions. The generalisation procedure allow to invert to generalisation to a specialisation to the given solution. Universal programming [82] and generic solutions [109] use generation facilities for deriving an essential part of a solution from already existing more general ones.

3.4   Tools for Model-Based Development

The fundamental idea behind MetaCASE and its incorporation to a sophisticated tool support for modelling [23] is the separation of models from their visual representations. MetaCASE is a layered database architecture consisting of four OMG layers: signature, language, model and data.

The computational environment for the approach can be based on systems ADOxx, CoreEAF, Eclipse, Eugenia, GMF, Kieler, mathematical problem solvers, MontiCore, and PtolemyII [30,47,54,57,60,66,87,88]. The two case studies mentioned below have been discussed in [53,69,78,104]. More examples on models in science are discussed in [103].

The compiler-compiler approaches [17,43,49,72] are far more powerful. They have been developed for domain-specific languages (at that time called 'Fachsprachen') since 1973. This approach is our main background for modelling as programming. It can be combined for 'brownfield' development (migration, modernisation) with the strategies in [62]. The directive and pragma approaches have been developed already for FORTRAN and have been extensively used for C, C++, and especially ADA [98]. The layered approach used in this chapter follows the realisations already known and widely applied for programming languages since COBOL and ALGOL60. Layering is also the guiding paradigm behind LaTeX and TeX [63,71] with a general setup layer, the content layer, the adaptable device-independent layer, and the delivery layer. The compiler-compiler approach additionally integrates generic models [11,92,106,109], reference libraries [37,107], meta-data management [68], informative models [102], model-centric architectures [76], and multi-level modelling [40].

3.5   The Background: Model Suites

Modelling should follow the *principle of parsimony*: Keep the model as simple and as context-independent as possible.

Models that follow this principle provide best surveyability and understandability. Context-dependence would otherwise require to consider all other models and origins together with the model. The result would be a model that is not really ready for use.

Another principle is the *separation of concern*: Instead of considering a holistic model which allows to consider all aspects and functions, we use a number of models that concentrate on few aspects and support few functions.

This second principle requires consideration according to aspects such as structure, functionality, behaviour, collaboration as the triple (communication, cooperation, coordination), interactivity, infrastructure, storage, and computation. The classical co-design approach to database system development follows this principle by integrated consideration of database structure models, functionality and behaviour models, viewpoint models, and realisation models. The principle can also be based on the W*H separation [24], i.e. who (relating to user profile, habits, personal culture), where (wherein, wherefrom, which orientation), what (whereof, wherefore, wherewith), why (whence, whither, for what, whereto), in what way (how, by what means, worthiness, which pattern, on which basis), when (at what moment and time frame), whom (by whom, whichever), and whereby (which enabling system, infrastructure, languages with their own obstinacy and restrictions ...). Separation of concern enables to consider from one side inner and implicit models as deep models and from the other side outer and explicit models as normal models. Deep models are typically stable and will not change. Normal models are more tightly associated with the origins that are really under consideration.

Following the two principles, we use a collection of models. The entire picture is then derived from these models similar to the global-as-view approach [117]. These models do not need to be entirely integrated. It is only required that the models in the collection are coherent. Utilisation of several models requires support for co-existence, consistency among abstractions, and integration of deep and normal models. Models in such collections or ensembles are also partially governing other models, i.e. we can use a synergetic separation into master and slave models. This separation provides a means to use control models for master models. We do need control models for slave models.

Coherence becomes then a main property of such model collection. This coherence must be maintained. The simplest way for support of coherence is to build explicit associations among these models. Associations can be build on general association schemata. In this case we can develop tracers and controllers for the model association. The association represents then the architecture of the model collection. Associations among models may also based on association among sub-models or on substitutability of a submodel by another submodel or on composers of models.

A *model suite* is a coherent collection of models with an explicit association schema among the models, tracers for detection of deviations from coherence, and controllers for maintenance of the association.

3.6   The Trick: Layered Model Development

The model suite in Fig. 4 will be layered into models for initialisation and landscaping, for strategic intrinsic set-up, for tactic extrinsic reflection and definition, for customisation and operationalising including adaptation, and for model delivery. Figure 4 displays layering for greenfield development. Brownfield development is based on revision for modernisation, integration, evolution, and migration. It uses also reengineering of models that become additional origins with their normal models, deep models, mentalistic and codified concepts. Heritage development does not follow layering in this way.

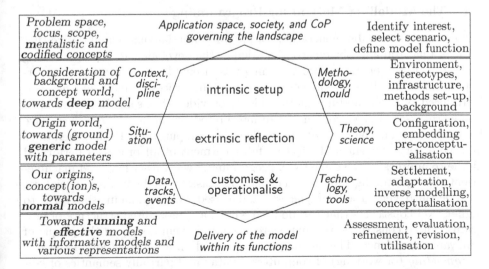

Fig. 4. The layered approach to model suite development and program generation (revised and modified from [53])

We use the W*H characterisation for *landscaping* as initialisation of a layered model suite. Figure 4 separates from one side supporters such as sources, grounding and basis on the left side and from the other side enablers such as methodology, theories, techniques on the right side.

4 Model-Based Thinking

Model-based thinking is going to integrate modelling into programming. Models can be used for 'semantification' of programs. Model-based thinking is different from programming since it uses models of humans together with models of the computing infrastructure. These models can be oriented on the way of programming, controlling, and supporting infrastructure. The way of modelling allows to concurrently consider several variants and alternatives for a solution, to use preference assessment for 'good' solutions, and to separate concerns by well-associated with each other models.

Models are used in everyday life as mental prospect or idea. In this case they are less precise than those used in system construction scenarios. Program development needs a higher level of accuracy and precision. We concentrate here on high-quality models, i.e.

- with potential extensibility, adaptability, replaceability, efficiency, stability, validatable, testable, analysable, exactness, error-proneness, reliable spacial and temporal behaviour, dependability, maintainable, etc. from one side of external quality and
- with inner coherence, tolerable redundancy, constructivity, modularisation, coherence, and efficiency, etc. from the other side of internal quality.

4.1 The Modelling Method for Programming

Let us briefly remember generations of programming languages and derive that M2P is a natural and obvious continuation of the development of programming languages. First generation programming was oriented on executable processor-dependent code. The second generation brought processor independence and introduced symbolic and mnemotic code. It provided thus some hardware independence. Assembling programs were interpreted by an assembler. They have been oriented on the *way of controlling* the computation. Both generations allowed a very efficient and effective full treatment of all processes performed at the computer. At the same time, programming was rather low level machine-oriented programming and, thus, a challenging task for well-educated specialists.

The third generation languages standardised Von Neumann constructs to higher level constructs that can be used within a standardised structure of programs. These constructs are context-reduced and exempted from the plague of firmware dependence. The languages are oriented on an abstraction of the *way of computing* (or working) of computers. Syntax and partially semantics of languages became standardised and well-defined. Meanwhile, these constructs are near to very basic constructs of human languages. Third generation programming became somehow independent on the enabling infrastructure. Structuring of programs has been standardised and component-backed. The main enablers for third generation languages are compilers, debuggers, linkers, and editors. Compilers incorporated also optimising programs for generation of efficiently executable code at the level of second or first generation languages. Programming could be thus performed by everybody who got computer engineering education.

Fourth generation languages provided implementation and groundware independence, e.g. data storage and management independence and management system independence. These languages are macro-based instead of command-oriented and are often script languages. Optimisation is now available for a bunch of concurrently executed programs. Groundware independence can nowadays also be provided in networked computation. Third and fourth generation programming can be based on a number of different paradigms such as object-orientation, parallel computing, functional programming, imperative or procedural programming, symbolic computation, collection-oriented (e.g. set- or bag-oriented) programming, event-driven programming, and declarative programming.

Fifth generation languages raised the hope for program development in computational environments that could 'think' for themselves and draw their own inferences using background information. The approach was mainly based on representing programs as massives of formulas in first-order predicate logics. One of the reasons that this program failed is this restriction to first-order predicate logics. Another reason is that the target audience, able to express everything in predicate logics, is very limited. Other reasons are: "it was highly dependent on AI technology, it did not achieve an integration of AI and human-computer interface techniques, ... it tried to provide a universal solution for any kind of programming, it routed granularity to basic program blocks, and it was oriented on one final solution instead of coherent reasoning of coherent variants of final solutions depending on the focus and scope of a user" [53].

Our vision is to integrate the way of programming and the way of modelling. Models are typically model suites and allow to concentrate on certain aspects while not loosing the association among the models in the suite. This approach decreases the complexity of reasoning to a level that a human can easily capture it. Since the model suite is integrated, this reduction does not mean to loose the entire view on a program. Model-based thinking is also based on approximate reasoning since a model can be an abstraction of another more precise or more accurate model. Models incorporate their explanations, the necessary knowledge from the application domain, and the reasoning and thinking approaches of users. If models and model suites can be transformed to programs then maintenance of such programs can be transferred back to maintenance odf models.

4.2   The Near Future M2P: The Modelling_To_Program Initiative

M2P is based on a consolidation of the body of knowledge for models, modelling activities, and modelling. The renaissance of modelling towards a real art of modelling allows to use modelling as a matured practice in Computer Science and Computer Engineering, esp. for system development and software system development. The previous chapters contributed to this development. M2P can be understood as a technology for model-based development and model-based reasoning.

Model-based reasoning and thinking is the fourth dimension of human life beside reflection and observation, socialising and interacting, acting and fabricating (e.g. engineering), and systematising and conceptualising (typical for scientific disciplines). Programs reflect a very specific way of acting with a machine. Programming is so far bound to Von Neumann machines. It will be extended to other machines as well, e.g. to interaction machines [42,115]. Model-backed development coexists with programming since its beginning, at least at the idea and comprehension level. Documentation or informative models are developed after programming. Modelling_to_program is coordinated modelling within program development and design processes. It enhances programming, contributes to quality of programs and enables in model-oriented and purposive maintenance, change management, and system modernisation. Model and systems complement one other using separation of concern and purpose. Non-monolithic programs and systems use a variety of languages. Their coherence and integration is far simpler if we use model suites and if programs are also following architecture principles similar to the associations in the model suite.

M2P requires high-quality models. Models must be precise and accurate. They must not reflect the entire picture. They can be intentionally incomplete. These models may use dummies and hocks for code injection by the translator, e.g. similar to stereotype and pattern refinement [5]. Models may already contain directives and adornments as hints for translation. In most cases, we use an interpreter for transformation. A typical example is the ADOxx+ transformation for HERM++ interpreters discussed in [67]. In this case, views are represented by dummies. Late logical code optimisation is necessary after translation. M2P requires refinement and adaptation of the translated code. Models intrinsically incorporate deep models. Modelling is then mainly normal model development. An early variant of this approach is the RADD toolbox for database structure design and development [99]. Website generation [92] is another typical example of this approach.

Modelling has now reached the maturity to properly support programming at the intentional level. It is also going to be used at the meta-reasoning level [22] for guiding methodologies and methods. Modelling becomes an enabler for development of large and complex systems. It is already a commonly used technique for user-oriented and internet-based web information systems [92]. These systems support a wide variety of user frontend systems according to business user's needs. They integrate a number of different backend systems.

Modelling-to-program does not mean that programs have to be developed only on the basis of models. Models can be the source or pre-image or archetype or antetype of a program. Still we also program without an explicit model. M2P eases programming due to its explanation power, its parsimony, and comprehensibility.

4.3   From Literate Programming to Literate Modelling

Literate programming co-develops a collection of programs with their informative models [102] that provide an explanation of the programs in a more user-friendly way. It can be extended by approaches to MaP with proper compilation of source code on the basis of small programs, program snippets, and a model suite. Programs and the model suite become interwoven. The first approach to literate programming has been oriented on programs with derived libraries of user interfaces and informative models [64]. It became far more advanced. Nowadays programs are interspersed with snippets of models. Most of these models are, however, documentation models. In this case, models formulate the meaning and understanding of programs. They connect this documentation to the program code at a high level and mostly in natural language. Documentation models integrate the code documentation with the developer idea documentation, the usage documentation, and the interface documentation. Literate programming thus overcomes the habit that the documentation is going to live in the program itself. The program is going to live in the documentation model. In a similar way, interface and informative models can be handled.

Literate programming can be based on models for the central program and models for interfacing and documenting. Since the central program is the governing program, literate modelling will essentially be a global-as-design approach for a model suite. Different users might use different models for the same application case.

Literate modelling is essentially modelling with integrated vertical and horizontal model suites. Horizontal model suites consist of models at the same abstraction level. A typical horizontal model suite in the global-as-design approach is the conceptual database structure model together with the view(point) external models for business users. Vertical model suites integrate models at various abstraction and stratification levels. Software development is often based on some kind of waterfall methodology. Models at a high level of abstraction are, for instance, storyboard and life case models. They are refined to models representing data, events, processes, infrastructure, and support systems. Modelling the OSI communication layer structure results in a typical vertical model suite.

Literate modelling incorporates a variety of models such as representation and informative models in a natural language into program development. It provides a high level abstraction and is thus program-language independent. The meaning of programs is provided prior to coding. Many-model thinking [83] can be developed towards model suite thinking. There are high-level introductory models such as informative models. These models are refined to models that reflect certain aspects of an application and to models that serve as origins for implementation models.

4.4 MaP: Towards Second Generation – Modelling as Programming

A central challenge of (conceptual) modelling is to facilitate the long-time dream of being able to develop (information) systems strictly by (conceptual) modeling. The approach should not only support abstract modelling of complex systems but also allow to formalize abstract specifications in ways that let developers complete programming tasks within the (conceptual) model itself. It thus generalises the model-driven and modelling_to_program approaches and develops a general approach to modelling as high-level programming.

Modelling is an activity guided by a number of postulates, paradigms, principles, and modelling styles. Already nowadays, we use paradigms such as global-as-design and principles such as meta-modelling based on generic and reference models. MaP is however dependent on deep models and the matrix. Next generation programming will also allow to be flexible in the postulates and paradigms.

Modelling can be organised in a similar way as structured programming, i.e. following a well-developed methodology and framework within an infrastructure of supporting tools. Models may be based on refinement approaches such as pattern-oriented development [5]. They contain enactor hocks for integration of source code.

Similar to system programming, modelling will be based on literate programming and literate modelling. For MaP, literate modelling becomes essential. Modelling_as_programming is oriented on development of complex systems. model suites Model suites can be developed on the basis of different frameworks as mentioned above,

A number of tools are going to support MaP:

- Sophisticated editors and frameworks have to be developed for this approach as extension and generalisation of existing ones, e.g. ADOxx, Kieler, CoreEAF, MontiCore, and Ptolemy II.
- Code generation for the general MaP programme is still a matter of future development. There are already parts and pieces that can be used for generation and compilation: the RADD workbench realisation (Rapid Application and Database Design) [99], database programming by VisualSQL tool [52], performance management and tuning (e.g. [95,108]), advance high-level workflow specification [14], integrated web information systems design, and co-design.
- The implementation approach to MaP may be inspired by three solutions that are already common for programming languages:
  - Transformation and compilation is based on standardised combinable components. These components can also be reflected by specific models within a model suite.
  - Each specialisation can be enhanced by directives for compilation and by pragmas for pre-elaboration, convention setting, and exception handling like those in C++ and ADA. Model directives configure and pre-prepare a model for compilation. Models can be enhanced by default directives or by adornments detailing the interpretation of model elements. Pragmas are used to convey "pragmatic information" for compiler controllers,

adapters, context enhancers. There are language-defined pragmas that give instructions for optimization, listing control, storage, import of routines from other environments, extenders for integration into systems, etc. An implementation may support additional (implementation-defined) pragmas.

- MaP afford programming-language independence. In this case, it has to be supported by multi-language compilers or compiler-compiler technology. For instance, database model suites are going to be mapped in a coherent and integrated form to object-relational, network, hypertext, etc. platforms. The association among various structuring of data structure is governed by the association schema of the model suite.

MaP requires a proper education for modellers. They have to master modelling, system thinking, programming techniques, reflection of models in various ways, communication with the application experts, and design of model suites. MaP knowledge and skills will become a central module in Computer Science similar to algorithmic thinking and programming. Model suites will become the mediating device between applications and their needs from one side and the system realisation from the other side. Already programming can be understood as an experimental science and as empirical theories by means of a computing device. Modelling continues this line. MaP thus needs a proper development of a theory and technology of modelling. Continuous model quality management will become a challenging issue.

5   Towards True Fifth Generation Programming

True fifth generation programming will be based on models which are considered to be programs due to generation of program code from the models without programming at the level of 4PL or 3PL. Compilers or compiler-compilers are transforming the model suite directly to the target environment that can be compiled in the classical approach. A high-quality model suite is used as a program of true fifth generation, becomes the target environment over host languages, and will be mapped to programs in host languages of fourth or third generation.

A new generation of modelling languages as programming languages has to support a large variety of application areas since computers became an essential element of modern infrastructures and proper program support is necessary for all these areas, disciplines and daily life. We might try to develop a very large number of domain-specific languages. In this case, domain experts in a singleton domain are supported within their thought pattern. However, if application is of a cross-domain nature with a wide variety of cultures, habits, and approaches, model suite enable collaborative work. The literate modelling approach seems to be an alternative. In this case, model suites will thus become high-level programs and thus will be the basis for true fifth generation programming in true fifth generation programming (5PL).

One potentially applicable realisation strategy is based on a layered approach discussed below similar to successful approaches such as LaTeX. We shall use this strategy in onion meta-model specification approach.

MaaP should also by partially independent on programmer's postulates, paradigms, and principles. It should also be tolerant and robust against changes in the target environment thus providing a programming language independence. At the same time, MaaP needs to be robust against a deviations from the normal application situation. We currently observe that application development is based on some kind of 'normality' in the application without at all taking into consideration potential but tolerable deviations from the normal case. At the same time, it must be supported by a specific MaaP education.

5.1   Ideas for 5PL on the Basis of MaaP

5PL have to be based on a revision of principles of computer science (e.g. the reconsideration in the style of [26]). These principles are, however, not yet commonly accepted and well-developed. The classical categories of computing [27] must be extended for 5PL: communication and coordination towards integrated collaboration, computation towards computation infrastructures, recollection towards data and information management at many levels of detalisation, evaluation towards assessment at the SPICE level, automation beyond compilation, dynamic optimization depending on system usage and environment, and design as sophisticated modelling. Computer Science was for a long time the study of phenomena observed for computers and computation. These principles can be combined with the four paradigms of sciences (rephrasing them from [46]): empirical sciences, intellectual sciences, computational sciences, and data science (data-intensive scientific discovery). Data science can be understood as a kind of computational science.

At the same time, almost everybody in our area was and is an avid modeller at least at the intentional level. There is a fifth (or fourth after reconsideration) paradigms we need to consider: daily life collaboration at least on the level of handicraft or art. All paradigms are supported by models. A paradigm that is so far neglected is approximation, esp. for complexity reduction and manageability. Modelling and models add a number of additional principles, issues, and concerns. 5PL must then integrate these principles, paradigms, experience, and "shortcut" decisions.

Models are often developed as normal models that inherit implicit deep models together with corresponding methodologies, techniques, and methods, i.e. its matrices. Normal models directly reflect origins according to the focus used for shaping the scope and non-scope of the model, functions that the model play in application scenarios, and analogy to be used for representing the origins. The surface is, however, only the direct visible part. Alike the iceberg, the essential part of the application is hidden and not explicitly elicitable by a programmer or somebody from our area. Instead of hunting down this experience, it is far simpler to use the models from the application area. Justification and the quality sufficiency characteristics are often injected by deep models. Therefore, 5PL has to neatly integrate insights from the application area.

Moreover, complex applications remain to be complex also in the case that a model suite is going to be used. Complexity is not easy for humans. Systems consist of components that again depend on the system. So, the sum of the components does not define the system. Components can be captured by models. Their combination requires a proper coherence and integration management, i.e. association schemata within a model suite.

Modern applications are also interdisciplinary and are developed by many professionals in teamwork which follow very different postulates, paradigms, and principles. They are not entirely harmonisable. They co-exist, however, in daily life. And daily life is coherent. We claim that this co-existence can be expressed on the level of models but not on the level of programming languages. Model capsules [105] allow maintenance of associations in a model suite on the basis of sub-models of models in the model suite. This approach supports proper life of models within a model suite as a society of models.

Model suites will bond the applications, the domain and the computer support. They will become mediators between the application and the supporting infrastructure. Models are at the same time a means, an intermediary, and the medium for expressing separatable aspects of an application. Model suite will play the role of a "middle-range theory".

A model suite comes with its architecture and meta-model of the model suite. We may also use steering and governing models within a model suite. Some models in a model suite can be considered to be guiding ones since they are refined to more specific ones. A model suite can incorporate also quality-supporting meta-models (called checksum models) in order to provide means for quality control and for coherence support. Model suites incorporate also user-oriented interfacing models. We expect that these models will be developed as external and informative models for issues important for different users. In this case, models can be narrative as long as the association schema supports that. Synergetics approaches allow to develop master and slave models. Slave models are entirely dependent from master models. Master models can be configured and adapted by control models. In this case, we need to build sophisticated editors for model suites.

5PL need a new generation of editors. These editors have to support at the same time high-level informative modelling, exploration and explanation models, domain-situation models, prescription models with compiler pragmas and directives, usage models for the system to be generated, steering models as instruction books for the modelling process, and guidance models. The editors could be based on the same principles as the compilers for program generation from a given model suite. It seems that the development of such editors ware not feasible. In the next Subsect. 5.2, we consider the onion meta-model for model suite composition. Editors should also include supporting means for check, control, and debugging.

Separation of concern can be based on application profiles, application demand models, and application portfolio [61]. The application profile is based on an application analysis space that represents interests, scenario, processing and data demand, excort processing and data, correction and calibration approaches, explanation pattern similar to 5D techniques, and the application context. Application demand models represent the application situation, suppositions, application concept spaces, phenomena, actors with their profiles and abilities, and termination and goal test. The portfolio represents the data and the processing spaces. We ned thus models that allow to represent these different concerns. These models can be used for derivation of requirement models. Before that we need, a sophisticated mould or several methodologies for support of separation of concern.

A trick in programming is the development of a program library. Such libraries can be imported whenever some of their programs are useful. Programs to be imported can also be customised to the given environment. Production lines are already used for orchestrated, syndication, adaptation, and configuration. We may use a similar trick based on generic models and heritage model suites. These model suites represent the book of knowledge gained so far. They can be adapted and specialised to diverse situations. 5PL integrate libraries of injectable deep model suites for landscaping and intrinsic strategic consideration steps. In a similar way, we use normal model suites for the given application case. Programming in 5PL is going to be far simpler than programming in 3PL or 4PL.

The development of programming languages has been based on building abstract program blocks, their standardisation and introduction of shortcuts for these blocks. Languages provided an environment for sophisticated usage of such blocks. Reasoning on programs became stereotyped and standardised. 5PL based on model suites is now going to be based on an art of programming with model suites. They have their foundation in "natural" human perception, as opposed to an academic perspective on data computation. Since model suites are more natural and humanised than programs, model-based thinking and reasoning allows to tackle complex applications, e.g. interdisciplinary projects. We need, however, a proper underpinning and development of this art.

The delivered model (suite) is then going to be *compiled* to a program. The compiler has to transform the model to platform-dependent and directly executable programs after an optimisation phase. The compiler will typically be a 4-pass compiler (lexical analysis, semantical analysis, transformation and optimisation of intermediate code, target coding).

Computer scientists often turn up one's nose at results of laymen programming. Laymen bring their own application knowledge. They work from a complete knowledge and insight into the application domain. Their experience is captured in application-domain and domain-situation models beside their specific experience-based models. Most of these models are not explicitly expressed. Also, deep models reside inside the application as tacit knowledge. Insiders follow principles in the application that are only partially explicit but part of their tacit, habitual and cultural behaviour. 5PL is going to augment programming by insider's mental modelling power. Laymen programming lifts this treasure, maintains coherence in applications, and will result in less defective code and simple program maintenance.

Von Neumann and Turing style of programming is only the beginning of a new era of development of computerised support mechanisms. This programming style does neither entirely reflect how humans reason and work nor represent the way how cultures, organisations, and societies act and evolve. We often map some kind of understanding to a program system and expect that the world outside computation is going to behave this way. Very soon after installation of such system it is going to be changed. Paradigms like programming-in-the-small and programming-in-the large can not be easily extended to programming-in-the-society or programming-in-the-world. The software and the data crises are essentially a result of the endeavour to ortho-normalise and to conquer the world by means of computer systems.

The simplest approach to change this situation is Models_as_a_Program that reflects human way of working and thinking as well as the understanding of a society. We develop a new generation of models as a new generation of programs.

5.2   One Potential Solution: The Onion Meta-model Specification Approach

MaaP can be based on a stereotyped model suite specification. This specification may follow the style of LaTeX document specification onion in Fig. 5. One typical solution (however only one of many) for system and also model suite development is vertical layering: (1) specify the surface and foundation; (2) provide an understanding of mechanisms of functions, processes, and operations; (3) develop means that the system functions; (4) develop the basis for functioning; (5) develop variants for a solution within a variation spreadsheet with

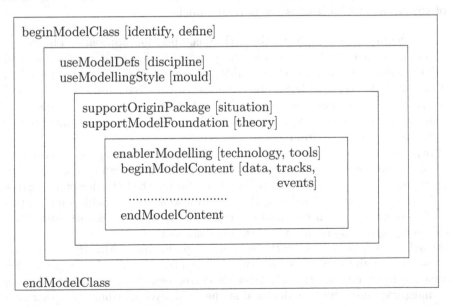

Fig. 5. The onion approach to model suite specification (modified from [104])

adaptation facilities. This approach supports development and application of well-structured and composable models suites which are governed by the kind of model.

Model class: Models are used as instruments and thus depend on the scenario in which the function. Different kinds of models can be stereotyped. This stereotypical categorisation can be used for the definition of the model class. The model class becomes the outer shell of the model specification onion. Model classes are based on the internal shell for model formating and general initialisation.

Model style and pattern: Depending on the model class, we may incorporate various libraries and methodological moulds at the model-style-and-discipline shell of the onion.

Model generics and foundations: Models consist of an internal deep model and of a normal model. The deep model is typically not completely revised. Its essential element is the model background. The grounding is accepted without any revision. The basis can be slightly extended and modified. The background forms the model foundation. The model foundation will be supported by a model package for representation of the specifics of the model situation. Additionally, generic models may be used as a basis for the normal model. These models may be collected in a library of generic models.

Model embedding and tools: The fourth shell is the support shell. Compilers are tools as well as a specification workbench. Technology support is a matter of convenience. A specific support is given for the combination of the given deep model with the normal model.

Normal model specification: The main part that is represents the specifics of the given set of origins is the normal model.

The specification setting follows the LaTeX compilation approach. The generation of the target model suite and the programs will result in a number of auxiliary elements similar to symbol tables for compilers of the first generation. The intermediate result of the transformation is a realisation-independent and infrastructure-independent model suite. The final result is then a realisation-dependent and infrastructure-dependent model suite or a program that may be executed in the given environment.

Pragmas and *model directives* are essential elements that we use for enhancement of conceptual models for system realisation. Pragmas can be considered as a language feature that allows adjusting or fine-tuning the behavior of a program compiled from a model. Model directives might also be used as additional control units for compilation. An essential element of a compiler is the *precompilation* based on a *prefetching* strategy of compiler-compilers.

Model correction is an essential element of prefetching. Already in the case of consistency maintenance for integrity constraints, we realised that models for translation must be correct. Schema-wide correctness is often neglected since most integrity constraints are declared at the local level. Cardinality constraints are a typical example which global correctness is partially based on local and type-based correctness. Since databases have to be finite and schemata are connected then we may derive implications for a given set of integrity constraints. We have to validate whether these implications are correct. Moreover, a set of cardinality constraints may be fulfilled only in infinite databases or in empty databases. Models must have a sufficient quality that is evaluated on the basis of corresponding evaluation procedures. If a model or a model suite is not correct then we have to improve the quality of a model before translation.

This approach is already currently realisable. Let us consider in brief two case studies [53, 69, 78, 104]:

MaaP for Database System Design and Development

Database structure modelling often uses extended entity-relationship models such as HERM [99]. HERM can also be extended to HERM+ with a specific algebra for database functionality and view collections. It is already well-known how to translate an existing entity-relationship schema to a so-called logical (or implementation) schema. ER schemata can be enhanced by directives for this translation.

Rule-Based OR compilation of HERM schemata and models uses the theory of extended entity-relationship models. In the case of extended entity-relationship schemata and of VisualSQL as a query and functionality specification language, we may use a rule system consisting of 12+1 translation phases for transformation. The phases for a compilation are the following ones:

0. Configuration of the HERM compiler, preprocessing, prefetching according to the model directives;
1. Schema and operation lexical analysis;
2. Syntactic analysis for schema and operations;
3. Semantical analysis schema and operations;
4. Generation of intermediate code that is also used as the ground schema for VisualSQL query, view, maintenance specification;
5. Preparation for schema and operation optimisation (or normalisation);
6. Schema tuning (operational optimisation);
7. Introduction and injection of controlled redundancy;
8. Redefinition and revision of generated types and operations (also UDT);
9. Recompilation for quantity matrix (Mengengerüst) (big and huge DB);
10. Toughening for evolution and change in data dictionary;
11. Derivation of support services and view towers;
12. Generation of data dictionary entries.

We can enhance this translation to more specific compilation and embedding into the corresponding platforms. Practitioners use in this case pragmas at least at the intentional level for object-relational technology. The translation includes also translation of view collections. Furthermore, HERM+ can be extended by VisualSQL that allows to declare queries at the level of HERM schemata. This translation results then directly in a performance-oriented structure specification at the level of physical schemato. We may envision that this approach can also be extended to other platforms such as XML or big data platforms.

Figure 6 specialises the general Fig. 5 for database modelling as sophisticated database programming for a sample application (booking and financing issues in business applications based on the global-as-design specification approach).

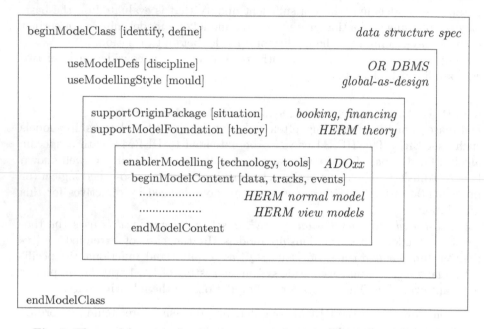

Fig. 6. The model-centric database structure development based on HERM+

MaaP for Workflow Derivation From Storyboards

The second case study is going to discuss solutions if the deep models are not similar. In this case, we either normalise the source models in such a way that they can be transformed to the target models or programs or generate the full variety of potential target models or programs. The last approach is feasible if the generated models or programs are not changed on their own. All changes to them must be changes at the level of the source model suite. Web information system development has already successfully used this approach. Normalisation of source models is driven by well-formedness rules that are applied to the models.

Storyboarding and BPMN-based workflow specification are based on different deep models, i.e. we observe a deep model mismatch. The differences are similar to those observed for impedance mismatches between parallel database processing and sequential program computation. Therefore, the model transformation needs also approaches to overcome this mismatch. BPMN is strictly actor-oriented and based on a strict local-as-design paradigm. Storyboarding is more flexible. We might use global-as-design or partial local-as-design combined with global-as-design techniques. Storyboarding provides some freedom on the flow of activities. BPMN mainly uses a more strict form where diagrams are given with a static flow of activities. Diagrams are not adapted to the changes in user behaviour. Dynamic workflow specification is still based on flexibility at design time and on stability during runtime.

SiteLang specification allows to define scenes with plots for activities within a scene by different actors. This interaction among actors must be mapped to communication interaction between diagrams based on collaboration diagrams, to choreography diagrams among, or to conversations among actors. Scenes in a SiteLang specification can be visited by all enabled actors and completed by some of them. This freedom of task completion is neither achievable for normal BPMN diagrams nor for dynamic ones. Generic BPMN diagrams can however be used for adaptation to the actual actor behaviour at runtime.

The transformation of a storyboard can be based on language transformation rules. Typical rules are the following ones:

- An actor storyline is directly transferred to a BPMN pool.
- An atomic scene without atomic plots is transferred to a BPMN activity.
- A story sequence is represented by a sequence of BPMN activities. A well-formed story split with its own join (Fitch structure[1]) is transformed to the corresponding BPMN gateway structure. Optional scenes can be transformed to corresponding BPMN gateway structures. Iterations of simple stories can also be directly transferred to BPMN.
- Complex scenes are transformed to either BPMN diagrams or to complex activities or to sub-scenes.
- Story entries and completions are transferred to events in BPMN.
- Communication is based on BPMN communication pattern among diagrams, e.g. a link-scene-link combination among different actors.

The storyboard should also be normalised or transformed in some kind of well-formed storyboard. Parallel links between scenes are normalised either by introduction of intermediate scenes or by merging into a complex scene including plot transformation or link merging. The decision which next scenes are going to be chosen is integrated into the plot of the source scene. The naming of scenes is unified according to a naming scheme. Stories in a storyboard can be encapsulated into units with a singleton task. The storyboard is separated into mini-stories that will become workflows. The stories in a storyboard are decomposed into relatively independent mini-stories with starting and completing points. A mini-story must be representable by a singleton BPMN diagram if the actor in the mini-story does not change. Otherwise, we use superflow diagrams which call subflow diagrams as subprograms.

[78] introduced a small example for a storyboard of a trail system. The normalisation process leads directly to a diagram in Fig. 7 that restricts the freedom and reduces the enabled actors to actors with encapsulatable behaviour within a mini-story.

---

[1] Each split must has its join in the diagram and each join has only its split what is a one-to-one association of splits and joins.

32   B. Thalheim

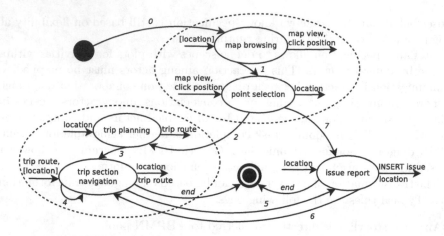

Fig. 7. The storyboard from [78] after refinement and normalization

There are several techniques and rules for storyboard conversion including
data structure development:

Refinement preprocessing orients on data view mapping for each actor, on
strict actor and role separation, on strict start-end flow, on session separation,
and on additional communication.

Restriction of freedom is based on selection of the most essential flows since
he storyboard that allows too much freedom. It downsizes the storyboard by
restricting the flow of activities to the essential ones and by removing the
rest.

Restricted and well-formed parallelism must yield to Fitch structuring.

Normalisation of the storyboard arrives at well-formed BPMN diagrams.

Plot integration for scenes with potential actor and role separation of these
scenes into separate scenes with singleton actors.

We apply graph grammar rules to the stories since storyboarding uses a graphical
language. The storyboard contains also the data viewpoint. This design information must be supported within a co-design approach to data structuring and
workflow specification.

A normalised storyboard is now the basis for a BPMN diagram that displays
only the visitors' viewpoint. The flow of activities is restricted to the most essential ones. Nothing else is supported. This transformation is information-loosing.
A partial diagram after this transformation is displayed in Fig. 8.

5.3   5PL Research and Challenges

We feel certain that the models_as_a_program approach is feasible. So far, we have seen only few examples that demonstrate realisability and feasibility of this approach. It has, however, its lacunas, research and realisation challenges, and theory misses we should be aware of. There are inevitable gaps between what we know and master so far, what we are able to do in our environments, what kind of failures and risks we have to accept or to master by ourselves, and why programs are partially wrong or provide only incomplete solutions.

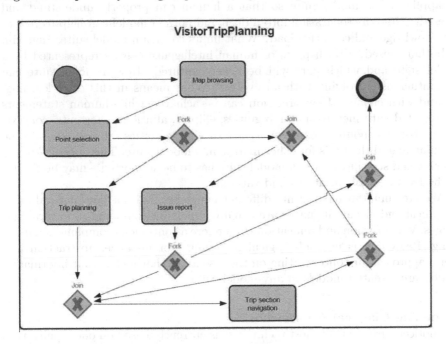

Fig. 8. Translation of the storyboard from [78] to some BPMN process

Let us summarise some of them. The list seems to long and seems to be killing the 5PL programming vision. But all of these problems can be solved – at least in a pragmatic way as humans do in daily life. Since there is no universal world formula we shall not find the least and ultimate solution. We will, however, be able to find a reasonable and acceptable solution.

The Model Suite Transformation Challenge

Model suites should be the central basis for program generation. So we have to answer questions such as: What are possible architectures and organisations of compilers and compiled code? How model suites will be properly implemented in computational environments? What languages we shall use for model suites that will allow to effectively and efficiently to specify what the computer has to do? What kinds of semiotics and logics have to be used for these languages?

How we can check and control the correctness of translations in various 3PL and 4PL settings?

Humanising Model Suite Programming

Humans have their limitations and at the same time cognitive abilities far beyond what a computer can handle. Separation of concern is a technique that also reduces complexity. But what are the basic steering and guiding models in a model suite that represent cognition? What kind of focusing and scoping can be applied for a model suite so that a human can properly understand and digest it? How the separation into a deep and normal model can help to reduce the knowledge and cognitive load? What limits constrain model suites that aim to be humanised? Which parts of human intelligence can be represented by a model suite and which part will be never captured? How a model suite can be continuously evolving with an evolver? What means in this case 'learning' for and with change? How precision can be achieved while human statements are repleted with metaphors, ambiguities, ellipses, allusions, shortcuts, context, pragmatism, economy of expression, and specific semiotics. Models may also be speculative and the basis for other models in a model suite. This specific kind of layering and stratification in a model suite has to be supported – may be similar to the treatment of variations and variants.

We are simultaneously using different languages and not only natural ones. Graphical and visual languages are equally important compared to natural languages. Visualisation and reification is therefore a continuous companion in modelling. Reasoning is not only logical reasoning. For instance, abstraction is a useful approach for concentrating on the essential. That means that informative models are essential models in any model suite.

Extending Classical Approaches

We noticed already that most technology is currently based on one architecture of a computing system. We have to develop approaches to other architectures and overcome limitations of Von Neumann computing. We should obtain from random proliferation of 3PL and 4PL languages. Rather we need to restrict the transformation to those parts of these languages that are really useful and definitely essential and relevant. This challenge would also require a novel approach to model suites.

Performance and energy consumption is a problem for all computerised systems at present and in future. What will be then a green energy and highly performing program? Which model suite approaches exist for sustainable and well-performing systems?

Systems are and will be build for the use of their users. Challenging and unauthorized users should be redlined and thus excluded from access and usage. Biological systems act in a different way in their normal (health) mode: Anything what is really needed at the given moment is accepted and anything else is discarded. Can we integrate the two different paradigms to a new kind of programs?

Engineering of Model Suites

Engineering should consider all four intertwined aspects and perspective: the model suite, the knowledge and technology to be used, the activities of cooperating and competing teams for development and utilisation, and last but mostly importantly the expression of human or society needs and desires. We need a proper methodology for an integrated and holistic but manageable development of model suites. Engineering follows methodologies and is based on a mould. Therefore, a model suite should also contain meta-models as guiding and steering models for metareasoning [22].

Other open issues are: What are the principles behind the development of 5PL solutions? How one can prove that a model suite provides a proper solution? How we extend the normal case known to everybody to a solution that integrates also the deviations? What means robustness and error tolerance in such specifications? How evolution and modernisation can be supported without revolution, i.e. cannibalisation combined with killing existing problematic solutions? What impact has a modification and change to the model suite and the compiled program? What kind of mould best support understandability, modifiability, and parsimony of model suites? What mould and methodology reduces the complexity in a model suite?

Model Suite Theory and Practice Support

Model suites should follow a proper composition and architecture. Whether we have to follow successful design or to develop a completely different way to consider constructors, components, and compositions is an open question. It seems that application-domain-driven standardisation offers a solution for the first step.

The architecture of a model suite is so far based on a separation of concern. Are there other architectures that are proper at least in some application areas? Can we use some partial context-freeness among models in a model suite?

Sciences – such as empirical, intellectual, or computations ones – follow different paradigms, postulates, and principles. Models also reflect these various sciences and are therefore different in structure and function. The theory of model suites must thus be adaptable to the kind of science as well to the kind of engineering or practical task. The human side has to have proper theory support for expression of human or society needs and desires. That means, social sciences must be used for enhancement of a formal theory of model suites.

So far, the theory of models suites makes extensive use of mathematics and theoretical computer science. It uses mathematical solutions from (logical) reasoning, category theory, discrete mathematics, representation, algebra, probability theory, and geometry. There are many other mathematics branches which are going to be useful. Also branches of theoretical computer science and artificial intelligence provide parts and pieces to the theory of model suites.

Model suites should support precise and accurate statement at least as this is necessary and required. We do not need 100 % precision and accuracy. We need something similar to the 90 % principle. The theory and practice has to find a way to include quality assessment, quality improvement, and quality management. Models have their potential and their capacity based on their essential quality characteristics.

Towards Industrial Development On the Basis of Models
Mechanical engineering became a success story after standardisation of machinery building components. Machines have been manufactured at one location, sold to another one and got repaired and modernised by third party. Componentisation and standardisation became the Ansatz in modern manufacturing industry. Building components are developed at various standardised and controllable quality levels. A theory of design supported systematic and feasibility-oriented planing of products according to the job definition. The design process is based on functional structures, functional modules, principal solutions, general and product-neutral design processes in line with restrictions, minimality of lists of components, cost-reduced construction, and solutions in line with application restrictions. All this enabled industrialisation and engineering as effective and efficient way 'turning ideas into reality' with design against failure[2].

Comparing this success story with the state-of-art in Computer Science and Computer Engineering we have to admit that we need a completely different way of solution development. Development and design must be based in future on standardisation, rigid and forceful componentisation, design synthesis of generic components, design of compositions and connections, principles such as structural and functional integrity of computing systems, and consideration of economic, social, and environmental problems and issues.

One way to achieve all this is true fifth general programming based on the models_as_a_program paradigm. It can be supported by a mould and methodology of design and construction of solutions. Model suites with a proper architecture of the suite and corresponding translation machines can be the basis of industrial software and computing system development.

CAM, CAD, and CAx provide a successful support for mechanical and other engineering branches. The development of environments and an infrastructure is also a task for 5PL. These environments support collaborations and teamwork in work processes. A fundamental challenge comes from these infrastructure requirements.

6   M2P, MaP, MaaP: Summarising

The M2P, MaP, and MaaP approaches revise, combine, and generalise efforts and projects for model-driven development. We discussed some of those projects

---

[2] Engineering is the art of building with completely different success criteria (see [90]: "Scientists look at things that are and ask 'why'; engineers dream of things that never were and ask 'why not'." (Theodore von Karman)).
"Engineers use materials, whose properties they do not properly understand, to form them into shapes, whose geometries they cannot properly analyse, to resist forces they cannot properly assess, in such a way that the public at large has no reason to suspect the extent of their ignorance." (John Ure 1998, cited in [90]).

while knowing that model-driven design and development became already a major trend in software engineering. The trend became possible due to the maturity of our discipline. Different branches in computer science and engineering got their separate professional identity and groups. At the same time, it has resulted in a huge number of success stories. Researchers, programmers, and developers share a common base of computer science and computer engineering.

All professionals are avid modellers. Many of them claim not to be modellers. They are, however, widely and intensively using models in a variety of ways: (1) as conception, notion, vision, image, view, concept, picture, basic orientation, performance, comprehension, representation; (2) as less rigid but useful mental models, e.g. idea, imagination, perception, prospect as a mental picture, belief, conceivability, vision, imagination; (3) as models in manufacturing, e.g. as template, pattern, reference, presentation, prototype, origin for production, master copy, sample. So, our discipline is already model-backed, model-based, and model-driven.

We add to this a approach model-based thinking as the main form for extraction of necessary essentials from applications into solution development on the basis of computational infrastructures. Modern applications such as interdisciplinary research crusade and require representation of various disciplinary backgrounds. They need to go far beyond the perspectives of various actors. These field have a substantial overlap and also a challenging non-integration. They infuse solutions to other areas and resist at the same time injection of conceptions from these other areas. We live then in a coherent world while being on our own. Providing a solution in a monolithic form is not only infeasible but impossible. So, new program solutions should enable us to live in this variety. One potentially fruitful solution is to use model suites and to translate the solution-oriented precise and accurate models into a program. True fifth generation programming can be realised this way.

The MaaP, MaP, and M2P approaches will are based on a complete model suite that becomes the source for the code or program of the problem solution and for the system to be built. We discussed the layered approach to model suite development and proper utilisation (see Fig. 4). This layered and stratified approach can be based on the onion architecture depicted in Fig. 5. Some potential deliverables have already been discussed in [53, 78, 104].

MaaP, MaP, and M2P will also enable laymen to develop their own computational solution without being forced to program it. We close thus the gap, ridge, and disaccord among disciplines, e.g. in interdisciplinary research clusters. Everybody who can express thoughts and ideas will be able to develop a program solution. This ability results in quicker, effective, and efficient solutions. Experts can skillfully articulate their ideas for solutions without being forced to program them. They will also be able to understand the solution within their thought and experience worlds. The computer will then be used used as a solution-proposer or solution-generator instead of being used as the solution-forcer or -maker.

Finally we ask ourselves why we should target on true fifth generation programming. A number of reasons force us to use next generation programming:

- Computer engineering has not yet reached the level of being a science. It has not got its culture. Education is mainly education for handicraft work.
- Programming is more and more often performed by laymen, outsiders, casual users, non-specialists, self-made programmers, etc. They need a proper support.
- Apps and modern facilities are often developed without CS education. The uncontrolled growth worsens this situation.
- Users have not been the main concern for programmers. Operator and administrator thinking is still THE common sense understanding of the area.
- Migration, integration, maintenance, and modernisation are still a real nightmare. Half-life time of systems and software is far lower than lifespan of software deployment. New systems use new paradigms without downgrading features.
- Documentation is often luxury. Documentations are often generated from code (without inner documentation, without thoughtful architecture, with "monster" classes, only once and never after modification) because of it is otherwise not economic, it seems to be side work, it disturbs delivery in time, and there is no urgent need in better ones. Modernisation and maintenance becomes then a real vexation.

We finally complete this paper with a citation to a Genicore poster presented at ER'2017: "Modelware is the new software", i.e. domain-situation models instead of models of software [54,55].

References

1. Adam, K., et al.: Model-based generation of enterprise information systems. EMISA Forum **38**(1), 56–60 (2018)
2. Aiso, H.: The fifth generation computer systems project. Future Gener. Comput. Syst. **4**(3), 159–175 (1988)
3. Aiso, H.: 25 years of MITI and its influence on computing research in Japan. IEEE Comput. **24**(9), 99–100 (1991)
4. Aiso, H.: Discussion on achievements, challenges, solutions, and problems of the 5th generation PL project, Nov. 13: Evening with B. Thalheim and colleagues from Keio University, Yokohama, Japan (2016)
5. AlBdaiwi, B., Noack, R., Thalheim, B.: Database structure modelling by stereotypes, pattern and templates. In: Proceedings of EJC 2014, KCSS, Kiel, Germany, vol. 2014/4, pp. 1–19, June 2014. Department of Computer Science, Faculty of Engineering
6. AlBdaiwi, B., Noack, R., Thalheim, B.: Pattern-based conceptual data modelling. In: Information Modelling and Knowledge Bases, Volume XXVI of Frontiers in Artificial Intelligence and Applications, vol. 272, pp. 1–20. IOS Press (2014)
7. Albrecht, M., Altus, M., Buchholz, E., Düsterhöft, A., Thalheim, B.: The rapid application and database development (RADD) workbench — a comfortable database design tool. In: Iivari, J., Lyytinen, K., Rossi, M. (eds.) CAiSE 1995. LNCS, vol. 932, pp. 327–340. Springer, Heidelberg (1995). https://doi.org/10.1007/3-540-59498-1_257

8. Baresi, L., Garzotto, F., Paolini, P.: Extending UML for modeling web applications. In: HICSS (2001)
9. Becker, J., Delfmann, P. (eds.): Reference Modeling: Efficient Information Systems Design Through Reuse of Information Models. Springer, Heidelberg (2007). https://doi.org/10.1007/978-3-7908-1966-3
10. Berztiss, A., Thalheim, B.: Exceptions in information systems. In: Digital Libaries: Advanced Methods and Technologies, RCDL 2007, pp. 284–295 (2007)
11. Bienemann, A., Schewe, K.-D., Thalheim, B.: Towards a theory of genericity based on government and binding. In: Embley, D.W., Olivé, A., Ram, S. (eds.) ER 2006. LNCS, vol. 4215, pp. 311–324. Springer, Heidelberg (2006). https://doi.org/10.1007/11901181_24
12. Börger, E.: A practice-oriented course on principles of computation. Programming and systems design and analysis. In: CoLogNet/Formal Methods Europe Symposium, TFM 2004, Gent (2004)
13. Börger, E., Raschke, A.: Modeling Companion for Software Practitioners. Springer, Heidelberg (2018). https://doi.org/10.1007/978-3-662-56641-1
14. Börger, E., Sörensen, O.: BPMN core modeling concepts: inheritance-based execution semantics. In: The Handbook of Conceptual Modeling: Its Usage and Its Challenges, Chapter 9, pp. 287–334. Springer, Heidelberg (2011). https://doi.org/10.1007/978-3-642-15865-0_9
15. Börger, E., Stärk, R.: Abstract State Machines - A Method for High-Level System Design and Analysis. Springer, Heidelberg (2003). https://doi.org/10.1007/978-3-642-18216-7
16. Börger, E., Thalheim, B.: A method for verifiable and validatable business process modeling. In: Börger, E., Cisternino, A. (eds.) Advances in Software Engineering. LNCS, vol. 5316, pp. 59–115. Springer, Heidelberg (2008). https://doi.org/10.1007/978-3-540-89762-0_3
17. Bormann, J., Lötzsch, J.: Definition und Realisierung von Fachsprachen mit DEPOT. Ph.D. thesis, Technische Universität Dresden, Sektion Mathematik (1974)
18. Brambilla, M., Comai, S., Fraternali, P., Matera, M.: Designing web applications with WebML and WebRatio, pp. 221–261 (2008)
19. Brassard, G., Bratley, P.: Algorithmics - Theory and Practice. Prentice Hall, London (1988)
20. Brenner, J.E.: The logical process of model-based reasoning. In: Magnani, L., Carnielli, W., Pizzi, C. (eds.) Model-Based Reasoning in Science and Technology, pp. 333–358. Springer, Heidelberg (2010). https://doi.org/10.1007/978-3-642-15223-8_19
21. Conallen, J.: Building Web Applications with UML. Addison-Wesley, Boston (2003)
22. Cox, M.T., Raja, A. (eds.): Metareasoning - Thinking About Thinking. MIT Press, Cambridge (2011)
23. Dahanayake, A.: An environment to support flexible information modelling. Ph.D. thesis, Delft University of Technology (1997)
24. Dahanayake, A., Thalheim, B.: Co-evolution of (information) system models. In: Bider, I., et al. (eds.) BPMDS/EMMSAD-2010. LNBIP, vol. 50, pp. 314–326. Springer, Heidelberg (2010). https://doi.org/10.1007/978-3-642-13051-9_26
25. Daly, T.: Axiom: the scientific computation system (2018). http://axiom-developer.org/axiom-website/
26. Denning, P.J.: Computer science: the discipline. In: Encyclopedia of Computer Science, vol. 32, no. 1, pp. 9–23 (2000)

27. Denning, P.J., Martell, C.H.: Great Principles of Computing. MIT Press, Cambridge (2015)
28. Deransart, P., Jourdan, M., Lorho, B.: Attribute Grammars. LNCS, vol. 323. Springer, Heidelberg (1988). https://doi.org/10.1007/BFb0030509
29. Draheim, D., Weber, G.: Form-Oriented Analysis. Springer, Heidelberg (2005). https://doi.org/10.1007/b138252
30. Eclipse project web site. http://www.eclipse.org
31. Edwards, M.: A brief history of holons (2003). Unpublished essay. http://www.integralworld.net/edwards13.html
32. Ehrig, H., Ermel, C., Golas, U., Hermann, F.: Graph and Model Transformation - General Framework and Applications. Monographs in Theoretical Computer Science. An EATCS Series. Springer, Heidelberg (2015). https://doi.org/10.1007/978-3-662-47980-3
33. Embley, D.W., Liddle, S.W., Pastor, O.: Conceptual-model programming: a Manifesto. In: Embley, D., Thalheim, B. (eds.) The Handbook of Conceptual Modeling: Its Usage and Its Challenges, Chapter 1, pp. 1–15. Springer, Heidelberg (2010). https://doi.org/10.1007/978-3-642-15865-0_1
34. Embley, D.W., Mok, W.Y.: Mapping conceptual models to database schemas. In: Embley, D., Thalheim, B. (eds.) The Handbook of Conceptual Modeling: Its Usage and Its Challenges, Chapter 5, pp. 123–164. Springer, Heidelberg (2010). https://doi.org/10.1007/978-3-642-15865-0_5
35. Ershov, A.P.: The transformational machine: theme and variations. In: Gruska, J., Chytil, M. (eds.) MFCS 1981. LNCS, vol. 118, pp. 16–32. Springer, Heidelberg (1981). https://doi.org/10.1007/3-540-10856-4_71
36. Feigenbaum, E.A., McCorduck, P.: The Fifth Generation - Artificial Intelligence and Japan's Computer Challenge to the World. Addison-Wesley, Boston (1983)
37. Fettke, P., Loos, P. (eds.): Reference Modeling for Business Systems Analysis. Hershey (2007)
38. Fiedler, G., Jaakkola, H., Mäkinen, T., Thalheim, B., Varkoi, T.: Application domain engineering for web information systems supported by SPICE. In: Proceedings of SPICE 2007, Seoul, Korea. IOS Press, May 2007
39. France, R.B., Ghosh, S., Dinh-Trong, T., Solberg, A.: Model-driven development using UML 2.0: promises and pitfalls. Computer 39(2), 59–66 (2006)
40. Frank, U.: Multilevel modeling - toward a new paradigm of conceptual modeling and information systems design. Bus. Inf. Syst. Eng. 6(6), 319–337 (2014)
41. Garzotto, F., Paolini, P., Schwabe, D.: HDM - a model-based approach to hypertext application design. ACM ToIS 11(1), 1–26 (1993)
42. Goldin, D., Srinivasa, S., Thalheim, B.: IS=DBS+Interaction: towards principles of information system design. In: Laender, A.H.F., Liddle, S.W., Storey, V.C. (eds.) ER 2000. LNCS, vol. 1920, pp. 140–153. Springer, Heidelberg (2000). https://doi.org/10.1007/3-540-45393-8_11
43. Grossmann, R., Hutschenreiter, J., Lampe, J., Lötzsch, J., Mager, K.DEPOT 2a Metasystem für die Analyse und Verarbeitung verbundener Fachsprachen. Technical Report 85, Studientexte des WBZ MKR/Informationsverarbeitung der TU Dresden, Dresden (1985)
44. Harel, D.: Algorithmics: The Spirit of Computing. Addison-Wesley, Reading (1987)
45. Harel, D., Marelly, R.: Come, Let's Play: Scenario-based Programming Using LSCs and the Play-Engine. Springer, Berlin (2003). https://doi.org/10.1007/978-3-642-19029-2

46. Hey, T., Tansley, S., Tolle, K. (eds.): The Fourth Paradigm: Data-Intensive Scientific Discovery. Microoft Research, Redmond (2009)
47. Hölldobler, K., Jansen, N., Rumpe, B., Wortmann, A.: Komposition Domänenspezifischer Sprachen unter Nutzung der MontiCore Language Workbench, am Beispiel SysML 2. In: Proceedings of Modellierung 2020, LNI, vol. P-302, pp. 189–190. Gesellschaft für Informatik e.V. (2020)
48. Houben, G.-J., et al.: HERA, pp. 263–301 (2008)
49. Hutschenreiter, J.: Zur Pragmatik von Fachsprachen. Ph.D. thesis, Technische Universität Dresden, Sektion Mathematik (1986)
50. Isakowitz, T., Stohr, E.A., Balasubramanian, P.: RMM: a methodology for structured hypermedia design. Commun. ACM **38**(8), 34–44 (1995)
51. Jaakkola, H., Mäkinen, T., Thalheim, B., Varkoi, T.: Evolving the database co-design framework by SPICE. In: Information Modelling and Knowledge Bases, Vol. XVII, Series Frontiers in Arificial Intelligence, vol. 136, pp. 268–279. IOS Press, May 2006
52. Jaakkola, H., Thalheim, B.: Visual SQL – high-quality ER-based query treatment. In: Jeusfeld, M.A., Pastor, Ó. (eds.) ER 2003. LNCS, vol. 2814, pp. 129–139. Springer, Heidelberg (2003). https://doi.org/10.1007/978-3-540-39597-3_13
53. Jaakkola, H., Thalheim, B.: Model-based fifth generation programming. In: Information Modelling and Knowledge Bases, Vol. XXXI, Frontiers in Artificial Intelligence and Applications, vol. 312, pp. 381–400. IOS Press (2020)
54. Jonsson, T., Enquist, H.: CoreEAF - a model driven approach to information systems. In: Proceedings of CAiSE 2015 Forum, CEUR Workshop Proceedings, vol. 1367, pp. 137–144 (2015)
55. Jonsson, T., Enquist, H.: Semantic consistency in enterprise models - through seamless modelling and execution support. In: Proceedings of ER Forum 2017 and ER 2017 Demo Track, CEUR Workshop Proceedings, vol. 1979, pp. 343–346. CEUR-WS.org (2017)
56. Kalliamvakou, E., Gousios, G., Blincoe, K., Singer, L., German, D.M., Damian, D.: The promises and perils of mining GitHub. In: Proceedings of the 11th Working Conference on Mining Software Repositories, pp. 92–101. ACM (2014)
57. Karagiannis, D., Mayr, H.C., Mylopoulos, J. (eds.): Domain-Specific Conceptual Modeling, Concepts, Methods and Tools. Springer, Cham (2016). https://doi.org/10.1007/978-3-319-39417-6
58. Kelly, S., Rossi, M., Tolvanen, J.-P.: What is needed in a metaCASE environment? Enterp. Model. Inf. Syst. Archit. **1**(1), 25–35 (2005)
59. Kelly, S., Smolander, K.: Evolution and issues in MetaCASE. Inf. Softw. Technol. **38**(4), 261–266 (1996)
60. Website Kieler. Kiel Integrated Environment for Layout Eclipse Rich Client (2018). https://www.rtsys.informatik.uni-kiel.de/en/research/kieler. Accessed 29 July 2018
61. Kiyoki, Y., Thalheim, B.: Analysis-driven data collection, integration and preparation for visualisation. In: Information Modelling and Knowledge Bases, vol. XXIV, pp. 142–160. IOS Press (2013)
62. Klettke, M., Thalheim, B.: Evolution and migration of information systems. In: Embley, D., Thalheim, B. (eds.) The Handbook of Conceptual Modeling: Its Usage and Its Challenges, Chapter 12, pp. 381–420. Springer, Heidelberg (2011). https://doi.org/10.1007/978-3-642-15865-0_12
63. Knuth, D.E.: The METAFONTbook. Addison-Wesley, Boston (1986)
64. Knuth, D.E.: Literate Programming. Number 27 in CSLI Lecture Notes. Center for the Study of Language and Information at Stanford, California (1992)

65. Koch, N., Knapp, A., Zhang, G., Baumeister, H.: UML-based web engineering, pp. 157–191 (2008)
66. Kolovos, D.S., García-Domínguez, A., Rose, L.M., Paige, R.F.: Eugenia: towards disciplined and automated development of GMF-based graphical model editors. Softw. Syst. Model. **16**(1), 229–255 (2017). https://doi.org/10.1007/s10270-015-0455-3DD
67. Kramer, F., Thalheim, B.: Holistic conceptual and logical database structure modeling with ADOxx. Domain-Specific Conceptual Modeling, pp. 269–290. Springer, Cham (2016). https://doi.org/10.1007/978-3-319-39417-6_12
68. Kramer, F.F.: Ein allgemeiner Ansatz zur Metadaten-Verwaltung. Ph.D. thesis, Christian-Albrechts University of Kiel, Technical Faculty, Kiel (2018)
69. Kropp, Y., Thalheim, B.: Model-based interface generation. In: Proceedings of 29th EJC, Lappeenranta, Finland, pp. 70–87. LUT, Finland (2019)
70. Lakoff, G.: Women, Fire, and Dangerous Things - What Categories Reveal About the Mind. The University of Chicago Press, Chicago (1987)
71. Lamport, L.: LaTeX: A Document Preparation System. Addison-Wesley, Boston (1994)
72. Lötzsch, J.: Metasprachlich gestützte Verarbeitung ebener Fachsprachen. Ph.D. thesis, Dresden University of Technology, Germany (1982)
73. Magnani, L., Carnielli, W., Pizzi, C. (eds.): Model-Based Reasoning in Science and Technology: Abduction, Logic, and Computational Discovery. Springer, Heidelberg (2010). https://doi.org/10.1007/978-3-642-15223-8
74. Mahr, B.: Information science and the logic of models. Softw. Syst. Model. **8**(3), 365–383 (2009)
75. Marco, D., Jennings, M.: Universal Meta Data Models. Wiley Publ. Inc., Hoboken (2004)
76. Mayr, H.C., Michael, J., Ranasinghe, S., Shekhovtsov, V.A., Steinberger, C.: Model centered architecture. Conceptual Modeling Perspectives, pp. 85–104. Springer, Cham (2017). https://doi.org/10.1007/978-3-319-67271-7_7
77. Meliá, S., Gómez, J.: The WebSA approach: applying model driven engineering to web applications. J. Web Eng. **5**(2), 121–149 (2006)
78. Molnár, A.J., Thalheim, B.: Usage models mapped to programs. In: Welzer, T., et al. (eds.) ADBIS 2019. CCIS, vol. 1064, pp. 163–175. Springer, Cham (2019). https://doi.org/10.1007/978-3-030-30278-8_20
79. Moto-oka, T. (ed.): Fifth Generation Computer Systems. North-Holland, Amsterdam (1982)
80. Muller, P.-A., Studer, P., Fondement, F., Bézivin, J.: Platform independent web application modeling and development with Netsilon. Softw. Syst. Model. **4**(4), 424–442 (2005)
81. Nersessian, N.J.: Creating Scientific Concepts. MIT Press (2008)
82. Noack, K.: Technologische und methodische Grundlagen von SCOPELAND. White paper (2009). http://www.copeland.de
83. Page, S.E.: The Model Thinker - Waht You Need to Know to Make Data Work for You. Basic Books, New York (2018)
84. Pastor, O., Abrahao, S., Fons, J.: An object-oriented approach to automate web applications development. In: Bauknecht, K., Madria, S.K., Pernul, G. (eds.) EC-Web 2001. LNCS, vol. 2115, pp. 16–28. Springer, Heidelberg (2001). https://doi.org/10.1007/3-540-44700-8_2
85. Pastor, O., Molina, J.C.: Model-Driven Architecture in Practice - A Software Production Environment Based on Conceptual Modeling. Springer, Heidelberg (2007). https://doi.org/10.1007/978-3-540-71868-0

86. Pittman, T., Peters, J.: The Art of Compiler Design: Theory and Practice. Prentice Hall, Upper Saddle River (1992)
87. Podkolsin, A.S.: Computer-based modelling of solution processes for mathematical tasks. ZPI at Mech-Mat MGU, Moscow (2001). (in Russian)
88. Website PtolemyII. Ptolemy project: heterogeneous modelling and design (2018). http://ptolemy.berkeley.edu/ptolemyII/. Accessed 29 July 2018
89. Di Ruscio, D., Muccini, H., Pierantonio, A.: A data-modelling approach to web application synthesis. Int. J. Web Eng. Technol. 1(3), 320–337 (2004)
90. Samuel, A., Weir, J.: Introduction to Engineering: Modelling, Synthesis and Problem Solving Strategies. Elsevier, Amsterdam (2000)
91. Schewe, K.-D., Thalheim, B.: Co-design of web information systems. In: Texts & Monographs in Symbolic Computation, pp. 293–332. Springer, Vienna (2015)
92. Schewe, K.-D., Thalheim, B.: Design and Development of Web Information Systems. Springer, Heidelberg (2019). https://doi.org/10.1007/978-3-662-58824-610. 1007/978-3-662-58824-6
93. Schmidt, J.W., Matthes, F.: The DBPL project: advances in modular database programming. Inf. Syst. 19(2), 121–140 (1994)
94. Schwabe, D., Rossi, G.: The object-oriented hypermedia design model. Commun. ACM 38(8), 45–46 (1995)
95. Shasha, D.E., Bonnet, P.: Database Tuning - Principles, Experiments, and Troubleshooting Techniques. Elsevier, Amsterdam (2002)
96. Silverston, L.: The Data Model Resource Book, vol. 2, Revised edn. Wiley, Hoboken (2001)
97. Steeg, M.: RADD/raddstar - a rule-based database schema compiler, evaluator, and optimizer. Ph.D. thesis, BTU Cottbus, Computer Science Institute, Cottbus, October 2000
98. Taft, S.T., Duff, R.A., Brukardt, R.L., Ploedereder, E., Leroy, P., Schonberg, E. (eds.): Ada 2012 Reference Manual. Language and Standard Libraries. LNCS, vol. 8339. Springer, Heidelberg (2013). https://doi.org/10.1007/978-3-642-45419-6
99. Thalheim, B.: Entity-Relationship Modeling - Foundations of Database Technology. Springer, Heidelberg (2000). https://doi.org/10.1007/978-3-662-04058-4
100. Thalheim, B.: Codesign of structuring, functionality, distribution and interactivity. Aust. Comput. Sci. Commun. 31(6), 3–12 (2004). Proc. APCCM'2004
101. Thalheim, B.: The theory of conceptual models, the theory of conceptual modelling and foundations of conceptual modelling. In: Embley, D., Thalheim, B. (eds.) The Handbook of Conceptual Modeling: Its Usage and Its Challenges, Chapter 17, pp. 547–580. Springer, Heidelberg (2011). https://doi.org/10.1007/ 978-3-642-15865-0_17
102. Thalheim, B., Dahanayake, A.: Comprehending a service by informative models. Trans. Large Scale Data Knowl. Centered Syst. 30, 87–108 (2016)
103. Thalheim, B., Nissen, I. (eds.): Wissenschaft und Kunst der Modellierung: Modelle, Modellieren. Modellierung. De Gruyter, Boston (2015)
104. Thalheim, B., Sotnikov, A., Fiodorov, I.: Models: the main tool of true fifth generation programming. In: Proceedings of EEKM 2019 - Enterprise Engineering and Knowledge Management, Moscow, CEUR Workshop Proceedings, vol. 2413, pp. 161–170 (2019)
105. Thalheim, B., Tropmann-Frick, M.: Model capsules for research and engineering networks. In: Ivanović, M., et al. (eds.) ADBIS 2016. CCIS, vol. 637, pp. 202–214. Springer, Cham (2016). https://doi.org/10.1007/978-3-319-44066-8_21

106. Thalheim, B., Tropmann-Frick, M., Ziebermayr, T.: Application of generic work-flows for disaster management. In: Information Modelling and Knowledge Bases, volume XXV of Frontiers in Artificial Intelligence and Applications, vol. 260, pp. 64–81. IOS Press (2014)

107. Torge, S., Esswein, W., Lehrmann, S., Thalheim, B.: Categories for description of reference models. In: Information Modelling and Knowledge Bases, volume XXV of Frontiers in Artificial Intelligence and Applications, vol. 260, pp. 229–240. IOS Press (2014)

108. Tropmann, M., Thalheim, B., Korff, R.: Performance forecasting. 21. In: GI-Workshop on Foundations of Databases (Grundlagen von Datenbanken), pp. 9–13 (2009)

109. Tropmann-Frick, M.: Genericity in process-aware information systems. Ph.D. thesis, Christian-Albrechts University of Kiel, Technical Faculty, Kiel (2016)

110. De Troyer, O., Casteleyn, S., Plessers, P.: WSDM: web semantics design method, pp. 303–351 (2008)

111. Ueda, K.: Logic/constraint programming and concurrency: the hard-won lessons of the fifth generation computer project. Sci. Comput. Program. **164**, 3–17 (2018)

112. van de Riet, R.P.: An overview and appraisal of the fifth generation computer system project. Future Gener. Comput. Syst. **9**(2), 83–103 (1993)

113. Vela, B., Acuña, C.J., Marcos, E.: A model driven approach to XML database development. In: Proceedings of the 23rd International Conference on Conceptual Modeling (ER2004), Shanghai, China, pp. 273–285, November 2004

114. Webster, B.F.: Pitfalls of Object-Oriented Development: A Guide for the Wary and Entusiastic. M&T Books, New York (1995)

115. Wegner, P., Goldin, D.Q.: Computation beyond Turing machines. Commun. ACM **46**(4), 100–102 (2003)

116. Wilhelm, R., Seidl, H., Hack, S.: Compiler Design - Syntactic and Semantic Analysis. Springer, Heidelberg (2013). https://doi.org/10.1007/978-3-642-17540-4

117. Xu, L., Embley, D.W.: Combining the best of global-as-view and local-as-view for data integration. In: Proceedings of ISTA 2004, LNI, vol. P-48, pp. 123–136. GI (2004)

Research Papers

How to Catch a Moonbeam: From Model-Ware to Component-Ware Software Product Engineering

Ajantha Dahanayake(✉)

Lappeenranta-Lahti University of Technology, Lappeenranta, Finland
`Ajantha.Dahanayake@LUT.fi`

Abstract. Models are an integral part of software systems Engineering (SSE). In SSE, modeling is the activity of creating the artifact – the model. Models are created according to the method of the modeling approach. An SSE endeavor comprises multiple modeling techniques for supporting multiple models. The recent scientific literature exhibits a plethora of sophisticatedly articulated philosophies, principles, definitions, and theories for models and modeling. There is a gap in linking the model to software systems generation by-passing the programming allowing unskilled programmers to develop software products. Such an endeavor requires organizing the software systems engineering as the engineering activities of the development of model-ware and software product generation through off-the-shelf component-ware. It also requires to engineer systems engineering methodology flexible and adapting to the community that practices software product development.

This research presents the theory behind the computer-aided method engineering (CAME) approach that pioneered the engineering of models to generate component-based CASE (computer-aided software engineering) tools which are software products, by by-passing the programing or code generation. Paving way for unskilled programmers to design and develop software products. It enumerates the achievements of CAME and layout future directions for truly achieving model-ware to component-ware software plug and play product engineering as the potential technology for software systems engineering.

Keywords: Conceptual modeling · Method engineering · Component-based · Plug and play software product development · CAME · Model-ware · Component-ware

1 Introduction

A paradigm shift in software systems development is anticipated for some time. As such the software systems are developed from craft-based structures where user requirements are specified in models for custom solutions development, to a market-generated product-based approach. It is expected for some time that the users themselves will be able to select and arrange meaningful-to-them components as solutions to their requirements [1].

© Springer Nature Switzerland AG 2021
A. Dahanayake et al. (Eds.): M2P 2020, CCIS 1401, pp. 47–66, 2021.
https://doi.org/10.1007/978-3-030-72696-6_2

The emergence of such a disruption to present-day systems and software development needs to solve several underlying issues in the software system engineering methodology which is expensive, time-consuming, myopic, inflexible, and its software production technology making the shift towards componentized software product development.

Historically, humans have come to appreciate that a well-structured and well-planned approach leads to the successful completion of any complex task [2]. It is not a secret that software systems engineering (SSE) endeavors always follow an approach. This approach is called the SSE methodology. The methodology brings in the structure, planning, phases, controls, and built-in quality management to the engineering process to produce quality software systems. To handle the complexities of software engineering the process is branched into the systems engineering and software engineering sectors forming the main SSE communities, the soft and hard practices. Over time the soft and hard divider in the methodology followed suit with the division of systems engineering comprise of planning to systems design with the possible end product as the blue-print of the software system and software engineering comprise of programming and the realization of the software product.

At the same time, the methodology also evolved from structured databased oriented (Yourdon, Information Engineering), object and process-oriented (Rational Unified Method), to Agile, Extreme, Scrum, Rapid Application Development, Lean Development, Web-Based Systems Development, to Mobile App Development. Software systems and Applications domain evolved from business and industrial information systems, embedded systems, to applications of healthcare, medical, scientific, social media, e-commerce, citizens science, data science, big data, business intelligence, and many more. But still, software product development is treated separately from designing and modeling.

From an engineering perspective to reach the transition from models to componentized custom solutions development, to a market-generated, product-based approach in which users themselves select and arrange components, a radical change to the software systems engineering methodology must be perceived by:

- Modeling adapted to the community of practice and according to the adapted methodology.
- Plug and play components developed to generate software products according to models designed by the practicing community, the users, and unskilled programmers.

This paper enumerates the empirical evidence of how the above changes are achieved. First, the SSE methodology is introduced and its shortcomings and mismatch to fulfill the needs of a model-ware to component-ware transition are discussed followed by how models can be developed according to the method engineering concept to arrive at the SSE methodology of the practicing community. The CASE tool generation from the models of the modeling techniques and the plug-and-play component-based development is discussed showing how software products are generated without any programming or coding. Thus, supporting unskilled programmers to develop software products. Finally, future research directions of paving the way for unskilled programmers to design and develop plug-and-play software products are laid out for achieving model-ware to component-ware software product engineering transition as the potential future of software systems engineering.

2   Software Systems Engineering Methodology

SSE Methodology bundles the systems engineering and software engineering process management with a set of software systems design and development tools for engineering software products. The methodology as a total package must support both soft and hard SSE tasks and scenarios. The division of soft systems engineering and hard software engineering also shrouds the methodology [2]. The methodology adopted for the realization of software systems is dependent on the community at practice [2]. Figure 1 illustrates the dynamics between the software development community, the methodology, and the software product development.

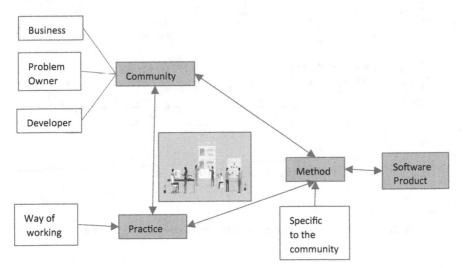

Fig. 1. The relationship between the software development community, practice and the methodology

The quality of the software system depends on the SSE methodology [2]. The SSE methodology builds quality assurance into the systems engineering process by integrating a set of modeling tools for multiple modeling scenarios at different phases of the SSE life cycle. The quality cannot be guaranteed at the point of the software quality testing phase. Adequate quality must be built into the SSE tools used for modeling and programming. Therefore, quality assurance is introduced at the early stages of the systems engineering process by integrating a set of modeling tools at different phases of the SSE life cycle during multiple modeling scenarios of Communication, Negotiation, Conceptualization, Description, Prescription, to Realization.

The systems development culture of the SSE community influences the models developed, the set of tools employed for modeling at different phases and life cycle scenarios, and the way of working and thinking of the methodology followed during software product development. Therefore, the methodology is represented as in Fig. 2 providing the required flexibility for the SSE community.

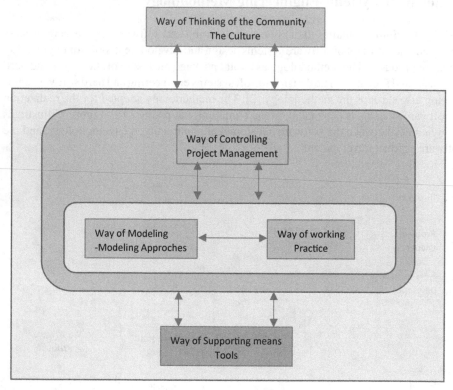

Fig. 2. SSE methodology framework adaptable to the community of practice

2.1 SSE Models and Modeling

SSE methodology is anchored in the two-stage balancing act of the soft and hard SSE practices of systems engineering and software engineering. From the SSE lifecycle point of view planning, analysis, and design phases belong to systems engineering while software product development activities of systems programming, testing, and production phases belong to software engineering.

The soft systems engineering stage is notoriously overloaded with creativity, intuition, and pragmatics supported by tools for modeling and model creations. Those model creation and use are dependent on the SSE methodology at the use and practicing community. Typically, modeling fulfills scenarios for model creation and the models fulfill functions specific to some context in the SSE life cycle. To complete the activity of modeling, modeling tools are engaged as instruments to create models that are adequate for that task at hand. Table 1 below gives an overview of this interpretation mapped into the usefulness, usability, and usage of models and modeling activities.

Table 1. Dependency of the engineering scenarios and their usefulness, usability, and usage.

Usefulness		Modeling Scenarios	Usability	Usage
The dependency of The Engineering domain	Practicing Community	Modeling Scenarios	Model's Context	Adequacy of modeling to complete activity: Tools/ instruments
SSE Methodology	Systems Engineering	Communication Negotiation	Planning	MS-Project Flow charts
			Analysis	Mind Map Ontology
		Conceptualization	Analysis	ERD, OM, BPM UML techniques Logical models Storyboarding
				Blueprints
		Description	Design	
	Software Engineering	Prescription	Generation	Database schema Relational tables Web components Software components Software/Object libraries Component hierarchies
		Realization	Production	Front End -Web sites/Pages
			Testing	-Web interfaces Back End
			Integration	-Databases -Software applications Middleware
			Migration	
			Maintenance	

- **Usefulness** is the quality of being useful models and modeling. The **usefulness** of a model is dependent on the practice of the community and the discipline or domain it is applied.
- **Usability** is the degree to which a model is able or fit to use. The **usability** of a model is specific to the modeling scenario and the context a model belongs to.
- **Usage** is the action of using a model or the fact of the model being used. The model is a product of the modeling activity supported by an instrument/tool that adequately defines its **usage**.

In software systems, engineering modeling is the activity that defines the Usage of models that are Useful, and Usable for engineering software systems for the practicing community and the engineering methodology [3].

2.2 SSE Models

The definition of a model then follows the formulation of [4].

- **A model** is a well-formed, adequate, pragmatic, and dependable artifact that represents origins and functions in the utilized scenario.
- **A model is characterized by** the model's adequacy, well-formedness, pragmatics, and dependability on the context and community it is using, as well as its function within the utilization scenario.
- **As an artifact,** the model is grounded in the community's methodology and is based on elements chosen from the practice.
- **The quality of the software system** depends on the quality of the models designed within the engineering methodology.

   A model is a **conceptual model** when it represents concepts relevant to the context within a utilization scenario [4]. **SSE models are conceptual models** and represent concepts relevant to the context within an application scenario.

2.3 Modeling Language

A **modeling language** consists of a basic set of concepts, constraints, and associated graphical representations of those concepts and constraints, and a set of basic operations for modeling and it is the method of the modeling tool [5] (Fig. 3). Some popular examples of modeling languages are Entity Relationship Diagram (ERD), Unified Modeling Language (UML), Predicator Set Model (PSM), and Higher-order Entity-Relationship Modeling (HREM).

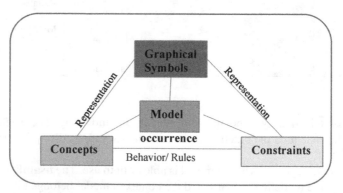

Fig. 3. The representation of modeling primitives

Modeling is the creative activity of using a modeling tool to create models according to the language of the modeling technique.

Modeling is always according to the underline modeling language of the CASE tools (computer-aided systems engineering tools).

- Examples of popular modeling languages: Entity Relationship Diagram (ERD), Unified Modeling Language (UML), Predicator Set Model (PSM), Higher-order Entity-Relationship Modeling (HREM).

CASE tools are computer-aided modeling tools, which are also software products for modeling **systems engineering** scenarios and are dependent on the modeling language.

Therefore, a **modeling language** can be described as an adequate set of modeling primitives consisting of:

- A set of concepts
- A set of constraints
- Associated graphical symbols of those concepts and constrains
- A set of basic operation for modeling

3 Models to Components Realization

3.1 Model-Ware and Component-Ware

Systems engineering communities use multiple modeling languages to design models during an SSE endeavor. They tend to choose modeling languages according to the function, context, scenario, and pragmatics of the methodology. A modeling tool's usage is defined with concepts logical to the interpretation of the specific way of thinking and way of modeling of the modeling language to fulfill a specific purpose in a given scenario. Some common examples where modeling takes place during systems engineering are brainstorming with MindMaps tool, project management with MSProject tool, data modeling with ERD tool, or Object-Relation-Modeling.

Modeling and modeling tools have never been popular among the hard-core software engineering community. CASE tools are heavily marginalized as drawing tools with the attitude of 'why bother'. Even after five decades of education, training, and research, the full potential of modeling and conceptual modeling is under-utilized in the software engineering community.

There are some valid reasons for this situation, in summary, those are such as:
- The lack of flexibility and tailor-ability to configure and streamline the models and modeling languages according to the practicing SSE methodology.
- SSE communities are notorious to follow their methodology.
- Pragmatism is part of the engineering disciplines and the approach for software systems engineering and the methodology, in general, is a mix and match modeling languages for the function and task of the software systems realization.
- The changing landscape of technology and applications needing agility in systems development methodology.

- Evolution of Technology: cloud, web-based, web services, middleware, Analytics, to name a few.
- The arrival of new applications areas: social media, Big data, marketing, AR, VR, crowdsourcing to name a few.
- Confusion and objectives of integration within modeling techniques not seriously addressed.

  - Integration issues are overlooked from modeling to application generation.
  - The integration of knowledge from one language to another is generally cumbersome and on average integration is conducted at an intuitive level to arrive at the description of a target model and eventual manual translation to the functional model(s).

- Highly competitive software product industry and time to market pressures
- SSE has yet to reach the level of engineering maturity. The culture of the SSE is hard to comprehend, and SSE education is artisan's education
- Programming often performed by non-professionals

  - Casual users, non-specialists, and self-made programmers.
  - Apps and mobile facilities worse this situation.

- Usability has become the main concern for software product acceptance but not the main concern for programmers.

  - Operator and administrator thinking - is still the common understanding.

- Migration, integration, maintenance is still a real nightmare

  - The half-life time of systems and software is far lower than the lifespan of software deployment. New systems use new paradigms without downgrading features.

- Documentation is luxury

  - Documentations are often generated from code without consistent development documentation, without thoughtful architecture, with "monster" classes, only once and never after modification because otherwise, it is not economical, it seems to be side work, it disturbs delivery in time, and there is no urgent need to do better.

  The SSE methodology and practices have failed to some extent to justify the usefulness of models and modeling to the software engineering community. The recent scientific literature exhibits a plethora of sophisticatedly articulated philosophies, principles, definitions, and theories for models and modeling. Pragmatic engineering justification of models and modeling to be useful for software engineering is not discussed in the literature. A pragmatic engineering endeavor requires rethinking software product development.

From a pragmatic engineering perspective, it is possible to consider systems engineering as building descriptions of models that can be called **model-ware,** the blueprint, or architecture. Then the prescription of those models is made up of constructions known as programming or coding to product realization packaged as **component-based** software products. This way of thinking transforms modeling and programming into **model-ware and component-ware**. Models are developed as model-ware and components are selected and plugged into generating software product realization. Component-ware is the industry behind programming and coding to develop packages of off-the-shelf components (Fig. 4).

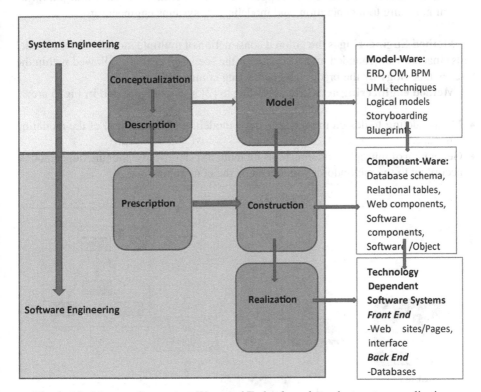

Fig. 4. Model-ware, Component-Ware, and Technology dependent systems realization

3.2 Flexible and Adaptable Models

The changing landscape of technology and applications demands adapting to tailorable and agile SSE methodology requiring time to market software products engineering i.e.:

- Tailor ability of methodology according to the software system being engineered
- Generation of multiple modeling tools according to the usage of the practicing community and useful according to the SSE methodology at the use

- Extending modeling of models and blueprints to the generation of software systems from models

For the above-mentioned purpose, the **Method Engineering** is coined in [6] and used in several types of research that contributed to several milestones [7]:

- The transition of CASE tools to the Meta CASE tool development.
- The engineering of multiple modeling tools to tailor the multi-model modeling support for systems engineering.
- Computer-aided environment to support design, generation of multi-tool platforms from modeling tool generation, and modeling for systems engineering.

Method Engineering is the tailored construction of multiple modeling tools (model suits) that are well-founded and adequate for the scenarios that are followed within the SSE methodology by the practicing engineering community.

Method engineering activities according to [2] **and as illustrated in** Fig. 5 are:

- Metamodeling to design the meta-model – modeling of the method of the modeling language.
- Generation of multiple modeling tools for modeling descriptive and functional models according to the methodology practiced by the community.

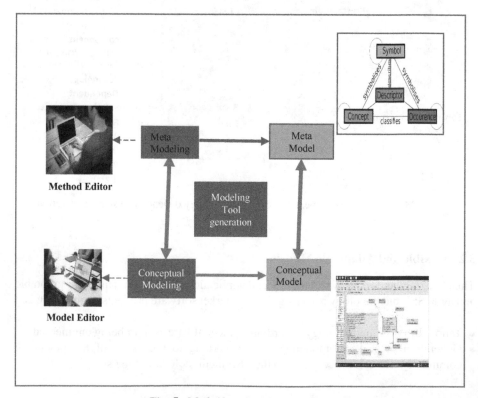

Fig. 5. Method engineering activities

Therefore, a **modeling tool** consists of

- A set of concepts,
- A set of constraints,
- Associated graphical symbols of those concepts and constrains
- A set of basic operations to facilitate the activity of modeling

In this respect, **Metamodeling** is also a form of modeling specifically engaged for modeling the modeling method of the modeling language.

To engage in Metamodeling a modeling language is required. Such a modeling language is called a Metamodeling language. **Metamodeling language** is a modeling language and it functions as a modeling foundation for metamodeling and conceptual modeling.

3.3 Separation of Concepts from Graphical Symbols

Metamodeling language to perform method engineering successfully, the modeling concepts require to be separated from their graphical symbols (Fig. 5). Then the same concepts at the metamodeling language level can represent different modeling techniques with different graphical representations (Fig. 6).

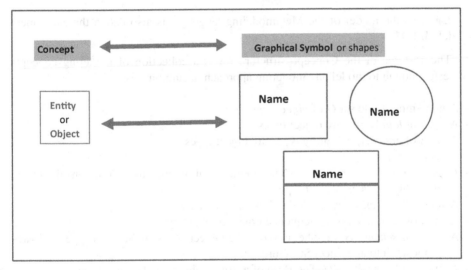

Fig. 6. Separation of concepts from their graphical symbols

3.4 Meta Modeling Language

A **Metamodeling language** is a modeling language and it functions as a modeling foundation for metamodeling and conceptual modeling and it is required to have the following characteristics [2]:

- Sufficient expressive power
- Formal foundation
- High level of conceptuality
- Adequately comprehensible
- Produce executable models

In this research, the Metamodeling language used is PSM (Predicator Set Modeling) language [8].

The Meta modeling language (L) is represented by a quadruple $\{CS, MC, GR, AO\}$ where

- CS is a 15-tuple Concept Structure,
- MC is a set of Modeling constraints,
- GR is a set of Graphical representations, and
- AO is a set of Atomic operations

L is also the model of the Metamodeling language, is also called the Meta-meta model (**MMM**).

The 15-tuple of the Concept Structure CS is a collection of modeling concepts powerful enough to model any modeling approach in summary is

- A non-empty finite set O of *object types*
- A set L of *label types* are object types
- A set E of *entity types*. Entity types are object types
- A set P of *roles*
- A *patriation F* of the set P. The elements of F are called relationship types. Relationship types are object types
- A set G of *collection types*. Collection types are object types
- A set A of *sequence types*. Sequence types are object types
- A set C of *schema types*. Shema types are Object types. A Schema type is always decomposed into an Object Structure
- A function Base : $P \rightarrow O$. The Base of a Role in the related Object type
- A function Elt: $G \cup S \rightarrow O/L$. This function yields the elements of collection types and sequence types
- A relation Schema $\subseteq C \times O$. This relation describes the elements in schema type
- Relation Spec $\subseteq E \times (O/L)$ on Object types expressing specialization
- Relation Gen $\subseteq E \times (O/L)$ on Object types expressing a generalization
- A many-sorted algebra $D = <D, F>$ where D is a set of concrete domains used to instantiate label types
- A function *Dom*: $L \rightarrow D$. This function yields the domain of the label types

The meta-model ML of a modeling language ML_i is the sextuple $\{CS_i, MC_i, GR_i, AO, Adeq_i, Dpd_{ij}\}$ where

- CS_i is the specific set of concepts of the modeling language ML_i
- MC_i is the specific set of modeling constraints of the modeling language ML_i
- GR_i is the specific set of graphical representations of the modeling language ML_i
- $Adeq_i$ is the acceptance of the adequacy of the modeling language ML_i for the scenario i by the SSE community U_i
- Dpd_{ij} is the dependence of the modeling language ML_i on the context j and scenario i
- AO is the set of atomic operations specific to modeling and model creation

Then the Meta model of the modeling language ML_i is a restricted population of Metamodeling language L.

- **Metamodeling** is the modeling activity that creates a Meta model ML from the concepts of the Metamodeling language L.
- Modeling with the use of a modeling tool is the creation of a Model (e.g. ERD model) during systems engineering within the practicing SSE methodology. This modeling is *conceptual modeling* and the modeling we are familiar with because;

A **Conceptual model** (CM_i) is a population of the metamodel (ML_i) which is a restricted population of L. The conceptual Model (CM_i) has the graphical representations GR_i of the modeling language ML_i (e.g. ERD model). The meta-model (ML_i) is the method of the modeling tool MT_i.

A **Metamodel** is a functional representation of how a modeling language's concepts and constraints behave as a modeling method. It describes the rules and the dynamics of modeling and justifies the adequacy, well-formedness, and dependence of the modeling language within the SSE methodology practiced by the community. The graphical representation of the meta-model (ML_i) is from the metamodeling language L. In this research, the Predicator Set Modeling (PSM) language is the L. Whereas the modeling tool MT_i's graphical representation GR_i is specific to the modeling tool MT_i.

For example, the meta-model (ML_{ERD}) of the Entity-Relationship Diagram (ERD) modeling tool MT_{ERD} is the description of the ERD modeling method represented with the graphical representations of PSM. The ERD modeling language ML_{ERD} uses the graphical representation (GR_{ERD}) particular to the ERD modeling tool. The conceptual model (CM_{ERD}) designed by the ERD modeling tool MT_{ERD} is an Entity-Relationship Model. This description and explanation are illustrated in Fig. 7.

3.5 Concepts to Graphical Symbols Coupling

The **Meta Model** (MM) of the modeling language L_i is a restricted population of Metamodeling language L. A modeling tool (T)'s modeling language is L_T *Where* GS_T *is the graphical symbols of tool* (T) - is a restricted population of graphic symbols of GS. **The graphical symbols of tool** (T) - is a restricted population of graphic symbols of GS. This generalization leads to the abstract representation and the relationship between PSM graphical symbols and conceptual modeling tools such as UML is illustrated in Fig. 7.

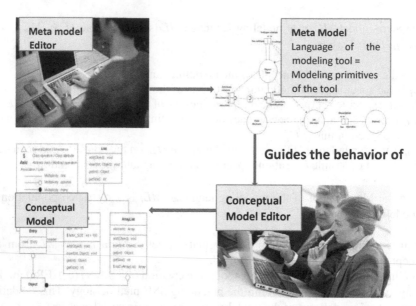

Fig. 7. Method Engineering, Meta Modeling, and Conceptual Modeling

4   Engineering Plug and Play Software Products

This section introduces how CASE tools are generated as plug-and-play software products. Such a CASE tool development environment is called a CAME (Computer-Aided Method Engineering) environment [2]. It allows systems engineers to design models of CASE tools and generate CASE tools by coupling components of graphical objects at run time. The design of the CASE tool's model is called metamodeling. Metamodels are designed using the PSM modeling techniques as explained in the earlier section. In Fig. 7 the meta-model editor is used to design the model of the Data Flow Diagram's (DFD) model in PSM, and later couples the graphical objects to DFD concepts to generate the DFD tool. Figure 8 illustrates how model-ware and the component-ware are orchestrated to generate a CASE tool. Figure 11 is a screenshot of this implementation.

In this case, model-ware are meta-models of the modeling tools and component-ware are the plug-and-play graphical objects. The details of this theory is available in [2, 9]. The generation of modeling tool editor by one click and supported by

- Plug and play software product (CASE-tool) generation (Fig. 9)
- Multiple tool generation supporting vertical and horizontal integration of concepts at meta-model level
- No coding at all as illustrated in Fig. 9
- Separation of concept from its graphic symbol and runtime coupling of graphical components (Fig. 8).
- Componentized implementation of CAME environment (Fig. 10)

This CAME environment has been implemented from an engineering perspective to reach the transition from models to componentized custom solutions development, a

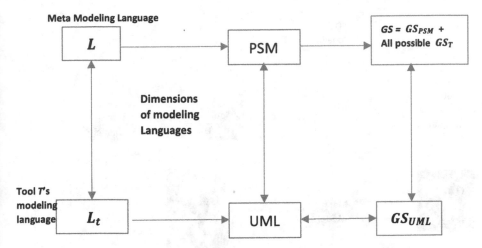

Fig. 8. Graphical symbols coupling to meta-model of UML

product-based approach in which users themselves can select and arrange components to generate CASE tools according to the methodology of the practicing community. It demonstrates how plug-and-play components are developed to generate the software product in this case the CASE tools according to models designed by the practicing community, the users, and unskilled programmers. As concluding remarks of this remarkable approach [2] can be summarized as follows:

- Tailor-ability for supporting modeling tools according to the practice of the SSE community
- From Model to Application generation of CASE tools without Programing
- Separation of Concept from Graphical symbol
- Seamless Multi-tool and multi-model support (or model suites) with vertical and horizontal model suite integration
- Tested and validated for Single and multiple method support (Yourdon, UML, DEMO) and large industrial production tool support
- Component-based implementation and architecture
- fully integrated modeling toolset support (model suites)
- Revolutionized the modeling tool building and generation with **the theory** that is pragmatic and from an engineering perspective

4.1 About MetaCASE

The tools that are generated based on a metamodeling language are known as MetaCASE tools. Also sometimes called modeling language workbenches or studios [3].

    MetaCASE tools **do not support integrated multiple modeling tools** (model Suits) in general. Tool generation is not provided to the customer. A customer buys a set of already configured tools. They are not of a componentized architecture or support plug and play tool development.

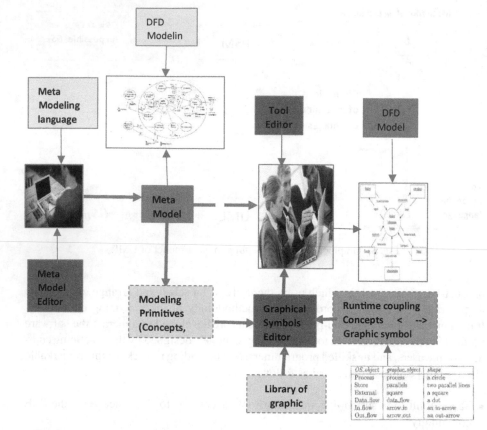

Fig. 9. Model-Ware construction and Component-Ware coupling to generate a CASE tool

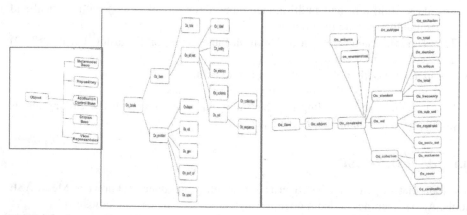

Fig. 10. Implementation of CAME as component libraries to accommodate plug and play product development

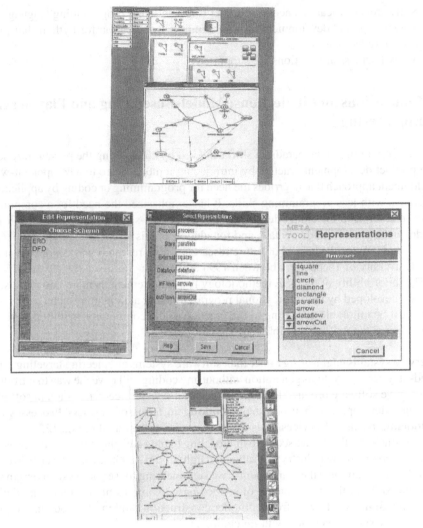

Fig. 11. Screenshot from the CAME environment on metamodeling of a DFD Technique and the plug and play generation of DFD editor

Commercially available typical **MetaCASE** products are:

- DOME, GME, MetaDONE, Obeo Designer, Whole Platform, ConceptBase
- **Visio** is a more sophisticated modeling tool suite that is also a MetaCASE
- Formally of Rational Rose and later acquired by Microsoft **Oracle DB products** is also supported by MetaCASE and accompanied by

  - Full package of development tools
  - **Uses the compiler approach,** not drag-drop application generation
  - Databases (multiple types)

- Software specifications need to be later tweaked to the programming languages
- Supports partial development of programming specification for Python, Java, and few more languages
- Many business applications are supported

5 Conclusions and Reflections: Model-Based Plug and Play Service Engineering

This research outlined the paradigm shift achieved by challenging the present-day software product development practice by introducing a model-ware to a component-ware development approach that overrides the need for programming or coding by application developers with less programming skills. It has emphasized the need for a component library marketplace for model developers to buy off-the-shelf component-ware. It has laid down the theory, fundamentals, and foundation of this scientific work in detail (see also [2] and [9]) for the benefit of future researches. The research was conducted at the Delft University of Technology between 1994 and 1997.

The tailor-ability of the SSE methodology is a requirement as more and more software are developed by non-professional programmers. In anticipating such future modeling must be tailorable according to the practice of the community. Within this vision following are some of the possible future directions:

- Service systems engineering rather than software systems engineering targeting plug-and-play service systems generation without any coding will pave the way to introduce disruptive software product development technology. Service-orientation in software product development then becomes **Thinking** in terms of business **Processes** and **Modeling** business **Services.** This future scenario is illustrated in Fig. 12.
- To truly achieve this future scenario of modeling to plug and play component coupling, the component-ware industry that saw some light in early 2000 must be re-energized. It needs to revolutionize the component-based engineering for service systems engineering investing in the development of service-based component catalogs. Stimulating the **Paradigm Shift** away from compiler construction thinking to modeling to plug and play service generation with **no coding** at all.
- Re-think modeling to accommodate modeling to plug and play service software product development with new types of modeling approaches to capture model-component-service modeling with

  - Pragmatic, engineering perspective, Intuitive and small-scale modeling
  - Bottom-up approach: final service/product as the starting point for guiding modeling
  - Adapting to application domains (e.g. Mobile Apps, business services, etc.,) and according to the methodology employed by the product development community (e.g., Agile modeling, Extreme modeling, etc.)

- Re-think service engineering by considering model-based service systems engineering by directing research initiatives for arriving at:

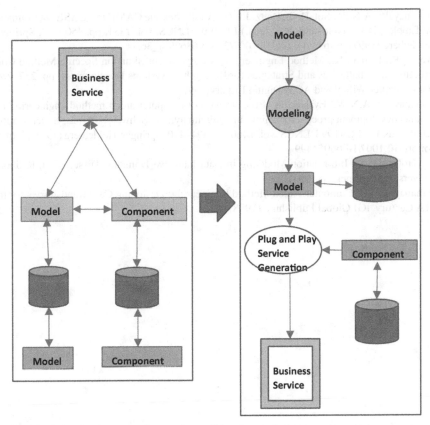

Fig. 12. Modeling business services and coupling plug-and-play components to promote users or non-professional programmers to develop software products

- New modeling techniques for model-component-service modeling
- New tools
- New development environments

References

1. Welke R. (1994) Shifting Software Development Paradigm. In: DATABASE, vol 25, no 4, pp 9–16
2. Dahanayake, A.: CAME: An Environment to Support Flexible Information Modeling. The dissertation Delft University of Technology (1997)
3. Keen, P., Sol, H.: Decision Enhancement Services: Rehearsing the Future for the Decisions that Matter. IOS Press, Amsterdam (2008)
4. Thalheim, B.: Conceptual Models and Their Foundations. In: Schewe, K.-D., Singh, N.K. (eds.) MEDI 2019. LNCS, vol. 11815, pp. 123–139. Springer, Cham (2019). https://doi.org/10.1007/978-3-030-32065-2_9

5. Dahanayake, A.N.W., Sol, H.G., Dietz, J.L.G.: A fully flexible CAME in a CASE environment. In: Embley, D.W., Goldstein, R.C. (eds.) ER 1997. LNCS, vol. 1331, pp. 450–463. Springer, Heidelberg (1997). https://doi.org/10.1007/3-540-63699-4_36
6. Welke, R., Kumar, K.: Method Engineering: A Proposal for Situation Specific Method Construction. In: Challenges and Strategies for Research in Systems Development, pp. 257–269. Book Chapter Willey and ACM Digital Library(1992)
7. Dahanayake, A.N.W.: Evaluation of the strength of computer aided method engineering for product development process modeling. In: Quirchmayr, G., Schweighofer, E., Bench-Capon, T.J.M. (eds.) DEXA 1998. LNCS, vol. 1460, pp. 394–410. Springer, Heidelberg (1998). https://doi.org/10.1007/BFb0054499
8. Ter Hofstede, A.: Information Modeling in Data Intensive Domains. Dissertation, Radboud University of Nijmegen (1993)
9. Dahanayake, A.: Computer-Aided Method Engineering: Designing Case Repositories for the 21st Century. IGI Global Publishing (1998)

Models Versus Model Descriptions

Joachim Fischer[1] , Birger Møller-Pedersen[2] , Andreas Prinz[3](✉) ,
and Bernhard Thalheim[4]

[1] Department of Computer Science, Humboldt University, Berlin, Germany
fischer@informatik.hu-berlin.de
[2] Department of Informatics, University of Oslo, Oslo, Norway
birger@ifi.uio.no
[3] Department of ICT, University of Agder, Grimstad, Norway
andreas.prinz@uia.no
[4] Department of Computer Science, University Kiel, Kiel, Germany
bernhard.thalheim@email.uni-kiel.de

Abstract. In the development of computer-based systems, modelling is
often advocated in addition to programming, in that it helps in reflecting the application domain and that it makes the design and experiment activities of development more efficient. However, there is disagreement about what models are and how they can be used in software
systems development. In this paper, we present the Scandinavian approach to modelling, which makes a clear distinction between models and
model descriptions. This paper explains the connections between models,
descriptions, systems, and executions. Combining the Scandinavian approach with the Kiel notion of model, we establish that both descriptions
and executions are closely connected instruments with different roles.
The paper argues that (program) executions are the models of dynamic
systems, not their descriptions in terms of diagrams and text. So in a
general sense programming is about writing descriptions for systems. In
particular the paper clarifies when programming is also modelling.

Keywords: Model · System · Description · Execution · Semantics

1 Introduction

The development of computer-based systems brings together different areas
of experience, methods and terminology. Therefore, it is not surprising that
terms have different meanings in different contexts. Surprisingly, even very basic
terms such as system, model, model description, modeling and programming are
affected. In the development of computer-based systems, three methodologically
different computer-related disciplines meet. First, there are engineers who use
computer models to design new technical systems, simulate and test them before
actually building them. Second, there are IT experts who design software systems from abstract models by means of extensive transformations. Third, there
are other IT experts who design and implement systems directly using specific

© Springer Nature Switzerland AG 2021
A. Dahanayake et al. (Eds.): M2P 2020, CCIS 1401, pp. 67–89, 2021.
https://doi.org/10.1007/978-3-030-72696-6_3

programming languages and techniques. Each of these three groups use programming and modelling, and all of them have slightly different understanding of what a model is. The discrepancy in the conceptual perception remains with modellers and programmers even for development of pure software systems.

As part of system development, *programmers* produce running systems. They do this by programming, that is writing programs. Often, they do not subscribe to the idea of modelling as this typically implies the creation of diagrams that do not contribute to the making of programs and quickly become obsolete.

Modellers handle different kinds of *models* (domain models, requirements and design models) in a mixture of diagrams and text. It can be argued that programmers are to a certain extent also modelling, and modellers are programming. We will look at these two activities and explain how they are similar and how they are different. In this paper, we present the Scandinavian approach to modelling as a shared understanding between modellers and programmers using an understanding of models as illustrated in Fig. 1.

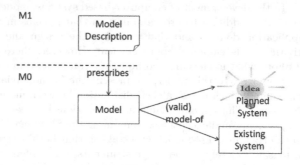

Fig. 1. Overview of the Scandinavian Approach to Modelling

The approach presented in this paper is called the Scandinavian Approach to Modelling. The Scandinavian Approach was started in the design of the language SIMULA (Dahl and Nygaard 1965; Dahl and Nygaard 1966), and developed further with the languages Delta (Holbæk-Hanssen et al. 1973), Beta (Madsen et al. 1993), and SDL-2000 (Union 2011). There are several articles describing aspects of the Scandinavian approach, see (Nygaard and Dahl 1978; Scheidgen and Fischer 2007; Madsen and Møller-Pedersen 2010), as well as (Fischer et al. 2016; Gjøsæter et al. 2016; Prinz et al. 2016), and finally also (Madsen and Møller-Pedersen 2018).

The paper evolves around the concept of a system, see the bottom of Fig. 1. This is quite natural as systems development is about producing systems. Systems can be existing physical systems, or imagined and planned systems. Systems can be made using various kinds of *descriptions*, e.g. *programs*. These descriptions imply executions, i.e. systems. There is a dotted line in Fig. 1 between the world of systems, called M0 (below the line) and the world of descriptions, called M1 (above the line).

The Scandinavian approach considers a *model* to be a (model) system, which is a model of another system called *referent* system. This referent system is an existing system in case of simulation or a planned system in case of system development. The (model) system is created by a (model) description, which is the diagram or code that describes the (model) system.

In this paper, we will focus on dynamic models. This restricted view on models helps to keep the discussion focused. Still, this is the prominent use of models in computer science and in system development. We combine the Scandinavian approach with the Kiel notion of model (Thalheim et al. 2015), which also provides a general definition of the term model.

The distinction between models and model descriptions has been made before in (Madsen and Møller-Pedersen 2018) and in (Fischer et al. 2020). Here we apply the argument to the MOF architecture (Kleppe and Warmer 2003) (see Fig. 2), and we conclude that models are systems at level M0.

M3	meta-language	Example: MOF
M2	language	Example: UML
M1	model description	Example: UML diagrams for library system
M0	model execution	Example: running library system

Fig. 2. OMG four level architecture

The paper is structured as follows. In Sect. 2, we discuss the notion of systems as a starting point for the discussion. This is extended in Sect. 3 with the role that descriptions have in creating systems. Then we continue with discussing the notion of models in Sect. 4. We bring all these parts together in Sect. 5 and compare with the Kiel notion of model. We discuss the Scandinavian approach in Sect. 6, and summarize in Sect. 7.

2 Systems

Modelling and programming are used in system development, so we start by defining the concept 'system'. Interestingly, although UML claims to be a language for the modelling of systems, it does not define what a system is. In general, programming languages do not define the term system, either. However, the UML standard mentions 'running system' when talking about interactions. Thus the UML idea of systems is running systems.

System development is about making dynamic systems, i.e. systems that inherently change over time. Figure 3 shows a sample system: a room with a control system for cooling and heating. Systems are composed of parts, and the interacting parts are changing, thus bringing about the system state changes[1]. We call the system state changes the *behaviour* of the system.

---

[1] The state changes can be continuous or discrete. We call the systems discrete versus continuous systems, or combined systems, if both kinds of state changes appear.

Fig. 3. Systems

The parts of a system can be existing entities, like a chair in the room, and they can be planned (imagined) parts, for example the controller of the heating system. We apply the perspective of object-oriented modeling and programming, so the parts of a system are objects. The parts of a system can be systems themselves.

The system structure itself can be static or subject to dynamic changes. Of course, there is the extreme case where a system only has existing parts, for example when we create a model in order to *understand* reality. Another extreme case is a system that only contains planned parts, most often in the process of creating something new. This brings us to our definition of system, compiled mainly from (Fischer et al. 2016; Bossel 2007).

Definition 1 (System). *A system is a purposeful collection of executing objects interacting with each other and with entities in the environment. It is a whole and loses its identity if essential objects are missing. A system has structure (existing and imagined objects having properties) and behaviour (executions by means of object behaviour).*

This way, a system is a set of possible executions, i.e. a set of object configurations that exist at different points in time. It has purpose, identity, structure, behaviour, and interaction with the environment.

An essential part of systems are their objects. We follow the ideas of SIMULA and UML for the definition of objects.

Definition 2 (Object, adapted from (OMG 2017)). *An object is an individual thing with a state and relationships to other objects. The state of an object identifies the values of properties for that object. Objects may have passive behaviour in terms of methods that can be called. An object may be active, meaning that it has some autonomous behavior.*

When we want to work with a system, it is important to know what we can observe. This is given by the system *state*, which in turn is based upon the system *structure*. The structure of a system is a dynamic collection of interacting objects, each with their properties that contribute to the state of the system. With the state we can observe the system by capturing snapshots of its progression.

Systems are just some part of reality. Typically, they have *interaction* with other parts of reality, which we call *environment*. If they do, we call them open (non-autonomous) systems. If systems can exist on their own, then they are closed systems. In many cases, a system with only planned parts is an open system. In this case, it is possible to close the open system by introducing an abstract part for the environment of the system, which is an existing part. In this paper, we are mostly talking about open systems, where the system reads inputs from the environment and writes outputs to the environment.

By Definition 1, not all parts of reality are systems; we have to consider a given part of reality as a system, and we abstract away unimportant parts and features of reality. There are two abstraction levels. First, we have a discourse, i.e. a way we look at reality in general, see Fig. 4. The discourse starts with our understanding how reality is composed in general. For our considerations and for this paper, we consider reality to be composed of objects, following an object-oriented discourse.

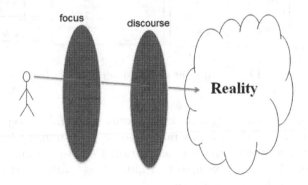

Fig. 4. Viewpoints and discourse

In addition to the discourse, the *purpose* of the system will add another level of abstraction. This is our focus when looking at the system, and it reduces the aspects to look at. The set of five ODP-RM viewpoints (ITU-T 1995) is an example of a high-level classification of the purpose of systems for a special class of complex system.

System identification always requires an abstraction of reality, which depends on the purpose of the system. This means that, with a completely identical system purpose, different systems can be created as object configurations. For example, the content of a boiler can be measured by the filled volume or by the water level.

All in all, we conclude that systems are part of reality (really existing or hypothetically assumed), and this means they are placed on OMG level M0.

3   System Descriptions

After we have clarified the notion of system, we will ask ourselves where the systems come from. In many cases, systems are created by making descriptions of them. In this section, we discuss these system descriptions.

3.1   Systems and Descriptions

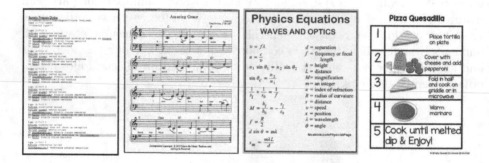

Fig. 5. Different system descriptions

Many systems are based on system descriptions, see Fig. 5. A typical example is a system that is based on a program in some programming language. The program is the description, and the description leads to a running system on a real hardware. A similar example is a music sheet that describes, i.e. is a description of, a musical performance.

The system described by the description can also be an imaginary system, as for example given by physics formulae. Their meaning creates a virtual world, i.e. a virtual system. In a similar sense, a recipe (description) creates an imaginary sequence of steps for a dish that can be used to create the real dish. In all these cases, the various kinds of *system descriptions* result in running systems, see Fig. 6. As discussed before, the running systems consist of executing objects.

All these examples show that the description is not a system in itself: it is not composed of objects and it does not have behaviour. The system related to a description is implied by the semantics of the language of the description and thereby the meaning of the description. It has become customary to call this connection between the description and the system for "prescribe", and then the description is rather a prescription, see again Fig. 6. A similar approach is used in (Seidewitz 2003). This allows us to define programming.

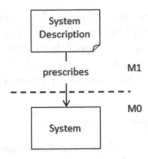

Fig. 6. Prescriptions

Definition 3 (Programming). *Programming is the activity to produce descriptions (prescriptions) in order to produce systems. In a narrow sense, programming is concerned with prescriptions in the form of computer programs. In the general sense, programming means to construct a description in order to create a system, as designing recipes, composing music, or inventing physics formulas.*

There is a vast body of knowledge as to which steps to take in order to create good descriptions, and computer engineering explain how to do this for computer systems. In this article, we are not concerned how the description comes about, but it is essential to agree that the description is created in order to create a system.

Coming back to the OMG architecture, we notice that a description is placed on level M1, independent of the kind of description. The description then implies a number of possible executions consisting of a changing structure of objects according to the prescription. These objects, i.e. the implied system, will be on M0. The objects behave according to their prescription of behaviour as part of the description on M1.

This approach divides the world into descriptions and objects, as shown in Fig. 7. Below the line, on M0, there are objects, there are states of objects, and there are state changes resulting from the behaviour of the objects.

M3	Descriptions and prescriptions, in
M2	terms of diagrams, text, or combined
M1	
M0	Objects, with behaviours, states and
	links between objects

Fig. 7. Descriptions and objects

Above the line, on M1[2], there are *no* objects, there are *no* states, and there are *no* state changes. However, there are *prescriptions of objects* (e.g. by means

---

[2] There are also descriptions and prescriptions on M2 and M3, but this is out of the scope of this paper.

of classes), there are *prescriptions of states* (e.g. descriptions of attributes of objects), and there are *prescriptions of state changes* (e.g. assignments).

In the following, we will use the term description for both description and prescription, except in cases where it is essential to distinguish. The main difference is between objects (on M0) and descriptions of objects (on M1–M3).

3.2   Semantics and Meaning

As already stated in (Fischer et al. 2016), it is the semantics of the language of the description defining the system belonging to the system description. Semantics is not about formality in the first place, even though system engineering is most interested in formal description languages and programming languages with a precise semantics.

In the OMG architecture, this is the move from descriptions on level M1 to objects and executions on level M0. This way, semantics is a *vertical* relation (crossing levels). The description is executed in some abstract machine. In reality, there might be several transformations (horizontal semantic steps) before the vertical step appears. In the world of computers, the most common way to provide transformation semantics is using a compiler, which is essentially replacing one description by another, more executable description.

Still, at the end we need to come to a description that can be executed, i.e. that can cross the level. We define the idea of semantics as follows.

Definition 4 (Semantics). *Semantics is the relation between a (system) description and its prescribed possible executions (the system)*[3]*. In our context, semantics is the same as the prescribe relation.*

The semantics of a specification is given by the language it is written in; it is not a property of the specification itself. The semantics as given by the language (on level M2) connects the system specification on level M1 to the implied system on level M0.

In this consideration, it is irrelevant whether the semantics is formal or not. The important point is that there is a system implied by the description. A programming language provides more formality than a music sheet, where the conductor can add some interpretation. In both cases, the description has a meaning.

Semantics provides two parts: structural semantics and dynamic semantics. *Structural semantics* details which structure the system implied by the description has, i.e. which objects and which properties it has. Each system state is then characterized by this same structure.

---

[3] The DELTA language report used the neutral term 'generator' that generates a system based upon a system description, i.e. provides the vertical relation. A generator could be a machine or a human being, or a mixture. In MDA, a generator is most often understood as a tool generating a new low-level description out of the original high-level description. This would amount to a horizontal generation and is not what semantics is about here.

There will be different realizations of these system structures, depending on the underlying reality that is used to run the system. For example, there will be different ways to represent Java objects depending on the underlying machine, but on the abstraction level of the execution, these are the same. This is given by the abstraction property of system as discussed in Fig. 4. In a similar sense, a musical sheet will have different realizations depending on the musical instrument it is played on.

In our object-oriented discourse, we can observe the system behaviour using *snapshots*, i.e. collections of objects with the values of their properties. Such a snapshot is a complete description of the current state of the execution of the system as defined by the execution semantics[4]. A snapshot includes information about all relevant runtime objects.

Experiments with systems, like testing and simulations, are experiments with an execution, not with descriptions. In (Exner et al. 2014), it is well documented that even prototyping is experimenting with systems in varying degrees of completeness, not experimenting with descriptions.

4   Models

After discussing systems and (system) descriptions, we are prepared to look into the definition of models. The UML standard uses the following definition (OMG 2017). Note the distinction between existing and planned systems (parts).

> A model is always a model of something. The thing being modeled can generically be considered as a system within some domain of discourse. The model then makes some statements of interest about that system, abstracting from all the details of the system that could possibly be described, from a certain point of view and for a certain purpose. For an existing system, the model may represent an analysis of the properties and behavior of the system. For a planned system, the model may represent a specification of how the system is to be constructed and behave.

4.1   The Model-of Relation

We start with a condensed definition from Webster, Collins, Wikipedia, UML, (Bossel 2013), and a general understanding of model.

> A model refers to a small or large, abstract or actual, representation of a planned or existing entity or system from a particular viewpoint and with a specific purpose.

Observe that this definition of model always defines a relation between the system acting as the model, and the system being modeled, see Fig. 8.

---

[4] A debugger is a tool that can show the current state of execution in some notation.

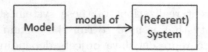

Fig. 8. Models are in a model-of relation with their referent systems.

Keep in mind that a model is related to some other entity or system, and that this means that being a model is always the same as being in a relation with something we call referent system. This relation is usually called *model-of*. Furthermore, a model is something that can represent the referent system, as stated in (Podnieks 2010): "a model is anything that is (or could be) used, for some purpose, in place of something else." Given the terms introduced so far, a model is a system itself, which means it can be executed in some sense. This leads to our definition as follows.

Definition 5 (model). *A model is a system, that is in a model-of relationship to a referent system, existing or planned. A model resembles the structure and the behavior of its referent system by a model-of relation. A model might be created using a model description (e.g. a diagram, a formula, or code).*

This way, a model is a special kind of system, which implies that a model description is a special kind of system description. The model description is used for creating the model, but it is not the model itself, see Fig. 9, which combines Fig. 6 connecting description and system (here with the special case of a model), and Fig. 8 connecting model and referent system. The combination yields a combined relation between the description and the referent system. This relation is most often called a describe relation. It is a bit weaker than the prescribe relation, but it is also relating a description to a system.

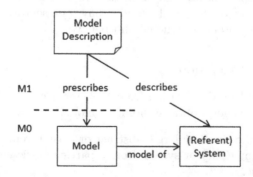

Fig. 9. Model, description, and referent system

A system description always leads to a system (a set of possible executions). The system does not need to be a model if there is no related referent system.

Note that both physical and mathematical models are systems, because it is their behaviour (their executions) that makes them models. Scale models are also concrete representations, but typically with an object structure that does not change over time.

Let us look at the small example in Fig. 10 to see what this definition implies. There are specifications (descriptions) of books in UML and in Java for a library system. The Java description might be derived from the UML description (blue arrow in the figure), but this connection is not important at the moment. The UML class allows a book object to be created at runtime, in the same way as the Java class allows a book object to be created at runtime. These runtime objects contribute to form a system, i.e. a library system. These two objects are typically models of the real book object existing somewhere in a library.

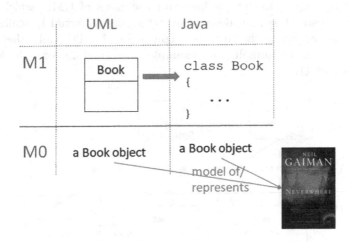

Fig. 10. Models of books (Color figure online)

Libraries are systems with changing sets of books and loans. Models of libraries with the purpose to understand libraries or to make computer-based library systems must be systems of objects representing real books and loans. The model, in this case, is an actual representation.

Now that we know what models are, we can define modelling as follows.

Definition 6 (modelling). *Modelling is the activity to create a model based on a purpose. There are two ways to create a model.*

1. *Create the model directly as a system (scale model or physical model).*
2. *Create a description that implies a system which is the model (mathematical, computer, design models).*

The Scandinavian approach fits well with the process of modeling technical or environmental systems. Authors like (Schmidt 1987; Pritsker 1979; Hill 2002) identify three iterative phases of this process. The first phase establishes a model problem resulting from the system purpose, and a model is derived, the validity of which has to be verified experimentally for the purpose of the investigation. The model is described (programmed) in the second phase as an executable simulation model. Instead of experimenting with the original, we are now experimenting with the (executable) model. The third phase is dedicated to targeted experimentation. A distinction is made between experiments to prove the model validity of the simulator and experiments to solve the model problem. The phase is concluded by the intellectual transfer of the model results into the world of the original.

4.2   Correctness

The model-of relation allows us to discuss correctness of models, see Fig. 11. An example for the figure are interactions and use cases of UML, which provide some kind of abstract system description by giving a partial formalization of ideas about the system as shown to the right of Fig. 11. Typically, they need to be extended with more formality, for example class diagrams or code, as shown to the left of Fig. 11.

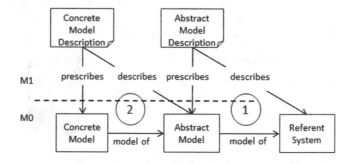

Fig. 11. Correctness

The right part of Fig. 11 named ① shows the same situation as Fig. 9. In this part, the relation between abstract model and referent system decides whether the model is correct. This is not a formal exercise as the referent system does not exist in a formal way. Validation is the process of finding out whether a system has the right model-of relation to an existing or planned real system, i.e. whether their executions match. In order to prove that the model system can represent the original system for the desired model purpose, i.e. that the model-of relation can be recognized as valid, according to (Bossel 2013), the validity must be proven with regard to four different aspects: behavioral validity[5], structural validity[6],

---

[5] It must be shown that for the initial conditions and environmental effects of the original system that are fixed within the scope of the model, the model system produces the (qualitatively) same dynamic behavior.

[6] It must be shown that the effect structure of the model (for the model purpose) corresponds to the essential effect structure of the original.

empirical validity[7], and applicability[8]. Validation by prototyping is the process of finding the system that is the desired model of a planned system.

As the match between model and referent system is already part of the definition of model, an incorrect model would not be a model at all. If the model is able to reflect the behaviour of the referent system under certain conditions, it might still be a model for a restricted purpose. Correctness is very important for the existing parts of the system. They start with a physical system and provide the model of it later. For the new parts, the referent system is imagined and the model is the first physically existing system.

In the diagram part named ②, we see again a similar diagram as in Fig. 9, where the referent system is given by the abstract model. Therefore, in addition to the description for the concrete model, there is also a description for the abstract model in the role of the referent system. This means we can formally compare the semantic implications of the two descriptions and determine whether the two systems match. This approach, called verification, uses the semantics of the two descriptions to compare the syntactic structures without going into the running systems. This way, the question of correctness is lifted to the level M1.

In a system with existing parts, we can simulate the system using the models of the existing parts. This way, we can *experiment* with the models instead of with the real systems and deduce properties. This is the typical development phase, where we use a model for the existing parts and the controller is changing rapidly due to better understanding of the system. Once the controller works well in the simulated environment, we can move to the real environment. The description is still the same, but now the existing parts are exchanged with their referent systems, i.e. the existing parts themselves. This means we do now deploy the new parts onto the real referent system.

5   Relation to the Kiel Notion of Model

In this section, we relate the concepts introduced in the previous sections to the Kiel notion of models (Thalheim et al. 2015). The Kiel notion of model is a very general notion capturing models from all areas of science. The Scandinavian approach is geared towards dynamic models in computer science. Still, as our approach is quite general as well, the two approaches can be compared. We start with an introduction to the Kiel model, then we summarize our approach, and finally we compare the two.

---

[7] It must be shown that in the area of the model purpose, the numerical results of the model system correspond to the empirical results of the Originals under the same conditions, or that they are consistent and plausible if there are no observations.

[8] It must be shown that the model and simulation options correspond to the model purpose and the requirements of the user.

5.1   The Kiel Notion of Model

The Kiel notion defines a model as follows.

Definition 7 (Kiel Model (Thalheim et al. 2015)**).** *A model is a well-formed, adequate, and dependable instrument that represents origins. Its criteria of well-formedness, adequacy, and dependability must be commonly accepted by its community of practice within some context and correspond to the functions that a model fulfills in utilisation scenarios and use spectra. As an instrument, a model is grounded in its community's subdiscipline and is based on elements chosen from the sub-discipline.*

In addition, (Thalheim et al. 2015; Thalheim and Nissen 2015) as well as (Thalheim 2019) give more detail to the criteria as follows.

– A model combines an intrinsic deep model and an extrinsic normal model. The deep model is based on the community's subdiscipline and has its background, e.g. paradigms, assumptions, postulates, language, thought community. Models are typically only partially developed as normal models which properly reflect the chosen collection of origins.
– An instrument is a device that requires skill for proper use in some given scenario. As such it is (i1) a means whereby something is achieved, performed, or furthered, (i2) one used by another as a means or aid, (i3) one designed for precision work, and (i4) the means whereby some act is accomplished for achieving an effect. An instrument can be used in several functions in scenarios.
– The criteria for well-formedness, adequacy, and dependability depend on the function that an instrument plays in the given scenario. Due to the function a model plays, it has a purpose and satisfies a goal. The (p) profile of a model consists of its functions, purposes and goals. A well-formed instrument is adequate for a collection of origins if (a1) it is analogous to the origins to be represented according to some analogy criterion, (a2) it is more focused (e.g. simpler, truncated, more abstract or reduced) than the origins being modelled, and (a3) it sufficient to satisfy its purpose. It is dependable if it is justified and of sufficient quality. Justification can be provided (j1) by empirical corroboration according to its objectives, supported by some argument calculus, (j2) by rational coherence and conformity explicitly stated through formulas, (j3) by falsifiability that can be given by an abductive or inductive logic, and (j4) by stability and plasticity explicitly given through formulas. The instrument is sufficient by (q1) quality characteristics for internal quality, external quality and quality in use. Sufficiency is typically combined with (q2) some assurance evaluation (tolerance, modality, confidence, and restrictions).
– The background consists of (g) an undisputable grounding from one side (paradigms, postulates, restrictions, theories, culture, foundations, conventions, authorities) and of (b) a disputable and adjustable basis from other side (assumptions, concepts, practices, language as carrier, thought community and thought style, methodology, pattern, routines, commonsense).
– A model is used in a context such as discipline, a time, an infrastructure, and an application.

Models function in scenarios for which they are build. The intrinsic deep model mainly depends on its setting: the function that a model plays in given scenarios, the context, the community of practice, and the background. Scenarios often often stereotyped and follow conventions, customs, exertions, habits. The scenario determines which instruments can be properly used, which usage pattern or styles can be applied, and which quality characteristics are necessary for the instruments used in those activities.

Therefore, we may assume that the deep model underpins any model within the same setting. As long as we only consider models within a given setting (Thalheim 2017) we may use simpler notions of model, as given in Wenzel (2000) as follows.

A model is a simplified reproduction of a planned or real existing system with its processes on the basis of a notational and concrete concept space. According to the represented purpose-governed relevant properties, it deviates from its origin only due to the tolerance frame for the purpose.

This definition already assumes the system background for simulation scenario in the context of production and logistics.

5.2   The Scandinavian Approach to Modelling

As a comparison, we have a look at the Scandinavian approach, see Fig. 12. The Scandinavian approach has the following properties.

- A system has a purpose, determining the properties of the system, with other properties 'abstracted away'.
- A system is abstracted from the reality in terms of a discourse.
- A model is a special kind of system.
- A model is in a model-of relationship with another system.
- A model can be created from a model description, which is a special case of a system description.
- A model description adheres to the system description language in which it is made.

5.3   Comparing the Approaches

Now we relate the elements of the two definitions, see Fig. 13.

Most of the connections are obvious, but some comments are in place.

1. The Scandinavian approach distinguishes between model description and model system, which is not explicitly done in the Kiel notion where a model may consist of several tightly associated models, i.e. a model suite. A bi-model suite may consist of a model and its representation or informative model. The latter is essentially a model description. This leads to the well-formedness being related to the model in Kiel and to the model description in the Scandinavian approach.

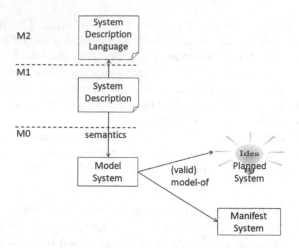

Fig. 12. Scandinavian model approach

Scandinavian Approach	Kiel Notion
A system has a purpose.	profile
A system purpose provides focus on essential system properties.	(a2)
A system is abstract in terms of a discourse.	(b), (g)
A model is a system.	specific instrument
A model is in a model-of relationship with another system.	origin-relationship, (a1), (a3), (g), (b)
A model can be created from a model description.	construction scenario
A model description adheres to the language it is written in.	well-formed

Fig. 13. Comparing the two approaches

2. The Kiel notion allows a description to be a model, which is not the case in the Scandinavian approach. The connection between description and model is further discussed in the next section.
3. The Kiel notion has much focus on purpose, usefulness, and the details of the model-of relation. This is has not been the focus of this paper, even though the Scandinavian approach has some ideas about it. Therefore, some aspects of Kiel do not appear in the table and many are grouped into the purpose and the model-of.
4. The Kiel notion is a generalisation of modelling practices in many scientific and engineering disciplines. It can be adapted to the Scandinavian notion by using specific adequacy and dependability criteria within a system construction setting.

As for the last point in the list above, the Scandinavian approach is based, not upon many scientific and engineering disciplines, but an understanding of application domains (or reality in general) consisting of phenomena (with measurable properties and behavior that changes these properties) and concepts classifying these phenomena. This is well-known from outside computer science, and when applied to modeling and programming, the short version is that objects model phenomena in the application domain, classes model concepts, and subclasses model specialized concepts. Composite phenomena are modeled by objects having part objects, the special case being the system containing parts. Objects have their own behaviour (not just methods), reflecting that in some domains there are phenomena (e.g. processes in a process control domain) that are active and exhibit parallel behaviour. The two approaches agree that analogy is a semantic property of the systems (executions). Analogy means in both approaches that elements of a model system represent (model) the corresponding elements in the referent system (origin). It is far more general than the mapping property that is often required for the model-of relation.

The idea of system and the idea of instrument do not match completely. This article defines system, but the notion of instrument is not defined in Thalheim et al. (2015). Apart from being a system, an instrument (or tool) also has some property of being useful, as stated in (g). Although system and instrument may not match, the Scandinavian notion of model matches the Kiel notion of instrument in the sense that both are used for the purpose of finding out more about the system to be modeled. Even the model description as an instrument does not collide with the Scandinavian approach: here the model description plays an important role in communication about the model. The name DELTA means 'participate' in Norwegian, and the idea behind the language was that the users of the final system should be able to participate in the 'system description' (the term for model description at that time) prior to its implementation. This later lead to the idea of 'participatory design', but now other means are used, like mock-ups, prototyping. However, a description (e.g. a program) still is an important instrument for developers.

6   Discussion

As explained before, the Scandinavian approach makes a clear distinction between a model and its description. This implies that a description is not a model.

We look into modelling and programming first, where we also discuss if programmers model. Then we consider code generation in the context of models and discuss why a description is not a model.

It might seem that the terms introduced and the details considered are not important in general. This is true, but still it is important to have the correct basic understanding in order to sort all the cases that might appear in programming and modelling practice.

6.1   Programming Versus Modelling

The Scandinavian notion of model applies to modeling and programming in general and would be the starting point of a combined modeling and programming language as proposed by several authors (Madsen and Møller-Pedersen 2010; Seidewitz 2016; Broy et al. 2017; Cleaveland 2018).

Markus Völter has compared programming and modelling in Völter (2011), Voelter (2018). He uses a definition of model-driven as follows.

> Model-driven refers to a way of developing a software system S where users change a set of prescriptive models M_i representing concerns C_i at an appropriate abstraction level in order to affect the behavior of S. An automatic process constructs a full implementation of S that relies on a platform P.

In this context, his conclusion is that modelling and programming are the same, and also coincide with scripting.

> Programming and modeling, in the sense of model-driven, where models are automatically transformed into the real system, cannot be categorically distinguished. However, the two have traditionally emphasized different aspects differently, making each suitable for different use cases.

He uses a similar definition of programming as we do, but he considers modelling to be creating a system description. This is of course the same as programming. However, a model description is not only a description of a system, but the system has to be related to a referent system using the model-of relation. Then all modelling by creating descriptions is also programming, but not all programming is modelling.

6.2   Do Programmers Model?

The question could be asked if programmers model? Of course, no programmer would want to write useless descriptions, so this kind of modelling they would avoid.

However, programmers *do* model, in the sense that they create systems that relate to reality, i.e. have a model-of relationship. They identify domain concepts and represent appropriate classes in the programs in line with the purpose of the system being developed. Objects of these classes are then model-of the corresponding phenomena. This is already discussed in Fig. 10.

This kind of modelling is not alien to programmers and can help programmers use modelling. Of course, a system might also contain platform- or implementation specific elements that are not models of anything.

In fact, on a more basic level, each programmer is following an idea of what the program is supposed to do and tries to write a description of a system that does the same. This is in the very core of modelling.

6.3   Code Generation and Models

Let us look into code generation, either manually or automatically, see Fig. 14. What is the relation between the high-level code (UML specification) and the low-level code (Java)? It is often claimed that the high-level code is a model of the low-level code. The same argument as before applies, in that the code itself is not a system. The connection between the two codes is given by the semantics of each of them. They both imply a system each via their respective semantics, and these systems can be related via the model-of.

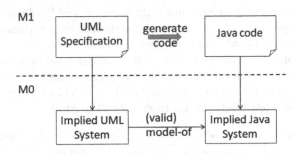

Fig. 14. Code generation and model-of

This indirect connection between the two kinds of code can be used to allow automatic code generation from the higher to the lower level. Please note that there might be different ways to create code from the higher level, and all of them can be correct as long as there is a match between the implied systems, i.e. they are semantically correct as discussed in Fig. 11.

6.4   Why is a Description Not a Model?

According to the arguments given before, a description is not a model, but implies a system which can be a model-of reality. But maybe it is possible to have also descriptions that are models?

Let's look at Fig. 15. It is often claimed that the UML specification or the database specification is the model of the system produced later on. This is not completely wrong, but the relation between the UML specification and the referent system is indirectly composed of two relations as shown in Fig. 15. There is a relation from the specification to the implied system, which is given by the semantics. The result of the semantics is then in the model-of relation to the system that is created. We have seen this combination already in the define relation, see Fig. 9. So the specification (which is a description) is not the model,

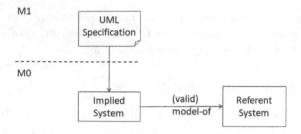

Fig. 15. Description to model

but the implied system is the model of the referent system. This is in contrast to the following text from (OMG 2017) on what a model is.

> A Model is a description of a system, where 'system' is meant in the broadest sense and may include not only software and hardware but organizations and processes. It describes the system from a certain viewpoint (or vantage point) for a certain category of stakeholders (e.g., designers, users, or customers of the system) and at a certain level of abstraction. A Model is complete in the sense that it covers the whole system, although only those aspects relevant to its purpose (i.e., within the given level of abstraction and viewpoint) are represented in the Model.

It is important to be precise that the description is not the model itself, but implies a system which is the model. This is also true for all model descriptions of database systems: A relationship diagram is not the model of the database, but it implies a system (mathematically) that is the model. In fact, the relationship diagram is then translated to code which again is a description. Running the code provides the system that is the model.

A similar situation relates to a model of the Mini (left in Fig. 16). Two alternatives, as presented by (Madsen and Møller-Pedersen 2018), are shown in Fig. 16. The same question arises: Is the description the model of the mini, or the implied result of the construction, i.e. the small Lego Mini? The answer is obvious - it is the small Mini - the system, not the description.

The connection between model system and real system is obvious when we look at experiments with the model. The Lego car allows to move forward and

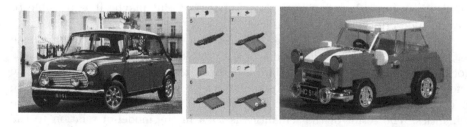

Fig. 16. Original, description, and model

backward, and to turn. The situation is different with the description, which only helps to generate the Lego car.

Another example was presented in an invited talk by James Gosling, Oslo, 2017. Sea robots were developed by testing them out in a simulation of the sea with waves, currents and obstacles. The simulation, that is the program execution (system) with the sea robots as objects, is the model of how it will be for real. It is not the simulation program and the programs of the sea robots that are models of the sea and of the real sea robots. The example also shows that the programs of the sea robots became part of the real sea robots, i.e. development by help of simulation. Note that these sea robots were simply programmed in Java without using a modeling language. Still, the simulation is a model of the sea with robots, and the sea robot objects are models of the real sea robots. Our definition of model as a system that is a model of another system is independent of which kind of language is used for making the model system.

7   Summary

This paper has discussed the relationship between models, systems, and descriptions. These terms were then compared with the Kiel notion of model. In this context, an executable model is the key instrument in the communication process about models and system development. It is also key in aligning the Scandinavian approach with the general Kiel notation of model. Other aspects of the Kiel modelling concept world that relate to the purpose, usefulness and details of the model-of relation are only partially discussed and should be deepened in further investigations. As the main result the paper has clarified the differences and similarities between modelling and programming. The paper has concluded as follows.

Systems Belong to the Modelling Level M0. The paper has argued that systems can be real or imagined, but that they exist on their own. Therefore, they are to be placed on OMG level M0.

Executing a System Description Leads to a System. System descriptions describe systems and lead to systems when their semantics is applied. Here it is irrelevant whether the semantics is formal or not. The description itself is not the system, but leads to it.

A Model is a System Being Model-of a Referent System. The model-of relation exists between two systems, which may or may not have a description. The description is the model, it is not involved in the model-of. Instead, the implied system of the description is the model.

Modelling is Programming Leading to a Model. Programming is about writing descriptions for systems. When the system produced is a model of a referent system, then the programming is also modelling.

Two Descriptions can Describe the Same System. When there are two descriptions of the same system, one high-level and one low-level, then both descriptions are related via their semantics, which may describe the same system on different levels of detail. The descriptions are not models of one another, because their syntax does not fit together, but the systems can be models.

With these clarifications it is easy to combine modelling and programming. There are far more aspects of models that are worthwhile to consider, which have been out of scope for this paper.

References

Bossel, H.: Systems and Models: Complexity, Dynamics, Evolution, Sustainability. Books on Demand GmbH, Norderstedt (2007)

Bossel, H.: Modeling and Simulation. Vieweg+Teubner Verlag (2013). https://doi.org/10.1007/978-3-663-10822-1

Broy, M., Havelund, K., Kumar, R.: Towards a unified view of modeling and programming. In: Proceedings of ISoLA 2017 (2017)

Cleaveland, R.: Programming is modeling. In: Proceedings of ISoLA 2018 (2018)

Dahl, O.-J., Nygaard, K.: Simula–a language for programming and description of discrete event systems. Technical report. Norwegian Computing Center, Oslo (1965)

Dahl, O.-J., Nygaard, K.: Simula: an algol-based simulation language. Commun. ACM 9(9), 671–678 (1966)

Exner, K., Lindowa, K., Buchholz, C., Stark, R.: Validation of product-service systems - a prototyping approach. In: Proceedings of 6th CIRP Conference on Industrial Product-Service Systems (2014)

Fischer, J., Møller-Pedersen, B., Prinz, A.: Modelling of systems for real. In: Proceedings of the 4th International Conference on Model-Driven Engineering and Software Development, pp. 427–434 (2016)

Fischer, J., Møller-Pedersen, B., Prinz, A.: Real models are really on M0 - or how to make programmers use modeling. In: Proceedings of the 8th International Conference on Model-Driven Engineering and Software Development - Volume 1: MODELSWARD, pp. 307–318. INSTICC, SciTePress (2020)

Gjøsæter, T., Prinz, A., Nytun, J.P.: MOF-VM: instantiation revisited. In: Proceedings of the 4th International Conference on Model-Driven Engineering and Software Development, pp. 137–144 (2016)

Hill, D.R.C.: Theory of modelling and simulation: Integrating discrete event and continuous complex dynamic systems: second edition by B. P. Zeigler, H. Praehofer, T. G. Kim, Academic Press, San Diego, CA, 2000. Int. J. Robust Nonlinear Control 12(1), 91–92 (2002)

Holbæk-Hanssen, E., Håndlykken, P., Nygaard, K.: System description and the delta language. Technical report, Norwegian Computing Center, Oslo (1973)

ITU-T. Basic Reference Model of Open Distributed Processing. ITU-T X.900 series and ISO/IEC 10746 series. International Organization for Standardization (1995)

Kleppe, A., Warmer, J.: MDA Explained. Addison-Wesley, Boston (2003)

Madsen, O.L., Møller-Pedersen, B.: A unified approach to modeling and programming. In: Petriu, D.C., Rouquette, N., Haugen, Ø. (eds.) MODELS 2010. LNCS, vol. 6394, pp. 1–15. Springer, Heidelberg (2010). https://doi.org/10.1007/978-3-642-16145-2_1

Madsen, O.L., Møller-Pedersen, B.: This is not a model: on development of a common terminology for modeling and programming. In: Margaria, T., Steffen, B. (eds.) ISoLA 2018. LNCS, vol. 11244, pp. 206–244. Springer, Cham (2018). https://doi.org/10.1007/978-3-030-03418-4

Madsen, O.L., Møller-Pedersen, B., Nygaard, K.: Object-oriented Programming in the BETA Programming Language. ACM Press/Addison-Wesley Publishing Co., New York (1993)

Nygaard, K., Dahl, O.-J.: The Development of the SIMULA Languages, pp. 439–480. Association for Computing Machinery, New York (1978)

OMG. Unified Modeling Language 2.5.1 (OMG Document formal/2017-12-05). OMG Document. Published by Object Management Group (2017). http://www.omg.org

Podnieks, K.: Towards a general definition of modeling (2010). https://philpapers.org/rec/PODTAG

Prinz, A., Møller-Pedersen, B., Fischer, J.: Object-oriented operational semantics. In: Grabowski, J., Herbold, S. (eds.) SAM 2016. LNCS, vol. 9959, pp. 132–147. Springer, Cham (2016). https://doi.org/10.1007/978-3-319-46613-2_9

Pritsker, A.A.B.: Compilation of definitions of simulation. Simulation **33**(2), 61–63 (1979)

Scheidgen, M., Fischer, J.: Human comprehensible and machine processable specifications of operational semantics. In: Akehurst, D.H., Vogel, R., Paige, R.F. (eds.) ECMDA-FA 2007. LNCS, vol. 4530, pp. 157–171. Springer, Heidelberg (2007). https://doi.org/10.1007/978-3-540-72901-3_12

Schmidt, B.: What does simulation do? Simulation's place in the scientific method of investigation. Syst. Anal. Model. Simul. **4**(3), 193–211 (1987)

Seidewitz, E.: What models mean. IEEE Softw. **20**, 26–32 (2003)

Seidewitz, E.: On a unified view of modeling and programming, position paper. In: Proceedings of ISoLA 2016 (2016)

Thalheim, B.: General and specific model notions. In: Kirikova, M., Nørvåg, K., Papadopoulos, G.A. (eds.) ADBIS 2017. LNCS, vol. 10509, pp. 13–27. Springer, Cham (2017). https://doi.org/10.1007/978-3-319-66917-5_2

Thalheim, B.: Conceptual modeling foundations: the notion of a model in conceptual modeling. In: Liu, L., Özsu, M.T. (eds.) Encyclopedia of Database Systems, pp. 9–71. Springer, New York (2018). https://doi.org/10.1007/978-1-4614-8265-9

Thalheim, B., Nissen, I. (eds.): Wissenschaft und Kunst der Modellierung: Modelle, Modellieren, Modellierung. De Gruyter, Boston (2015)

Thalheim, B., et al.: Wissenschaft und Kunst der Modellierung (Science and Art of Modelling) - Kieler Zugang zur Definition, Nutzung und Zukunft. De Gruyter, Berlin, Boston (2015)

Union, I.T.: Z.100 series, specification and description language sdl. Technical report, International Telecommunication Union (2011)

Voelter, M.: Fusing modeling and programming into language-oriented programming. In: Margaria, T., Steffen, B. (eds.) ISoLA 2018. LNCS, vol. 11244, pp. 309–339. Springer, Cham (2018). https://doi.org/10.1007/978-3-030-03418-4_19

Völter, M.: From programming to modeling - and back again. IEEE Softw. **28**, 20–25 (2011)

Wenzel, S.: Referenzmodell für die Simulation in Produktion und Logistik. ASIM Nachrichten **4**(3), 13–17 (2000)

Modeling and Implementing of Industrie 4.0 Scenarios

Albert Fleischmann[1]([✉]), Anton Friedl[2], Daniel Großmann[3], and Werner Schmidt[3]

[1] InterAktiv Unternehmensberatung, Dr. Albert Fleischmann & Partner, Pfaffenhofen, Germany
`albert.fleischmann@interaktiv.expert`
[2] Consulting for Automation and Digitalization, Herzogenaurach, Germany
`anton.friedl@herzonet.com`
[3] Technische Hochschule Ingolstadt, Ingolstadt, Germany
`{Daniel.Grossman,werner.schmidt}@thi.de`

Abstract. This paper describes the requirements on a modeling language of describing and implementing Industrie 4.0 systems. Based on those requirements PASS (Parallel Activity Specification Schema) as a subject oriented modeling language is investigated whether it would meet these requirements. It is shown that PASS allows a problem oriented specification of Industrie 4.0 scenarios based on the structure of natural languages and that PASS specifications can be implemented using OPC UA. OPC UA is a standard for implementing Industrie 4.0 scenarios.

Keywords: Industrie 4.0 · Industry 4.0 · Subject oriented modeling · Business process management

1 Introduction

In this paper we outline a concept for modeling entities in Industrie 4.0 systems including their communication with each other.

Industrie 4.0 means digitalization of industrial value chains by intelligent combinations of socio-technical-systems, including hardware, software, data, humans, and mechanical and/or electrical components that can autonomously interact with each other [13,44]. A value chain following the Industrie 4.0 philosophy involves humans, physical devices and IT-systems (hardware and software). These basic entity types can occur in any combinations. Most entities have a IT-component which is combined with physical components or with humans. IT combined with physical components are called Cyber-Physical Systems (CPS) and combinations of IT with human are called Cyber-Human Systems (CHS). IT-systems can be even combined with physical devices and humans. Then we get Cyber-Human-Physical-system (CHPS).

If an Industrie 4.0 system has to be designed the following major aspects have to be considered:

- the entities which are part of the considered system,
- data used by the entities and

© Springer Nature Switzerland AG 2021
A. Dahanayake et al. (Eds.): M2P 2020, CCIS 1401, pp. 90–112, 2021.
https://doi.org/10.1007/978-3-030-72696-6_4

– the communication between the entities.

Before implementing such a system a model needs to be created which defines the requirements of the final solution. The modeling concepts currently defined in Indus trie 4.0 include a model of an overall architecture of Industrie 4.0 solutions called Referenzarchitekturmodell Industrie 4.0 (RAMI) and the Asset Administration Shell for combining data with physical components. The communication between entities is only considered in a very basic way [10].

In this paper we show how the entities of an Industrie 4.0 system and their interactions can be modeled independently from the technology which is used for the implementation. In such model already existing Industrie 4.0 modeling approaches like Asset Administration Shell and OPC-UA can be embedded. The remainder of this contribution is structured as follows.

In the Sect. 2 we outline the basic philosophy on which our modeling approach is based. In Sect. 3 we describe typical Industrie 4.0 scenarios. Based on these scenarios the requirements for Industrie 4.0 models are derived. These requirements are used for defining the language Parallel Activity Specification Schema (PASS). The structure of this modeling language follows the basic structure of natural languages. In the last section this modeling language is combined with already existing Industrie 4.0 models.

2   Model of a Model

"You don't have to understand the world, you just have to orient yourself." According to Internet sources, this sentence is attributed to Albert Einstein. In order to orient ourself we consider only the part of the world in which we live or work in the current time. Which means that we create our mew world every day. Additionally our view on the domain we are interested in is subjective because we want to orient us.

In doing so, we identify the entities and the relationships between them that are essential for us. Such an abstraction of a part of reality is called a model [40]. Figure 1 shows the general approach for creating models.

The process for creating models follows three steps, mapping, reduction, and pragmatism [40].

In the mapping step, entities of the considered part of reality, which should become individuals of a model, are selected including the relations between entities which become part of the model. The selected entities and the relations between them are called attributes of a model. Since not all attributes of the original are captured by a model, a pragmatic dimension has been introduced in the broader sense. In the "broader sense" here means that not yet specific pragmatic-operational aspects are considered, according to which the attribute classes that are to be included in a model are selected. This initial selection of attributes is intuitive and arbitrary. In the narrower sense, the reduction is pragmatic only when the intentions and operational objectives of the model creator or user influence the selection of model-relevant attributes. The pragmatism step serves to check the intuitive selection of the attributes allows to achieve the intended purpose. Models are not clearly assigned to their originals. They serve as a replacement function for a specific interest group at a specific time for a certain purpose.

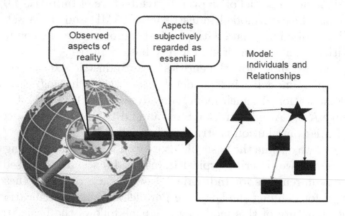

Fig. 1. Model of a model

It is also possible that the considered part of reality is already a model itself. This allows parts of an already existing model to be examined more closely resulting in a model of a model. This process can be repeated as many times as desired. This means there can be hierarchies of models. With each level a model becomes more abstract.

Models in computer science help developers to understand a certain problem identified by e.g. business people. Based on such models solutions will be developed. If these models are abstract which means in a solution, physical devices are not involved the identified problem is solved only ba software which should fulfill some quality requirements. "The methods used in software engineering aim to represent models of the real world with computational models used by computers" [35]. Computational models barely cover physical devices, and humans. UML the mostly used modeling language in software development considers the integration of physical devices and humans only in Use Case Diagrams [32]. Modelling systems for realtime applications cover the Cyber-Physical Systems e.g. MARTE [21] which is based on UML and SysML.

In [16,42] many other aspects of building models in software development and modeling approaches are considered but all of them consider mainly software aspects. In Industrie 4.0 scenarios software systems are embedded in an environment of physical devices and humans. Entities built of either of software, physical devices, humans and combinations of them interact with each other. In the following sections these particularities of Industrie 4.0 scenarios will be considered in more detail.

3   Characteristics of Industrie 4.0

3.1   Key Scenarios and Their Structure

Industrie 4.0 was announced to be the fourth industrial revolution based on Cyber-Physical Systems as a part of a smart and interconnected world [7]. Cyber-Physical Systems (CPS) were introduced by Edward A. Lee in 2008 [28] as "integrations of computation with physical processes". In CPS "embedded computers and networks monitor and control the physical processes, usually with feedback loops where physical processes affect computations and vice versa."

Industrie 4.0 embodies the introduction of the Internet of Things and Services to industrial production processes. Manufacturing and logistics will be based on CPS - "Cyber-Physical Systems comprise smart machines, storage systems and production facilities that are capable of exchanging information autonomously, triggering actions as well as of controlling each other independently" [7,20]. In Smart Factories components and machines autonomously manage production in a flexible, efficient and resource-saving manner. Smart Products are aware of their production status and the details of how they were manufactured or what the next production steps are.

Industrie 4.0 challenges all stakeholders to get connected as a collaborative community across all enterprise levels. The digitalization of industrial value chains and the real-time-capable, intelligent integration of humans, software and physical systems are crucial for Industrie 4.0. It is built upon four pillars:

- Digital integration of engineering across the entire value chain
- Horizontal integration through value networks
- Vertical integration in the production
- Resolution of the automation pyramid [7]

The digital integration of engineering across the entire value chain includes product design, production planning, production engineering, production execution and services. Digital models of products, production systems and production processes are created and managed in Integrated Product & Production Lifecycle Management Systems. Those digital models are called Digital Twins, as they represent every detail of the real-world entities. The digital models are continuously updated by real-time data to keep them up-to-date.

The horizontal and vertical integration of Industrie 4.0 (Fig. 2) integrates all entities (humans, software and physical systems) in the entire enterprise and across enterprises. Horizontal integration focuses on the collaboration across enterprise borders. It integrates suppliers and customers with producers via Supply Chain Management (SCM) and Customer Relationship Management (CRM) systems. Vertical integration takes place within the enterprise. It interconnects and integrates entities of all levels: Enterprise Resource Planning (ERP), Manufacturing Execution Systems (MES), systems and devices of the Shop Floor (SCADA systems, controllers, devices, sensors, actuators, ...). Horizontal and vertical integration implies integration into business processes, not just communication between the entities.

Industrie 4.0 is based on CPS, where CPS consist of autonomous entities (actors) that interconnect to dynamic and self-organizing networks without any hierarchical system control. This implicates that the classical hierarchically structured Automation Pyramid (Fig. 3) with its hierarchical communication and interaction structures will vanish gradually and will be replaced by a dynamic network of autonomous actors. The essential observation is that in dynamic value networks humans, software and physical systems act on data and/or physical entities and interact as autonomous actors with each other.

3.2   Industrie 4.0 Key Statement

In the proceeding sections the scenarios of Industrie 4.0 are outlined and which aspects have to be considered in Industrie 4.0 Models. In Fig. 4 the key statement of Industrie 4.0 modeling is shown.

There are active individuals which execute actions on passive entities. If we use natural languages to express that relation we use a simple sentence with subject, verb or predicate and object, e.g. "Customer fills out the order form". "Customer" is the active component, "fills out" the verb or predicate and the "order form" is the object.

In the world of Industrie 4.0 humans, software and physical devices are the acting elements and as such essential. We call acting elements subjects which are independent from their implementation. The term subject has manifold meanings depending on the discipline. In philosophy a subject is an observer and an object is a thing observed. In the grammar of many languages the term subject has a slightly different meaning. "According to the traditional view, subject is the doer of the action (actor) or the element that expresses what the sentence is about (topic)." [27] In the context of this paper if we talk about subjects, the meaning is close to the meaning in sentences. "The subject acts as the 'doer' or agent of an action" [5]. Because we think that the doer in an Industrie 4.0 context is the central aspect we call our modeling approach Subject-Oriented Modeling.

Subjects do something. This is expressed by a predicate or verb. A predicate is "a word or phrase that describes an action, condition, or experience. In grammar, it is the part of a sentence that contains the verb and gives information about the action normally executed by a subject" [4]. An action is executed on an object. "Objects normally follow the verb in a clause. A direct object shows who or what the action of the verb affects" [1].

As shown in Fig. 4 subjects do not only act on objects they also interact with each other. Interaction is realized by exchanging messages. Subjects synchronize their activities by sending and receiving messages. With the message exchange subjects do not only synchronize their work, messages also transport the data which must be known by a cooperation partner. In our modeling language we use the two special verbs "send" and "receive" to express these communication activities. When we talk about someone receiving something, we can express it using the typical word order: indirect object (io) + direct object (do) e.g. "The customer sends to the purchaser an order". If we want to bring more emphasis

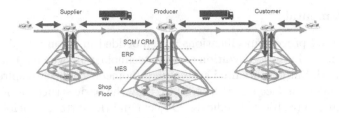

Fig. 2. Horizontal and vertical interactions

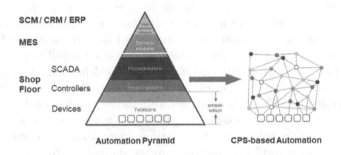

Fig. 3. From a hierarchical structure to a network

Industrie 4.0	Natural Language Grammar
Humans, software and physical systems	Subject
act on	Predicate
data and/or physical entities and	*Object*
interact as	interact
autonomous actors with each other	**Subject or indirect Object**

Fig. 4. Key statement of Industrie 4.0 scenarios

or focus to the recipient, we can use a prepositional complement (pc) instead of an indirect object, e.g. "The customer sends an order to the purchaser". The considerations above indicate that Industrie 4.0 scenarios can be described with two types of sentences:

– The subject acts as the 'doer' or agent of an action affecting an object.
– Subjects interact with each other by sending and receiving messages.

In the following Sect. 4 these basic considerations are formalized and a corresponding modeling language is derived.

4 Subject Oriented Modeling

In this section we introduce the formal foundations of a modeling language which we think is appropriate for describing and implementing Industrie 4.0 scenarios.

4.1   Fundamentals

Subject-oriented process specifications are embedded in a context. A context is defined by the business organization and the technology by which a business process is executed. Subject-oriented system development has been inspired by various process algebras (see e.g. [19,24,30,31]), by the basic structure of nearly all natural languages (Subject, Predicate, Object) and the systemic sociology developed by Niklas Luhmann [8,29] and Jürgen Habermas [22,38]. In the active voice of many natural languages a complete sentence consists of the basic components subject, predicate and objects. The subject represents the active element, the predicate the action and the object is the entity on which the action is executed. According to the organizational theory developed by Luhmann and Habermas the smallest organization consists of communication executed between at least two information processing entities (Note, this is a definition by a sociologist, not by a computer scientist) [29]. Figure 5 summarizes the different inspirations of subject orientation. The enhancements, such as the graphical notation, constitute the subject oriented approach and will be detailed in the following sections.

Particulary we describe how these various ingredients are combined in an orthogonal way to a modeling language for scenarios in which active entities have a certain importance like in Industrie 4.0. This language is called Parallel Activity Specification Schema (PASS).

4.2   Subject Behaviour and Interaction

Based on the basic ideas outlined in Sect. 4.1 a system consists of subjects acting on objects and interacting with each other. The objects on which a subject acts are owned by this subject and can not be seen by other subjects (in an extended version of subject orientation shared objects are also possible but are not considered here [18]). This means the first description layer shows the subjects of the considered system including their communication relationships. This specification is totally independent from the implementation of subjects, objects and the communication between subjects. This means subjects are abstract entities which communicate with each other and use their objects independent from possible implementations. The mapping to an implementation technology is done in a succeeding step. If an implementation technology is assigned to a subject it becomes an actor/agent e.g. software agent (for details see Sect. 4.5).

Figure 6 shows an example of such a subject interaction diagram (SID) for a street intersection control system. The boxes are labeled with the name of a subject and the arrows with the names of the exchanged messages. For example the subject "Car-detection-1-north" receives the messages "switch on" and "switch off" from the subject "Detected Car collector" and it sends the message "car detected" to that subject.

4.3 Structure of Subjects

The internal structure of a subject is built up by three parts.

- Input Pool: The input pool is the mailbox in which sending subjects deposit messages.
- PASS Graph: In the PASS Graph (Subject Behavior Diagram, SBD) it is defined in which sequence messages are sent, removed from the input pool or which local actions on which object are performed. A detailed description of PASS can be found in [19].
- PASS Graph Refinements: The PASS graph refinements encapsulate all the internal data of a subject and all the related operations allowed on the data.

The input pool specifies the synchronization type which is related to a message exchange. Figure 7 shows an example of an input pool specification. An input pool has a maximum size which defines how many messages can be stored in the input pool simultaneously. In the example the maximum size is two messages. The maximum size of messages can be detailed for example by defining how many messages from a specific subject and/or a specific name can be in an input pool. Additionally it can be specified what should happen if all spaces in the input pool are occupied. It can be defined whether the new message is discarded or a message in the input pool is replaced according to a specified strategy (details see [19]).

The input pool attributes allow to specify which messages are exchanged synchronously which means a sender waits till a receiver accepts the message or asynchronously which means that a message is deposited in the input pool.

Figure 8 shows an example of a PASS graph. A PASS graph can have three different types of nodes: receive nodes, send nodes and internal action nodes. If a subject is in a receive state several messages can be expected according to the Subject Interaction Diagram. If one of these messages is in the input pool it is removed from the input pool, Its payload (data) is copied into an internal object, and the transition to the subsequent state is executed. In Fig. 8 the start state (state with the triangle in the upper right corner) is a receive state. If the message "switch on" from the subject "Detected car collector" appears in the input pool, the next state is the state "Detect cars", which is an operation (action) on a local object. If this operation could be executed with the result "Car detected" the following state is "send state". In this state the message "car detected" is sent to the subject "Detected car collector". The next state will be again state "Detect cars". This is the loop in which the subject "Car detection 1 north" informs the subject "Detected car collector" about cars approaching the controlled intersection.

This loop is guarded by an exception handler. If the message "switch off" is detected in the input pool the main behaviour is interrupted and the subject follows the behaviour of the exception handler. In our case the exception defines that the end state is reached if the "switch off" message has been received.

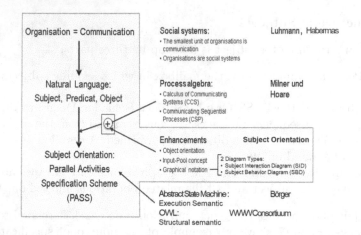

Fig. 5. Fundamentals of subject orientation

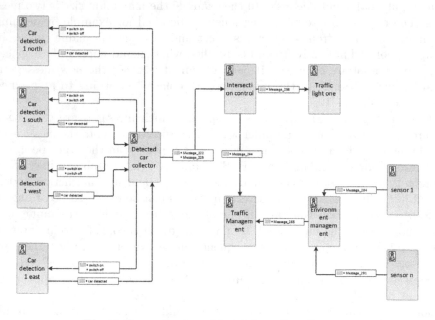

Fig. 6. Example of a subject interaction diagram

Each subject incorporates the objects it acts on. Objects are data structures and operations which are defined on the data structures. Objects are values in memory referenced by an identifier. This value can be changed or read by corresponding operations. In our example of an object "Detector device" incorporated in subject "Car detection 1 North" as shown in Fig. 9 there is a variable called "Car_detected". The operation "Detect cars" checks whether the variable "Car_detected" is equal 1. If this is true the operation returns the result "Car detected" and the value of the variable "Car_detected" is set to zero. Inside the object runs a loop which checks whether a car has been detected. If this is the case the variable "Car_detected" is set to one. The object "Detector device" is an abstract representation of a car detection device like an induction loop.

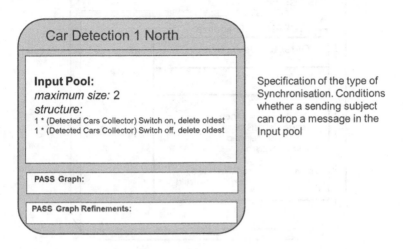

Fig. 7. Input pools in subjects

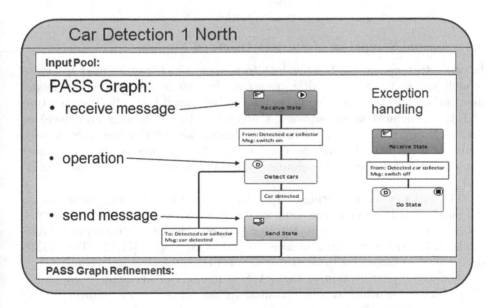

Fig. 8. PASS graph subject behaviour diagram

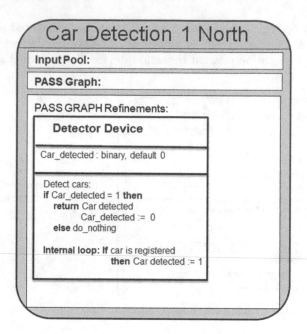

Fig. 9. PASS graph refinement

4.4   Formal Semantics of Subject Oriented Models

In order to keep models independent from tools which can be used to create models and to transform models in executable systems the structure of model descriptions and their interpretation have to be defined precisely. The structure of PASS is defined as an ontology. Using OWL (web Ontology Language) as defined in [6]. The ontology defines the description entities like state, transitions etc. and their relationships, e.g. the transitions between states. A detailed description and the complete definition of the PASS ontology can be found in [2] and [3].

The ontology allows editing of a model with any tool meeting the standard. An ontology only specifies the components of a model specification. It does not define the execution semantics. For that purpose, the interpretation of a PASS model with Abstract State Machine (ASM) is developed [11,12]. The ASMS define what actions have to be executed when an ontology is interpreted.

A detailed specification of the PASS semantic can be found in [3,45,46]. A complete code which can be executed on the coreASM environment can be downloaded from [47].

4.5   Implementation of Subjects

Subject oriented models address the internal aspects and structures of a system. They cover organizational and technical aspects. When implementing the models for execution, it is necessary to establish the relationship between the process model and the available resources [17]. Figure 10 shows the individual steps from a process model to the executable process instance.

In a system model, the subjects, the actions, their sequences and the objects manipulated by the actions are described. Actions (activities) can be performed by humans, software systems, physical systems or a combination of these basic types of actors. We call them the task holders. For example, a software system can automatically perform the "tax rate calculation" action, while a person uses a software program to perform the "order entry" activity. The person enters the order data via a form. The software checks the entered data for plausibility and saves it. However, activities can also be carried out purely manually, for example when a warehouse worker receives a picking order on paper, executes it, marks it as executed on the order form and returns it to the warehouse manager.

When creating a system model, it is often not yet known which types of actors execute which actions. Therefore, it can be useful to abstract from the executing entities when starting to describe processes. Instead of real actors abstract actors are introduced. An abstract actor is anything which is capabele to do something like human. A modeling language should allow the use of such abstractions. This means that when defining the process logic, no assertion should have to be made about what type of actor is realized. In subject oriented modeling, the subjects represent abstract actors. In the description of the control logic of a process, the individual activities are also described independently of their implementation. For example, for the action "create a picking order" it is not specified whether a human actor fills in a paper form or a form on a screen, or whether a software system fills out this form automatically based on some data in a database. As a consequence activities only describe what happens and not by what means the activities are carried out.

The means are of course related to the implementation type of the actor. As soon as it has been defined which types of actors are assigned to the individual actions, the manner of realization of an activity has also been defined. In addition, the logical or physical object on which an action is executed also needs to be determined. Logical objects are data structures whose data are manipulated by activities. Paper forms represent a mixture between logical and physical objects, while a workpiece on which the "deburring" action takes place is a purely physical object. Therefore, there is a close relationship between the type of task holder, the actions and the associated objects actors manipulate or use when performing actions.

Also the way of communication between subjects/actors depend on the implementation type of a subject. The way of communication between humans are implemented differently as between Cyber-Physical and Cyber-Human Actors.

A system model can be used in different areas of an organisation, e.g. for a process in the headquarters and in subsidiaries. The process logic can be uniquely applied in the respective areas. However, it may be necessary to implement the individual actors and actions differently. Thus, in one environment certain actions could be performed by humans and in another one the same actions could be performed by software systems. In the following, we refer to such different environments of use for a system model as context. Hence, for a process model, varying contexts can exist, in which there are different realization types for actors and actions.

A formal model how a subject oriented model is embedded in a certain organisational and/or technical environment can be found in [3,39].

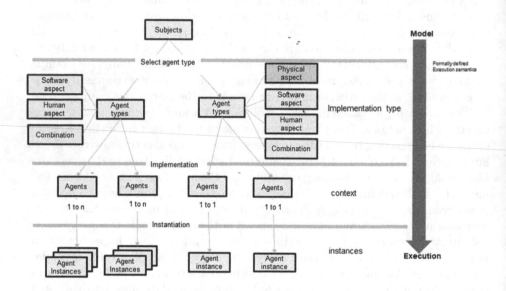

Fig. 10. Implementation hierarchy for subjects

4.6   Related Work

The subject-oriented approach is characterized by three dimensions:

1. Subjects as acting elements are in the center of the modeling approach.
2. Business objects, which are used by the subjects.
3. Implementation of the subjects and objects.

Other modeling languages for distributed systems do not clearly distinguish between these three dimensions. They mix logical with implementation aspects or neglect aspects.

BPMN [34], increasingly used as a language for describing business processes, allows to specify behavior aspects and implementation aspects in one diagram. Business objects are only covered marginally. Languages for designing software for embedded systems also integrate sensors and actuators in one model. Such languages combine subsets of UML with some special extensions [21].

Similar to languages for specifying embedded systems there exist languages to describe enterprises as systems consisting of people, organizational aspects and software. However, they do not consider physical devices and mix up logical and implementation aspects. An example of such a language is DEMO [15].

The authors of [41] give an overview of modeling methods for distributed systems being completely implemented in software. Programming languages for implementing distributed systems contain features for expressing concurrency, e.g. Erlang [26] or AKKA [48].

The investigated methods do not cover all the dimensions described above or lead to very complex languages when mixing dimensions in the specification.

5   Combining Industrie 4.0 Models with Subject Orientation

In this section we investigate the combination of Industrie 4.0 models with subject orientation. Firstly, in Sect. 5.1 the Platform Industrie 4.0 models RAMI and Asset Administration Shell and the IEC standard OPC UA are presented. It is shown that none of the models allows the specification of the behavior and interaction of components in terms of intelligent actors acting and interacting autonomously. As a solution, the combination of OPC UA with subject orientation is outlined in Sect. 5.2. OPC UA has been chosen for the combination with subject orientation because it is a widely used standard in automation and it already brings methods for information modeling in and communication between entities. Furthermore, some work already has been done on investigating how multi agent systems can be modeled using the OPC UA Client-Server mechanisms.

5.1   Industrie 4.0 Models

In April 2013 the professional German associations BITKOM, VDMA and ZVEI established the joint Industrie 4.0 Platform to promote the initiative and ensure a coordinated, cross-sectoral approach. In the Working Group "Reference Architectures and Standards" of the Industrie 4.0 Platform the technical concepts Reference Architectural Model Industrie 4.0 (RAMI 4.0) [23], the Industrie 4.0 Component and the Asset Administration Shell [9] for Industrie 4.0 components were defined.

The Reference Architectural Model Industrie 4.0 (RAMI 4.0) was published in April 2015. One of the fundamental ideas of RAMI is the grouping of highly diverse aspects in a common model in order to achieve a common understanding of what standards, use cases, etc. are necessary for Industrie 4.0. So, RAMI is a uniform architecture model as a reference, serving as a basis for the discussion of its interrelationships and details [43]. It joins the most important elements of Industrie 4.0 in a three-dimensional layer model providing a uniform structure and uniform wording and presenting the entire scope of I4.0. RAMI thus allows the relevant aspects of a particular asset to be shown at every point in time along its life cycle (Fig. 11).

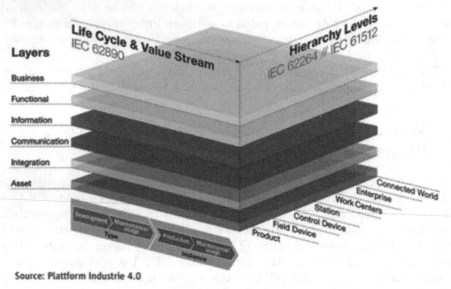

Source: Plattform Industrie 4.0

Fig. 11. Referenzarchitekturmodell Industrie 4.0

The "Hierarchy Levels" axis of RAMI structures the enterprise according to the automation pyramid levels (Product, Field Device, Control Device, Station, Work Centers, Enterprise, Connected Word). The "Life Cycle & Value Stream" axis represents the integrated product and production lifecycle. The six layers on the vertical "Layers" axis describe the properties of the assets in the digital world – broken down into layers (Asset, Integration, Communication, Information, Functional, Business). According to the RAMI model real-world assets can be classified in a unique way. RAMI is a high-level reference model for structuring Industrie 4.0, not a model that allows to describe the behavior of certain Industrie 4.0 assets or components.

For that purpose, in 2016 the concepts "Industrie 4.0 Component" and "Asset Administration Shell" for Industrie 4.0 components were introduced by the Platform Industrie 4.0 [9]. Figure 12 portrays the Industrie 4.0 Component and the Asset Administration Shell in a very high-level description. Every physical item to be integrated into Industrie 4.0 requires its own administration shell. The administration shell serves as logical representation of the asset in the digital world. The combination of asset and administration shell forms the so-called Industrie 4.0 Component [37].

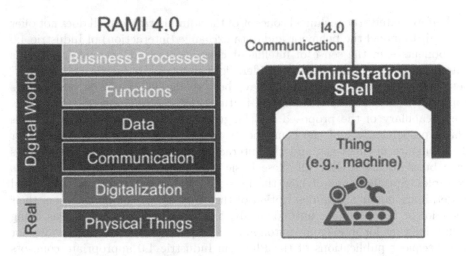

Fig. 12. Industrie 4.0 Component and Administration Shell

The Asset Administration Shell is the interface that connects physical items to Industrie 4.0 and consequently serves as the network's standardized communication interface. It stores all properties, data and functions of the asset in an information model (Fig. 13). Access to data is provided by the administration shell in an object-oriented way [9].

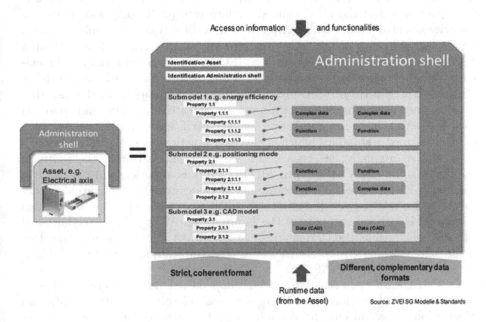

Fig. 13. Detailed model of the Administration Shell

Unfortunately, the technical concept of the administration shell does not offer methods to model the behavior and data exchange (interaction) of Industrie 4.0 components – in the sense of intelligent components that act and interact as autonomous actors. In [36] first considerations about an "Industrie 4.0 language" between Industrie 4.0 components have been made. The main purpose of this approach should be the exchange of features between components. Therefore, the vocabulary of the proposed I4.0 language has been described as features (data, properties, ...) of the components. Furthermore, very basic models for the structure of messages and the interaction protocols between components have been discussed. But all these basic models have only been outlined as examples. Specifications of how the messages and interactions are structured in detail are missing. The description of the "actions" of components, i.e. their behavior or how they act autonomously, has been recognized in [36] as being highly relevant for intelligent, autonomous components. But neither in [36] nor in subsequent publications of the Platform Industrie 4.0 appropriate concepts have been discussed or elaborated.

A well-known and widely used model and communication standard in industry is OPC UA, which stands for "Open Platform Communications - Unified Architecture". Already in 1996, the OPC Foundation released the first version of this communication standard under the name "OLE for process control" as it was built on Microsoft COM/DCOM technology. It acted like a device driver to enable PLC controllers to deliver data, alarms and historical data [33]. This today called "OPC classic" became de-facto standard for interoperable industrial communication. In 2003 the OPC Foundation started separating services from data and the OPC Unified Architecture (OPC UA) was created as a service-oriented architecture. After design, verification and implementation the first specification of OPC UA was released in 2008. Meanwhile, OPC UA is a full-fledged IEC standard known as IEC62541. With more than 750 members the OPC Foundation is the world's leading organization for interoperability solutions. The success of OPC classic and OPC UA comes from the fact that from the very beginning manufacturers, users, research institutes and consortia worked together in close cooperation on the specification and implementation and thus formed a standard which is effective, practicable and widely accepted.

OPC UA originally has been developed independently from the Platform Industrie 4.0 models. But in April 2018 the OPC Foundation and the German association ZVEI signed a "Memorandum of Understanding for mutual beneficial activities relating to "Industrie 4.0"". The first focus of this collaboration is an OPC UA based mapping of the Industrie 4.0 Asset Administration Shell (I4AAS). Meanwhile, the German association VDMA joined this initiative, too. In the joint Working Group "I4AAS OPC UA" they develop an OPC UA Information Model for the I4AAS.

OPC UA is an open standard without dependence on proprietary technologies or individual vendors. It delivers a secure, reliable transport of data and information across all enterprise levels. OPC UA is based on various types of standards and protocols like TCP for client-server communications (binary and

XML-based), MQTT and AMQP for cloud-based communications as well as UDP and specialized protocols like TSN or 5G for deterministic, real-time communication [33].

The heart of the OPC UA standard is a robust information modeling with an integrated address space in which process data, alarms and historical data together with function calls can be represented. OPC UA also defines the mechanisms needed to support dynamic discovery and access to information models. Key functions provided by OPC UA are browsing, read and write operations for current and historical data, method execution and notification for data and events.

OPC UA comprises two communication models, Client-Server communications and Publish-Subscribe (PubSub) mechanisms (Fig. 14). OPC UA Client-Server communications are based on the SOA design paradigm, where a service provider (server) gets requests from a client and sends back results together with the response to the client. To ensure interoperability between communication partners, OPC UA predefines generic standardized services. As a result, all OPC UA implementations are compatible and interoperable without the caller needing to have any special knowledge about the structure or behavior of a special service [33]. PubSub provides an alternative mechanism for data and event notification. Here multiple clients get broadcasted notifications from servers in a fire-and-forget fashion. While with Client-Server communications clients and servers directly exchange requests and responses, with PubSub publishers send messages to message-oriented middleware without any knowledge about the subscribers.

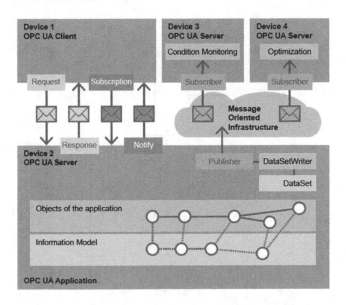

Fig. 14. OPC-UA communication models

OPC UA offers far more ways to exchange information between communication partners than the data-centric, feature based concepts of the Platform Industrie 4.0. The key functions browsing, read and write, method execution and notification allow a comprehensive data and message exchange and interaction between components. With the predefined generic standardized services OPC UA furthermore ensures interoperability up to a semantic level.

However, OPC UA still does not allow to model the behavior and interaction of components in the sense of intelligent components that act and interact dynamically as autonomous actors. The integration of Subject Orientation and OPC UA could perhaps be the solution for this challenge. In the following section ways to a corresponding approach will be introduced and discussed.

5.2 Integration Approach

Subjects are abstract entities. They are only defined by the interactions with other subjects and the objects they operate on. The way they are implemented is a separate decision. In this section we show how subjects can be implemented with the OPC-UA model. This is shown by a example based on an extract of the subject interaction diagram in Fig. 6. This extract is shown in Fig. 15. Because the problem is specified in a subject oriented way it can be also easily explained in natural language: The subject "Detected Car collector" sends a message "switch on" to the subject "Car Detection 1 North" and receives the message "car detected" from it. The subject "detected Car Collector" sends the messages "Message_222" and "Message_225" to the subject "Interconnection Control".

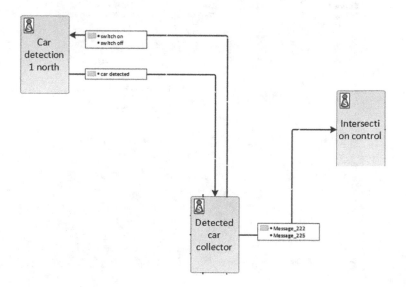

Fig. 15. Example: subject oriented solution structure

This problem-oriented specification is transformed into an implementation architecture based on OPC-UA. This architecture is shown in Fig. 16. The implementation architecture follows the approach to map a subject/agent to several OPC-UA servers and clients as it is described in [14] and [25]. Each subject is built by two servers and one client. The input pool and the PASS Graph Refinements are mapped to servers. The PASS Graph itself (Subject behavior diagram, SBD) is mapped to an OPC-UA client. This client sends messages by requesting the deposit operation of the input pool servers of the receiving subjects. The client receives messages by requesting the accepting operation of its own input pool server. This means the behavior client uses its own input pool server, all the input pool server of the subjects to which messages are sent and its server which incorporates all the internal objects. There must be at least one Refinement server but depending on the implementation complexity several servers can be applied.

The integration of Subject Orientation and OPC UA seems to be a win-win situation for both models. For OPC UA the extension by Subject Orientation allows to model the behavior and interaction of autonomous components, based on the standard information and communication models it comes with. Furthermore, as Subject Orientation is widely spread in business process modeling (S-BPM, Subject Oriented Business Process Modeling) it could be an opportunity for OPC UA to expand its area of application to upper levels of the enterprise like ERP, SCM or CRM, when its information modeling and communication methods are used in business process modeling and control. The value added for Subject Orientation when using OPC UA as a basis for information modeling and communication is on the one hand side the broad acceptance and distribution of this IEC standard IEC62541. On the other hand side, the multiple features of OPC UA (e.g. information modeling, integrated address apace

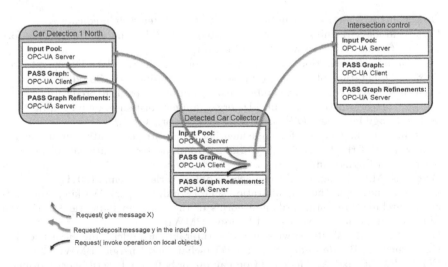

Fig. 16. OPC-UA based implementation of subjects

model, various use case specific protocol mappings, session services, integrated security by design) form an excellent basis for the implementation of Subject Orientation on all levels of the enterprise.

6 Conclusion

Appropriate modeling (behavior and interaction) of intelligent, autonomous Industrie 4.0 components is still an open issue in Industrie 4.0. The technical concept "Asset Administration Shell" of the Platform Industrie 4.0 is a data-centric and feature-based model. Specifications of how messages and interactions between Industrie 4.0 components (respectively their asset administration shells) are structured in detail do not exist up to now. OPC UA offers far more ways to exchange messages between communication partners. However, it still does not allow to model the behavior and interaction of intelligent components that act and interact dynamically as autonomous actors. The combination of OPC UA and the Subject-Oriented Paradigm, as proposed in this article, could be a solution for modeling and implementing intelligent and autonomous Industrie 4.0 components.

So far, this approach is only a first concept and multiple questions need to be answered in detail before it comes to an applicable modeling and execution solution. The authors of this article plan to launch a research project in which these questions are supposed to be answered. The goal of this project is an applicable solution for modeling intelligent, autonomous Industrie 4.0 components as well as a runtime system which ensures that Industrie 4.0 components act correspondingly to their modeling.

References

1. Object. https://dictionary.cambridge.org/dictionary/english/predicate
2. Pass ontology definition. https://github.com/I2PM/Standard-Documents-for-Subject-Orientation/tree/master/PASS-OWL
3. Pass standard definition. https://github.com/I2PM/Standard-Documents-for-Subject-Orientation/blob/master/Standard/Standardbuch-PASS.pdf
4. Predicate. https://dictionary.cambridge.org/dictionary/english/predicate
5. Subject. https://dictionary.cambridge.org/grammar/british-grammar/subjects
6. Web ontology language (OWL). https://www.w3.org/OWL/
7. acatech: recommendations for implementing the strategic initiative Industrie 4.0. Final report of the Industrie 4.0 Working Group. acatech - National Academy of Science and Engineering
8. Berghaus, M.: Luhmann leicht gemacht. Böhlau Verlag, Vienna (2011)
9. BMWi: Structure of the administration shell (working paper). Working group reference architectures, standards and norms of the platform Industrie 4.0. Federal Ministry for Economic Affairs and Energy (BMWi)
10. Bock, J., et al.: Weiterentwicklung des Interaktionsmodells für Industrie 4.0-Komponenten. Bundesministerium für Wirtschaft und Energie (BMWi) (2017)
11. Börger, E., Raschke, A.: Modeling Companion for Software Practitioners. Springer, Heidelberg (2018). https://doi.org/10.1007/978-3-662-56641-1

12. Börger, E., Stärk, R.: Abstract State Machines: A Method for High-Level System Design and Analysis. Springer, Heidelberg (2003). https://doi.org/10.1007/978-3-642-18216-7
13. Chukalov, K.: Horizontal and vertical integration, as a requirement for cyber-physical systems in the context of Industry 4.0. Int. Sci. J. Industry 4.0 **2**(4), 155–157 (2019)
14. Cupek, R., Ziebinski, A., Huczala, L., Grossmann, D., Bregulla, M.: Object-oriented communication model for an agent-based inventory operations management. In: INTELLI 2015: The Fourth International Conference on Intelligent Systems and Applications (2015)
15. Dietz, J.L.G.: Enterprise Ontology. Springer, Heidelberg (2006). https://doi.org/10.1007/3-540-33149-2
16. Embley, D.W., Thalheim, B.: Handbook of Conceptual Modeling. Springer, Heidelberg (2011). https://doi.org/10.1007/978-3-642-15865-0
17. Fleischmann, A., Oppl, S., Schmidet, W., Stary, C.: Contextual Process Digitalization. Springer, Cham (2020). https://doi.org/10.1007/978-3-030-38300-8
18. Fleischmann, A., Stary, C.: Dependable data sharing in dynamic IoT-systems - subject-oriented process design, complex event processing, and blockchains. In: Betz, S., Elstermann, M., Lederer, M. (eds.) S-BPM ONE 2019, 11th International Conference on Subject Oriented Business Process Management. ICPC Published by ACM Digital Library, Association of Computing Machinery (ACM) (2019)
19. Fleischmann, A., Schmidt, W., Stary, C., Obermeier, S., Boerger, E.: Subject-Oriented Business Process Management. Springer, Berlin (2012). https://doi.org/10.1007/978-3-642-32392-8
20. Friedl, A.: Meeting Industrie 4.0 challenges with S-BPM. In: Stary, C. (ed.) S-BPM One 2018 Proceedings of the 10th International Conference on Subject-Oriented Business Process Management. Communications in Computer and Information Science, Springer (2018)
21. Gooma, H.: Real-Time Software Design for Embedded Systems. Cambridge University Press, Cambridge (2016)
22. Habermas, J.: Theory of Communicative Action Volume 1, Volume 2. Suhrkamp Paperback Science (1981)
23. Hankel, M.: The reference architectural model Industrie 4.0 (RAMI 4.0)
24. Hoare, A.: Communicating Sequential Processes. Prentice Hall, Upper Saddle River (1985)
25. Hoffmann, M.: Adaptive und skalierbare Informationsmodellierung zur Ermöglichung autonomer Entscheidungsprozesse für interoperable reaktive Fertigungen. Von der Fakultät für Maschinenwesen der Rheinisch-Westfälischen Technischen Hochschule Aachen zur Erlangung des akademischen Grades eines Doktors der Ingenieurwissenschaften genehmigte Dissertation (2017)
26. Armstrong, J.: Programming Erlang. Pragmatic Bookshelf (2007)
27. Keenan, E.L.: Towards a universal definition of 'subject'. In: Charles, N.L. (ed.) Subject and Topic. Academic Press, New York (1976)
28. Lee, E.A.: Cyber physical systems: design challenges
29. Luhmann, N.: Social Systems. Suhrkamp Verlag, Berlin (1984)
30. Milner, R.: Communication and Concurrency. Prentice Hall, Upper Saddle River (1989)
31. Milner, R.: Communicating and Mobile Systems: The Pi-Calculus. Cambridge University Press, Cambridge (1999)
32. OMG: Unified Modeling Language® (OMG UML®). An OMG® Unified Modeling Language® Publication (2017)

33. OPC Foundation: OPC unified architecture - interoperability for Industrie 4.0 and the Internet of Things, version 07. www.opcfoundation.org
34. Open Management Group (OMG): Business Process Model and Notation (BPMN). http://www.omg.org/spec/BPMN/2.0
35. Pastor, O., Molina, J.C.: Model Driven Architecture in Practice. Springer, Heidelberg (2010)
36. Platform Industrie 4.0 in cooperation with ZVEI: Diskussionspapier I4.0-Sprache
37. Platform Industrie 4.0 in cooperation with ZVEI: Specification - details of the asset administration shell. Part 1 - the exchange of information between partners in the value chain of Industrie 4.0 (version 2.0)
38. Römpp, M.: Habermas leicht gemacht. Böhlau Verlag, Vienna (2015)
39. Schaller, T.W.: Organisationsverwaltung in CSCW-Systemen. Dissertation Universität Bamberg (1998)
40. Stachowiak, H.: Allgemeine Modelltheorie. Springer, Heidelberg (1973)
41. Sterling, L., Taveter, K.: The Art of Agent-Oriented Modeling. Massachusetts Institute of Technology (2009)
42. Thalheim, B.: The theory of conceptual models, the theory of conceptual modelling and foundations of conceptual modelling. In: Embley, D., Thalheim, B. (eds.) Handbook of Conceptual Modeling, pp. 543–579. Springer, Heidelberg (2011). https://doi.org/10.1007/978-3-642-15865-0_17
43. VDI/VDE: Working group reference architectures, standards and norms of the platform Industrie 4.0. VDI/VDE-Gesellschaft für Mess- und Automatisierungstechnik
44. Wan, J., Xia, N., Hong, J., Pang, Z., Jayaranab, B., Shen, F.: Editorial: key technologies for smart factories of Industry 4.0. IEEE Access: Special Section on Key Technologies for Smart Factories of Industry 4.0 (2017)
45. Wolski, A., Borgert, S., Heuser, L.: A CoreASM based reference implementation for subject oriented business process management execution semantics. In: Betz, S., Elstermann, M., Lederer, M. (eds.) S-BPM ONE 2019, 11th International Conference on Subject Oriented Business Process Management. ICPC Published by ACM Digital Library, Association of Computing Machinery (ACM) (2019)
46. Wolski, A., Borgert, S., Heuser, L.: An extended subject-oriented business process management execution semantics. In: Betz, S., Elstermann, M., Lederer, M. (eds.) S-BPM ONE 2019, 11th International Conference on Subject Oriented Business Process Management. ICPC Published by ACM Digital Library, Association of Computing Machinery (ACM) (2019)
47. Wolski, A.: ASM-pass-interpreter. https://github.com/I2PM/asm-pass-interpreter
48. Wyatt, D.: Akka Concurrency. Artima, Walnut Creek (2013)

Agile Generator-Based GUI Modeling for Information Systems

Arkadii Gerasimov, Judith Michael$^{(\boxtimes)}$, Lukas Netz, and Bernhard Rumpe

Software Engineering, RWTH Aachen, Aachen, Germany
{gerasimov,michael,netz,rumpe}@se-rwth.de
http://www.se-rwth.de

Abstract. We use two code generators for the model-based continuous development of information systems including its graphical user interfaces (GUIs). As our goal is to develop full-size real-world systems for different domains, the continuous and iterative model-based engineering of their GUIs comes along with challenges regarding their extension and modification. These challenges concern models, the languages they are written in and hand-written code. In this work we present four complementary approaches to allow extensions for GUIs that we encounter with the generator-based framework MontiGem to tackle these challenges. We discuss the four approaches in detail and present extensions of the framework in the grammar of the language, via atomic components, via hand-written amendments of generated models and by generating connections between the GUI and data structure models. These techniques can be used to create a flexible DSL for engineering information systems, adaptable for different domains and rapidly changing requirements.

Keywords: Information system · Modeling graphical user interfaces · Model-Based Software Engineering · Code generation · MontiGem

1 Introduction

Model-Based Software Engineering (MBSE) and code generators are well established technologies [30,31]. MBSE uses models as the basis for software engineering. They describe both problem and solution consistently and produce a solution that give comprehensive and verifiable answers to the system requirements posed by the problem [24]. These advantages provide significant support when seeking a solution to a software engineering problem.

MBSE and code generators can be used to create an Enterprise Information System (EIS) [2] using a multitude of Domain-Specific Languages (DSLs) [1]. Within this paper, we focus on the modeling of Graphical User Interfaces (GUIs) with a DSL and take a closer look on the needs for an agile iterative engineering process. In order to refine the target code, mechanisms to extend the generated code with hand-written amendments are introduced. This leaves us with two options to modify the application: Changing the model in order to generate new target code, or changing the hand-written code directly, for example

© Springer Nature Switzerland AG 2021
A. Dahanayake et al. (Eds.): M2P 2020, CCIS 1401, pp. 113–126, 2021.
https://doi.org/10.1007/978-3-030-72696-6_5

by extending the generated classes. In order to take advantage of the perks of MBSE and code generation, we intend to define as much as possible within the models. Therefore we have to consider a third option: Extending the grammar of a modeling language in order to facilitate the definition of further aspects.

Within this paper, we tackle three **challenges** regarding (1) the modification and extension of an EIS GUI (2) using an agile engineering approach (3) allowing for continuous re-generation (4) without adapting the hand-written code:

Challenge 1: Our GUI modeling language [1] is good enough for reuse in different generated EISs but *too generic and restrictive regarding addition of new components*. By extending the modeling capabilities of the language, we can integrate new components easily, generate more specific source code and reduce the amount of hand-written code in the resulting EISs.

Challenge 2: The current approach lacks support for *iterative, evolving GUI models* which can be reused. Similar to a pattern approach, a model should be usable as a template within another model of the same language.

Challenge 3: The current approach lacks support for *interweaving models from different languages*. Aspects already defined in a different model, *e.g.*, a data model, should be reusable to prevent redundancy in modeling. This requires composition of modeling languages.

To overcome these challenges, this paper addresses the **research question** *how we can extend and modify the GUI of an application created with MBSE methods without having to adapt the hand-written code for each particular generated EIS*. In this work we discuss *four approaches* to modify and extend the generated application and inspect options on how to adapt given models without having to adapt the hand-written code. The four (non-exclusive) options are:

(A1) Extension in the grammar: Introducing an approach to extend the grammar of the GUI-DSL enables the software engineer to define more problem-specific models and, thus, reduce the amount of hand-written source code (Challenge 1).

(A2) Extension via atomic components: A general GUI component in the grammar can be used to create and assemble new components and adds a new level of flexibility to the language (Challenge 1). This extension is similar to the first approach, but is more advantageous in particular cases.

(A3) Extension and modification via addition of hand-written GUI models: To modify GUI models by adding hand-written ones allows for model modifications despite continuous re-generation processes (Challenge 2).

(A4) Extension via data models and connections to the GUI models: Defining a connection between the two DSLs used to define the data structure and the GUI allows to generate view models from models of both types (Challenge 3).

Outline. The next section explains several prerequisites for agile and iterative GUI modeling of EISs. Section 3 presents our four approaches for GUI modeling. Section 4 discusses other GUI languages and how they handle the challenges described before. Section 5 concludes.

2   Prerequisites

MBSE relies on the use of models to reduce the complexity of developed applications and systems [17]. Engineers can use a variety of modeling languages for agile and model-based development of an EIS. In our case, these languages and their tooling are created with the modeling platform and language workbench MontiCore [18]. We use the generator framework MontiGem [2] and a newly developed DSL, called GUI-DSL, to create the resulting EIS [14].

2.1   The Language Workbench MontiCore

The MontiCore [18,22] language workbench facilitates the engineering of textual DSLs. It provides mechanisms to analyze, manipulate and transform the models of a developed DSL. The concrete syntax of a DSL is defined in extended context-free grammars and context conditions are programmed in Java for checking the well-formedness of models. MontiCore generates parsers, which are able to handle models of the DSL, and infrastructures for transforming the models into their Abstract Syntax Tree (AST) representation and for symbol table construction. The AST and symbol table infrastructures embody the abstract syntax of a modeling language. Once the parser gets a model as an input, it creates an AST for each model as well as a symbol table for further processing, *e.g.*, for code generation or analysis. The input AST can be transformed as needed. A template engine uses the output AST together with templates for the target language to create the resulting code [18]. MontiCore provides means for a *modular development* and *composition* of DSLs [18]. It supports language inheritance, embedding and aggregation [15].

Until now, a variety of languages, including a collection of UML/P [28] languages (variants of UML which fit better for programming) as well as the OCL, delta, tagging languages, SysML and architecture description languages are realized with MontiCore[1].

2.2   Creating Information Systems with MontiGem

MontiGem [1,2], the generator framework for enterprise management, creates an EIS out of a collection of input models and allows for hand-written additions. The parser, AST-infrastructure and the symbol table infrastructure of the framework are generated by MontiCore. Figure 1 shows the main generation process for an EIS using MontiGem.

MontiGem uses Class Diagrams (CDs) (domain and view models) and GUI-DSL models (views) as input (see A in Fig. 1). Additionally, it can handle OCL models, *e.g.*, for creating validation functions for input data, and tagging models, *e.g.*, for adding platform specific information to the domain model.

For code generation MontiGem uses two generators (B in Fig. 1): The data structure and the user interface generator. The data structure generator creates

---

[1] see http://www.monticore.de/languages/.

the database schema, back-end data structure and communication infrastructure for the back-end and front-end out of CD models and view models. The user interface generator creates TypeScript and HTML files for the front-end out of GUI models. The generator parsers check the input models for syntactical correctness and produce ASTs. The generators feed the ASTs and templates for the target languages (Java for the back-end and TypeScipt/HTML for the front-end) to a template engine, which generates the resulting code.

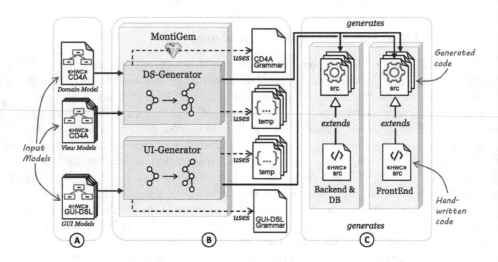

Fig. 1. The generation process using MontiGem

MontiGem can handle hand-written additions of the generated code. This is important for agile engineering processes and their need for continuous re-generation. For example, CSS classes are defined manually in separate files and can be referred to in the models. In other cases, the generated code needs to be extended by the hand-written code (HWC) directly, in which case the *TOP-mechanism* [18] is used. The main idea of the TOP-mechanism is to extend the generated code with the hand-written code using *inheritance*, while keeping artifacts separate (C in Fig. 1). This allows to extend the business logic of the information system and continuously re-generate code without losing the hand-written extension.

We have used the generator framework MontiGem for engineering of several applications, *e.g.*, a full-size real-world application for financial and staff control [13] and projects in the manufacturing [10], automotive and energy domain.

2.3 Roles for Language and Application Engineering

In practice, language and application engineering are separated processes, which involve people from different teams. Figure 2 shows roles related to the four approaches in Sec. 3. We distinguish six different roles that are involved in the application and generator engineering process: In order to define a model we need a DSL. A **Language Engineer** defines the grammar (Fig. 1Ⓑ) of the DSL and maintains it. These DSLs are used by the **Application Modeler** to define models (Fig. 1Ⓐ) that represent different aspects of the modeled application. Dependent on the DSLs, the Application Modeler does not require a background in programming, but should have good knowledge of the domain. Once a model is defined, it is parsed, interpreted and transformed into target source code (Fig. 1Ⓒ) by the generator. The generator itself (Fig. 1Ⓑ) is maintained and configured by the **Generator Customizer**. In small development teams, Language Engineer and Generator Customizer might be the same person, whereas in larger teams this might even be people from different teams. Hand-written parts (Fig. 1Ⓒ) of the resulting application are implemented by the **Application Programmer** who has coding skills. Predefined, not generated and not application specific components (Fig. 1Ⓒ) are implemented by the **Component Provider**. Finally, the **Tool Provider** configures and maintains libraries and components (Fig. 1Ⓒ) in the run-time environment of the application and the generator (Fig. 1Ⓑ).

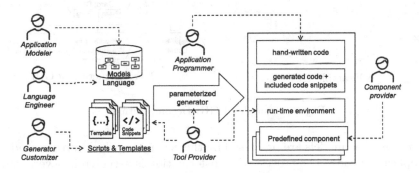

Fig. 2. Roles for language and application engineering

2.4 GUI-DSL, a Language for Defining User Interfaces

The GUI-DSL [14] is a textual modeling language aimed at describing an interactive user interface for data representation and management in an EIS. The DSL is part of a large collection of MontiCore languages and allows to create complex views by defining models, each of which is interpreted by the user interface generator and transformed into a web-page.

Grammar. As the web interface is a primary generation target, principles of web interface design are followed in the language and reflected in the structure of the grammar. The core concept of the grammar is built around the idea of constructing a view by combining and nesting GUI-components, which provide various data representations, *e.g.*, text, charts, tables, or are used to define the layout of the page. In the context of this work, a GUI-component is a software component with a graphical representation, defining a visual interaction unit and/or providing graphical representation of information. Another aspect handled by the language is the definition of data sources for the view, which includes minimal information about how and in what format the data is delivered.

Model. Each model of the language describes a web page and has a structure similar to an HTML document. The page definition describes a hierarchical view: A tree, where leaves provide the graphical representation of the data and intermediate nodes define the layout of the page, *e.g.,* Fig. 3b depicts the structure of the web page on Fig. 3a. The GUI-components are part of a `Card` container, where the head (blue top area of Fig. 3a) has a `Label` (text "Accountant details") and a `Button` (with a question mark). The body contains a `Datatable` (table of accounts). A distinctive feature of a GUI-DSL model is the data handling. The page definition includes information about the data as variables, which are used as an input for GUI-components.

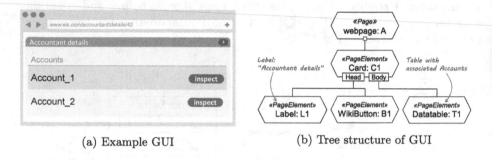

(a) Example GUI   (b) Tree structure of GUI

Fig. 3. Example of GUI Decomposition

Generator. The models are processed by the generator, which further produces the application code. The process of transformation is executed in several steps. First, the model is parsed and an AST of the model is created. The AST is further transformed into a form which closely resembles the structure of the generated code and is finally given to the template engine to construct the view and the logic of the page piece by piece. Optionally, the generated code is further formatted. This can be useful during the development as it makes the code more readable and helps to analyze the code.

In order to define a web-page with simple functionality, it is enough to create a GUI-DSL model to define the graphical representation and a data model to define the data being displayed on the page. We are also investigating approaches where only a CD is needed to create the first version of an application [14].

3   Approaches

During the agile development of an information system, several challenges arise for GUI modeling. We describe the challenge to be tackled in detail, propose a solution, define the roles involved in handling the challenge and analyze positive and negative aspects of the solution. The overreaching objective is to support the application programmer with MBSE by increasing the amount of generated code and decreasing the amount of hand-written code.

3.1 GUI-Extension via Grammar (A1)

A GUI model consists of GUI-components describing parts of a user interface. If a new GUI-component is implemented and used, it has to be reflected in the GUI model. Additionally, it has to be determined how the GUI-DSL needs to be changed and how it affects models of the language.

Challenge. Depending on the specification of data presentation in the user interface, various GUI-components are needed and new ones have to be implemented and integrated into the application (Challenge 1). In GUI-DSL, a page is described by a model which uses GUI-components. The GUI-components have to be included in the definition of the DSL to be useable in the model. The DSL is unaware of new GUI-components and they cannot be used in the model until its interfaces are described as a part of the DSL. It is also necessary to implement the transformation process in the generator in order to properly map the usage of a GUI-component in the model to its usage in the target code.

Roles. The adjustment of the current language is handled by a Language Engineer, whereas the generator is adjusted by a Generator Customizer.

Solution. A direct solution is to make both DSL and the corresponding generator extendable. This can be achieved with various kinds of language compositions, such as aggregation or inheritance [19]. The idea is to separately define a new DSL with its own generator, which can be combined with the existing one to allow usage of both DSLs in one model and produce a combined result. For example, a calendar GUI-component needs to be added to the user interface. We have to create a separate extension of the DSL and corresponding generator, which describes the calendar GUI- component and generate the code for it. Such approach requires a common ground for different kinds of GUI-components, an interface to consistently handle them and a reusable generator structure to mitigate the effort spent on implementation of mapping for the new component.

Advantages and Disadvantages. The solution is straightforward for both development roles involved and allows to embed the logic necessary for a proper operation of a GUI-component on a page directly into the generator. This is especially useful if the added component has a complicated structure and is heavily configurable. Specific syntax can be defined to simplify its definition in the model and let the generator handle the specifics. On the other hand, it takes considerable effort to integrate even the simplest GUI-components, as a new language and different generator parts have to be created and integrated with the existing ones.

3.2 GUI-Extension via Atomic Components (A2)

The previous challenge can be addressed from different angles and although the previous solution is valid, it has a considerable disadvantage regarding the effort.

Challenge. An ability to use a hand-written GUI-component in a model is important, but it is also important to provide this ability without spending a lot of effort on creating a DSL and a generator, especially if the added component is very simple and does not require additional specific behavior definition to be operable on a page (see Challenge 1). In such case, it is desirable to enable GUI-component definition in models, where a new component is defined in a model and conforms to a common structure. We will call these GUI-components atomic, which signify a smallest unit of view composition on a modeling level.

Roles. Since the problem is solved in a different phase, the responsibility to define new components moves from the Generator Customizer and Language Engineer to the Application Modeler.

Solution. Defining a GUI-component in a model means that a rule for such general definition of atomic components needs to be present in the language. This rule specifies how to create a new GUI-component, *e.g.*, by using the name of the component and its interface. The interface consists of configurable properties of the component, which then have to be defined in a model to allow instantiation and usage of the GUI-component in other models. Taking the example from the previous section, a calendar needs to be added to the user interface. This solution suggests to describe the calendar GUI-component in a model, which can be referred to from other models.

Advantages and Disadvantages. Introducing a new GUI-component in a model saves a lot of effort compared to DSL extension. If a simple component is implemented, this approach allows to quickly integrate it into the application models, and generate the corresponding code without penalty. Additionally, a uniform rule for component creation ensures consistency of GUI-component representation in models. However, if a complex component is created which requires additional logic to be used on web pages, either a mechanism for indirect generator manipulation needs to be defined and attached to the language or the generated code always has to be completed by a hand-written amendment. This solution amplifies the development effort proportional to the complexity of an introduced GUI-component: The more complex the component is, the more additional effort is required for its integration, whereas the previous solution implies the similar amount of effort regardless of the component complexity.

3.3   GUI-Extension and Modification via Hand-Written Model (A3)

Models can be generated or hand-written. Independently from the origin of models, modifications can be necessary and should remain during re-generation.

Challenge. In [14] we have introduced an approach to generate GUI-models from CDs. In such case, developers would like to change the appearance of the application which results either in adding larger amounts of hand-written code, changing the generated GUIs or changing the generated models. Whereas the first approach requires manual effort, any changes would be undone by the next generation cycle for the latter two. If not only code but also models are generated, changes in these models will get lost during re-generation processes. This requires an approach to handle changes for generated models.

Roles. The Application Modeler modifies models.

Solution. We can extend the GUI-DSL to allow for modification of a GUI model by adding another GUI model. This extension enables references between GUI models. The application modeler for example can be provided with a generated model, that displays data as a table. This approach enables him to replace the table with a bar chart by modifying the generated model with his handwritten one. As described in Fig. 3, a GUI model can be represented in a tree structure. With a simple set of tree manipulations, any GUI-model can be transformed into the one needed. Similar to the TOP-Mechanism [18], we use naming conventions to distinguish between and identify the generated and the hand-written model. The hand-written model itself is a valid model and replaces the generated one. This approach is discussed in [14] in more detail.

Advantages and Disadvantages. Extending models by further models, can lead to a lack of clarity considering where components are defined and configured. Hand-written models themselves can be modified multiple times leading to badly defined models. The alternative would be a modification within the generated source code, but depending on the size of the modification needed, an adaption of the model instead of the code might be easier to maintain and to comprehend for the developer while simultaneously generating consistent code.

3.4   GUI-Extension via Data-Models (A4)

Agile development requires additions and changes in the data structure. These changes will have effects on the graphical representation.

Challenge. The data structure of iteratively evolving software is very likely to be subject to change. The user interface presents and allows for interaction with the data, which is defined in the data structure. There is a strong dependency between GUI and data structure which should be reflected in a dependency between the GUI model and the domain model (Challenge 3).

Roles. The view is modeled by the *Application Modeler*, whereas the grammar of the GUI-DSL has to be adapted by the *Generator Customizer*.

Solution. In order to display data from the database in the GUI we use the MVVM pattern (Fig. 4). The Data-Model is defined by the domain model (a class diagram) and is used as an input for the generator. The View is defined by the GUI-model. We can use a combination of both to derive the View-Model. By referencing classes and attributes of the Data-Model in the View, we can derive the classes and attributes needed in the View-Model. An additional class diagram (View-Model) is generated for each GUI-model and provided to the data structure generator, which uses the Data-Model and all View-Models as an input. The dependency from Data-Model to View-Model can be used to load and transport the correct data to the View. For example, when defining a table in a GUI model, the data model could be referenced directly by the table entries.

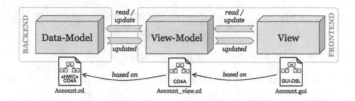

Fig. 4. MVVM pattern

Advantages and Disadvantages. Generated view-models can be less efficient than hand-written ones. This problem can be mitigated by allowing custom view-models, that are used instead of the generated ones. The advantage of generated view-models is that they always fit to the domain model. Changing the data structure will result in automatically changed view-models. Hand-written view-models become obsolete, which reduces developer effort.

4   Discussion and Related Work

MBSE for user interfaces has been addressed in different publications [5,20,23,25]. Different solutions address directly or indirectly the approaches discussed in this work, namely extensions (A1) in the grammar, (A2) via atomic components, (A3) via hand-written models and by generating models from models and (A4) by generating connections between the GUI and data-structure models. MontiGem in combination with MontiCore explicitly supports all four approaches.

GUI-Extension via Grammar (A1). The problem of extending the language to allow more flexible definition of the user interface is often set to the background [3,4,16]. The set of elements in the view is considered to be static and focused purely on information delivery. This can result in a need for language extension when the models are required to be applied for another domain. For example, the modeling language IFML [5] had to be extended in order to fit a different domain [7,8,26]. Similar to GUI-DSL, the language introduces interfaces and means for abstractions, which serve as a base for new GUI-components and provide a general description for components of the same type, although the adaptability of the language to a different domain is not considered directly. Aside from adding new GUI- components into the language, the extension is also possible using stereotypes, *i.e.*, additional information is attached to existing components with keywords, which specify the interpretation of a GUI-component. Such solution also requires implementation of a separate language and a generator and can be used if an infrastructure for this approach is available. Diep et al. [11] suggest several GUI modeling levels, starting from an abstract representation of GUI-components in general, followed by more specific element type, *e.g.*, button, text box, *etc.*, and ending with platform-specific elements, such as `StackPanel` for Windows Phone. The abstract models are transformed into more specific ones up to the generation of the target code. Having several levels of abstraction allows to add not only specific elements, but also a new category of GUI-components. However, adding a new category of components would still require the definition of the mapping to the more specific elements or target code.

GUI-Extension via Atomic Components (A2). Most approaches for user interface modeling use predefined sets of GUI-components [3,4,16]. There exist, however, some approaches which provide the ability to extend the variety of GUI-components. One option is to combine components from a predefined set into a new component and use it in models of the user interface [9,21,23]. Although it does not affect the visual appearance of an interface, it helps to reuse presentational patterns. An interesting take on the problem is discussed in [20], which defines a DSL based on a Groovy programming language. The DSL uses function calls similar to the rules for construction of GUI-components described in this work to build the view, *i.e.*, the GUI-component definitions are functions and new components can potentially be added by defining new functions. The key feature is that the pages and GUI-components are both described on the same modeling level. The GUI-components are functions, which are called in the body of a page function, thus constructing the whole view. This technique is similar to the presented one, but it is not designed to simplify the process of defining a GUI-component on a modeling level and does not guarantee the simplicity of GUI-component integration.

GUI-Extension and Modification via Hand-Written Model (A3). The concept of user interface derivation finds its place in [6], where the first step is to model the tasks with details such as task context, roles involved and manipulated objects. The user interface model is derived from the task model based on the dependencies between the tasks. As a result, the interface is updated when a task model is modified. [29] proposes model-to- model transformation in order to get models of user interface from models describing use cases, data structure and other models, which correspond to various aspects of an application. The approach considers only two options for modeling a user interface: it is either completely derived or completely modeled by hand. Our work goes one step further and enables flexible modification of the generated models.

GUI-Extension via Data-Models (A4). The possibility to reference the data structure in a user interface model has been recognized in [12,27,32]. The overall approach regarding the connection between view and a data structure is similar to the one in this work: The publications propose the usage of several models to tackle different aspects of a web application, where a domain model and presentation model are defined separately, but at the same time the presentation model refers to the domain model in order to define the content of a user interface. Using such concept allows to describe parts of application focused on specific problem separately and to bring these parts together by integrating fragments of a domain model in a presentation model to define their content.

In general, a DSL designed for GUI description tends to have a predefined set of GUI-components used to build a user interface. This allows a modeler to easily create a new GUI by simply choosing a suitable data presentation from a small set. However, this also implies that the language *restricts the variability* of the generated GUI, which is necessary if the language needs to be further reused and applied to a different problem domain. Making the language flexible by introducing extension mechanisms to integrate new GUI-components helps to cope with such challenge, but it still requires considerable effort to define a mapping between newly introduced component and the target code. If the language needs to be *heavily reusable and adaptable, e.g.,* to describe GUIs on different platforms or to target different users, it makes sense to introduce a creation rule for new GUI-components in the language to allow a modeler to create new building blocks for a user interface. Enhancements of a different kind, such as derivation of the GUI models, introduces the similar problem of restricting the variability of user interfaces by predefining the mapping from a non-GUI model to a GUI model. Major adjustments of a GUI on a modeling level would be confusing and difficult to maintain, while minor changes can be done manually and the problem can potentially be ignored. However, the benefits of a modeling approach would still be lost and it could be worth to create a simple set of operations to modify the generated GUI models. The last extension considered in this work is handling the connection between GUI and data. In case the data structure and GUI are modeled separately, establishing the connection between the models allows to generate a code for communication between a user interface and data provider, which enables building functional application prototypes.

The proposed solutions are designed to reduce the development time and to support the agile and iterative engineering of EIS. Typical engineering processes which consider MBSE and code generation include strong user involvement, agile reaction to changes and small product increments. The four approaches suggest adaptations on a language or a modeling level to delegate the task of changing huge parts hand-written code to a more abstract level, where the changes are minimal, thus reducing development time and effort.

5   Conclusion

MBSE and code generators allow for an agile development process of EIS. However, this comes along with the question where to make changes for changing requirements: In the models, in the grammar of the DSL the models are created with or in the hand-written code. The requirements can also imply different forms of changes, such as adding new code or adjusting the existing code. In this paper we have shown four approaches, which allow to extend and modify the GUI of an information system created with MBSE methods without having to adapt the hand-written code: (A1) in the grammar, (A2) via atomic components, (A3) via hand-written models and by generating models from models and (A4) generating connections between the GUI and data structure models. These techniques can be used to create a flexible DSL, adaptable for different domains and rapidly changing requirements with reduced manual effort.

It is important to enable extensions of GUIs using MBSE and code generation. The extendability is relevant not only for GUIs but on different levels and also for other model-based aspects of the application. Thus, further considerations have to be done to enable extendability of other generators for the application as well as the run-time environment.

References

1. Adam, K., Michael, J., Netz, L., Rumpe, B., Varga, S.: Enterprise information systems in academia and practice: lessons learned from a MBSE project. In: 40 Years EMISA: Digital Ecosystems of the Future: Methodology, Techniques and Applications (EMISA 2019). LNI, vol. P-304, pp. 59–66. Gesellschaft für Informatik e.V (2020)
2. Adam, K., et al.: Model-based generation of enterprise information systems. In: Enterprise Modeling and Information Systems Architectures (EMISA 2018), vol. 2097, pp. 75–79. CEUR-WS.org (2018)
3. Bernardi, M., Cimitile, M., Maggi, F.: Automated development of constraint-driven web applications, pp. 1196–1203 (2016). https://doi.org/10.1145/2851613.2851665
4. Bernardi, M.L., Cimitile, M., Di Lucca, G.A., Maggi, F.M.: M3D: a tool for the model driven development of web applications. In: Proceedings of the Twelfth International Workshop on Web Information and Data Management, WIDM 2012, pp. 73–80. ACM (2012)
5. Bernaschina, C., Comai, S., Fraternali, P.: IFMLEdit.org: model driven rapid prototyping of mobile apps, pp. 207–208 (2017)
6. Berti, S., Correani, F., Mori, G., Paternó, F., Santoro, C.: TERESA: a transformation-based environment for designing and developing multi-device interfaces, pp. 793–794 (2004). https://doi.org/10.1145/985921.985939
7. Brambilla, M., Mauri, A., Franzago, M., Muccini, H.: A model-based method for seamless web and mobile experience, pp. 33–40 (2016). https://doi.org/10.1145/3001854.3001857
8. Brambilla, M., Mauri, A., Umuhoza, E.: Extending the interaction flow modeling language (IFML) for model driven development of mobile applications front end. In: Awan, I., Younas, M., Franch, X., Quer, C. (eds.) MobiWIS 2014. LNCS, vol. 8640, pp. 176–191. Springer, Cham (2014). https://doi.org/10.1007/978-3-319-10359-4_15
9. Costa Paiva, S., Oliveira, J., Loja, L., Graciano Neto, V.: A metamodel for automatic generation of enterprise information systems (2010)
10. Dalibor, M., Michael, J., Rumpe, B., Varga, S., Wortmann, A.: Towards a model-driven architecture for interactive digital twin cockpits. In: Dobbie, G., Frank, U., Kappel, G., Liddle, S.W., Mayr, H.C. (eds.) ER 2020. LNCS, vol. 12400, pp. 377–387. Springer, Cham (2020). https://doi.org/10.1007/978-3-030-62522-1_28
11. Diep, C.K., Tran, N., Tran, M.T.: Online model-driven IDE to design GUIs for cross-platform mobile applications, pp. 294–300 (2013). https://doi.org/10.1145/2542050.2542083
12. Dukaczewski, M., Reiss, D., Stein, M., Rumpe, B., Aachen, R.: MontiWeb - model based development of web information systems (2014)
13. Gerasimov, A., et al.: Generated enterprise information systems: MDSE for maintainable co-development of frontend and backend. In: Michael, J., Bork, D., (eds.) Companion Proceedings of Modellierung 2020 Short, Workshop and Tools & Demo Papers, pp. 22–30. CEUR-WS.org (2020)

14. Gerasimov, A., Michael, J., Netz, L., Rumpe, B., Varga, S.: Continuous transition from model-driven prototype to full-size real-world enterprise information systems. In: Anderson, B., Thatcher, J., Meservy, R., (eds.) 25th Americas Conference on Information Systems (AMCIS 2020). AIS Electronic Library (AISeL), Association for Information Systems (AIS) (2020)
15. Haber, A., et al.: Composition of heterogeneous modeling languages. In: Desfray, P., Filipe, J., Hammoudi, S., Pires, L.F. (eds.) MODELSWARD 2015. CCIS, vol. 580, pp. 45–66. Springer, Cham (2015). https://doi.org/10.1007/978-3-319-27869-8_3
16. Heitkötter, H., Majchrzak, T.A., Kuchen, H.: Cross-platform model-driven development of mobile applications with md². In: SAC (2013)
17. Hölldobler, K., Michael, J., Ringert, J.O., Rumpe, B., Wortmann, A.: Innovations in model-based software and systems engineering. J. Obj. Technol. **18**(1), 1–60 (2019). https://doi.org/10.5381/jot.2019.18.1.r1
18. Hölldobler, K., Rumpe, B.: MontiCore 5 language workbench edition 2017. Aachener Informatik-Berichte, Software Engineering, Band 32, Shaker Verlag, December 2017
19. Hölldobler, K., Rumpe, B., Wortmann, A.: Software language engineering in the large: towards composing and deriving languages. Comput. Lang. Syst. Struct. **54**, 386–405 (2018)
20. Jia, X., Jones, C.: AXIOM: a model-driven approach to cross-platform application development. In: ICSOFT 2012 - Proceedings of the 7th International Conference on Software Paradigm Trends, pp. 24–33 (2012)
21. Koch, N., Knapp, A., Zhang, G., Baumeister, H.: UML-based web engineering: an approach based on standards, pp. 157–191 (2008)
22. Krahn, H., Rumpe, B., Völkel, S.: MontiCore: a framework for compositional development of domain specific languages. Int. J. Softw. Tools Technol. Transf. (STTT) **12**(5), 353–372 (2010)
23. Kraus, A., Knapp, A., Koch, N.: Model-driven generation of web applications in UWE. In: CEUR Workshop Proceedings, vol. 261 (2007)
24. Long, D., Scott, Z.: A primer for model-based systems engineering. Lulu. com (2011)
25. Marland, V., Kim, H.: Model-driven development of mobile applications allowing role-driven variants, pp. 14–26 (2019)
26. Morgan, R., Grossmann, G., Schrefl, M., Stumptner, M., Payne, T.: VizDSL: a visual DSL for interactive information visualization, pp. 440–455 (2018)
27. Ren, L., Tian, F., (Luke) Zhang, X., Zhang, L.: DaisyViz: a model-based user interface toolkit for interactive information visualization systems. J. Vis. Lang. Comput. **21**(4), 209–229 (2010). part Special Issue on Graph Visualization
28. Rumpe, B.: Modeling with UML: Language, Concepts, Methods. Springer, Cham (2016). https://doi.org/10.1007/978-3-319-33933-7
29. Seixas, J., Ribeiro, A., Silva, A.: A model-driven approach for developing responsive web Apps, pp. 257–264 (2019). https://doi.org/10.5220/0007678302570264
30. Selic, B.: The pragmatics of model-driven development. IEEE Softw. **20**(5), 19–25 (2003)
31. Stahl, T., Völter, M., Efftinge, S., Haase, A.: Modellgetriebene Softwareentwicklung: Techniken, Engineering, Management, vol. 2, pp. 64–71 (2007)
32. Valverde, F., Valderas, P., Fons, J., Pastor, O.: A MDA-based environment for web applications development: from conceptual models to code (2019)

Formal Model Checking and Transformations of Models Represented in UML with Alloy

Meriem Kherbouche[(✉)] [iD] and Bálint Molnár[(✉)] [iD]

Eötvös Loránd University, ELTE, IK Pázmány Péter 1/C, Budapest 1117, Hungary
{meriemkherbouche,molnarba}@inf.elte.hu
https://www.inf.elte.hu/en/

Abstract. Nowadays, information systems (IS) are making considerable efforts to create, develop, and build new and more advanced models capable of modeling all (or the mainstream) development trends in IS. The progress in IS is mainly related to three main points: document-centered approaches, modern database management systems and their applications, and new flexible models, which are more complex than existing models in most cases. The challenges of the modeling process are mainly the presentation of both the static and dynamic sides of the developed IS. The latter is directly influenced by the change processes of the business environment. In this paper, we use the properties of the Activity Diagram, represented by Alloy - an operationalizable specification language for software architecture - together with the underlying mathematical model to simplify the semantics of the models and to facilitate their analysis, verification, and validation.

Keywords: Model to program · Alloy · Formal modeling · Model checking · UML · Activity diagram · Verification · Transformation · Reliability of information systems

1 Introduction

UML (Unified Modeling Language) is a graphical modeling language that facilitates system modeling from the first stage of the design to the maintenance. It contains structural and behavioral diagrams and. The dynamic changes in the system are represented by behavioral diagrams. The architecture and structure of the system are represented by structural diagrams and . Business modeling is represented by the behavioral activity diagram. It shows the workflow from the starting activity to the final one, but it still needs to be verified to ensure the correctness of the behavioral specification of models. Alloy is a formal textual modeling language that combines formal specification and automatic analysis. Therefore, for more correctness, it is necessary to convert the UML AD diagram into a formal model. In our paper, we decide to transform UML-AD into Alloy

A. Dahanayake et al. (Eds.): M2P 2020, CCIS 1401, pp. 127–136, 2021.
https://doi.org/10.1007/978-3-030-72696-6_6

in order to benefit from the Alloy-Analyzer, which enables the analysis and verification of the model and increases the reliability of the system. In Sect. 2, we mention the related work to model transformations from UML models into formal models. In Sect. 3, we show the background and the preliminary work for our transformation. After showcasing the transformation from UML-AD into Alloy, and then showing the advantages of Alloy and its analyzer (Sect. 4), we draw a conclusion and present the concerns of future work.

2   Related Work

Plenty of research is done to transform UML models or other models like BPEL and BPMN models into other formal models to make their verification easier [19]. [22] present a detailed translation of a BPEL to BPMN covering all BPEL constructs and their semantics and [28] transformed BPMN models into BPEL. [5] is a formalization of Web Service orchestration (WS-BPEL) using a process algebra (CCS). Authors in [26] represent a formal transformation by integrating Z notation to UML Use Case, Class, Sequence Diagram for Representing the Static and Dynamic Perspectives of safety-critical system, then they analyzed and verified the output model using Z/Eves tool. Another transformation of UML state machine into FoCalize using Zenon automatic theorem prover of FoCaLiZe [1] that can be refined to generate executable code. A model transformation from UML SM to Discrete Event System Specification (DEVS) [27] is represented by Recker et al. [25], in the context of the Model-Driven Development (MDD) [7], to perform simulations using tools, they implemented transformation rules in Query/Views/Transformation (QVT) Relations language [12].

Transformed Activity diagram to YAWL, it simplifies the use of activity diagrams business process models as workflows [18]. [13] propose a transformation of activity diagram to Petri nets that enable behavior modelers to reduce the cost of verification before implementation. In some other previous work, UML diagrams are translated to BPMN for its clarity and importance [29]. The paper [20] uses UML and BPMN in modeling the integration of management systems that are dedicated to monitoring the reliability, maintenance, and various condition of operational systems, and they apply it in an application in an electric transformer system. In another paper, [15] integrating business process concepts into UML activity models, the authors extended the activity meta-model using a UML profile to make it able for modeling the business process. We focus on transformations between UML and Alloy [14]. [8] shows the utility of Alloy as a modeling language in the engineering domain, [4] propose a comparison of OCL, Alloy, and FOML as textual modeling languages and clarify the advantages of every language. There are various transformations of model specifications into format complying with Alloy, authors in reference [6] made a translation between Alloy specifications and UML class diagrams annotated with OCL like [11] a transformation from UML Protocol state machine to Alloy. [16] a transformation from UML Class diagram to Alloy and back from Alloy instances to UML class diagram. The features transformed in this paper are as follows directed associations, composite aggregations, interfaces, multiple-inheritance, enumerations, and classes.

The paper [10] propose a new approach for Visualization-Based Validation (VBV) to model transformation validation using compound F-Alloy specifications that are a sub-language of Alloy that allows the specification of functional Alloy modules [9]. Numerous translations between Alloy specifications and UML class diagrams are done [3,6] because UML is more referred to in the transformation fields, it captures different structural and computational aspects, furthermore, the behavior of the system in the form of Activity Diagrams (AD) and State machine (SM) [17].

3   Preliminaries

3.1   UML Activity Diagram

Unified Modeling Language activity diagram UML-AD is a useful behavioral diagram used to describe the behavior of control and data flows in complex systems. It describes the logic of the development of a use case. UML-AD notation is close to the state transition diagram in the presentation but different in interpretation. It is composed of an initial state and end with an ending point, activities, or actions, action flows or edges illustrate the transitions between activities and the decisions to represent a condition to move from an activity to another. Figure 1 shows the relevant components of UML-AD that we used in our transformation.

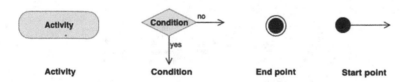

Fig. 1. Basic element of UML-AD.

UML-AD meta-model is needed in our work to determine the mapping rules from element to element. Figure 2 illustrate UML-AD meta-model [24]. In our Transformation we use meta-classes as follows: activity node, initial node, final node, fork node, etc.

3.2   Alloy

Alloy is one of the textual, declarative and formal modeling languages based on first-order relational logic. It expresses the behavior and structural constraints. An Alloy model contains paragraphs that can consist of *Signature* declaration. Every signature has a unique identifier signature id and signature body that contain a declaration expression composed of several expressions, and of facts that are always true in the model, predicates, and fields that represent a relation between signatures. Alloy couples formal specification and the automatic

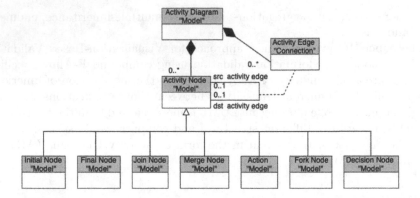

Fig. 2. Activity diagram meta-model.

analysis that is done by the Alloy Analyzer. Alloy analyzer uses an SAT solver to enable automatic model verification and to search for counterexamples. The model should satisfy the predicates, Boolean assertions, and the specified system constraints, or a counterexample falsify the model through breach of logic conditions. Figure 3 illustrates Alloy metamodel with more details.

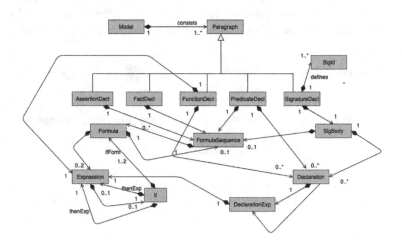

Fig. 3. Alloy metamodel.

4   Transformation from UML Activity Diagram to Alloy

There are former attempts of transformation of UML State Charts into process descriptions that are useful in Information Systems [17]. The various and flexible graph representations can be used for model checking, verification, and validation [23]. Various transformations from UML to Alloy or from Alloy to UML where they consider only Class diagrams in their transformation [2,3,6,16,21] as presented in Sect. 2. In our paper, we are transforming UML activity models to Alloy. In this section, we demonstrate an overview of our transformation. First, we represent a part of the Alloy metamodel used to represent the abstract metaclass signature declaration (SigDecl) (see Fig. 4 below) which is a portion of Alloy. A SigDecl can be used for subtyping as ExtendSigDecl or for subsetting as an InSigDecl signature. Every signature declaration has a signature body (Sig-Body). It can specify declarations (Decl) as well to define signature fields. To declare relation between signatures, declaration expression (DeclExp) is used. Then we define the mapping between elements used in the transformation from UML-AD to Alloy and finally we show a some transformed elements and the benefits of using Alloy for checking models with the SAT solver.

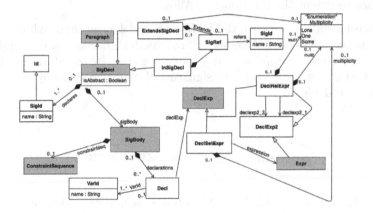

Fig. 4. Alloy signature meta model

From the UML activity diagram meta-model and the basic elements presented in Fig. 1 and Fig. 2 respectively, we define the UML activity diagram representation as follows:

Definition 1 (UML-AD representation) : From UML-AD meta-model presented in Fig. 2 we represent UML-AD model in a tuple $ActivityNodes = (N, W, D)$ where:

N can designate:

- AN which is an activity node or
- iN for the starting or initial node or
- fN for the ending or final node.

W represents the workflow, i.e. the flow of activities and the logical operations, the gateways, it can be:

- J join,
- M merge or
- F fork.

D represent the decision node.

From the Alloy meta-model presented in Fig. 1 we define the Alloy representation as follows:

Definition 2 (Alloy representation) : From Alloy meta-model presented in Fig. 3 we represent Alloy model in a tuple $AlloyM = (SigDecl, SigRel, ifFormula)$ where:

SigDecl represent the signature declaration,
SigRelrepresent the signature relations like extend between signatures.
ifFormula represent the if formula in Alloy.

In this transformation, we have the UML-AD model as an input which contains Nodes(Activity nodes, initial nodes or finale nodes), decision nodes and workflows. To create the appropriate Alloy model we start by transforming Activity nodes, initial nodes, final nodes to signature declaration in Alloy as shown in Fig. 5, Fig. 6 and Fig. 7.

Fig. 5. Transforming UML-AD action state into Alloy signature.

Fig. 6. Transforming UML-AD initial state into Alloy signature.

Fig. 7. Transforming UML-AD final state into Alloy signature.

Then we transform the part of decision nodes depending on the guards (the statement written next to a decision diamond) as represented in Fig. 8 are formulated by the *if formula* in Alloy to demonstrate the group of actions to be done in every case.

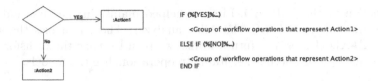

Fig. 8. Transforming UML-AD decision node and guards into Alloy if formula.

Afterward, we transform the links or workflows between signatures like a fork in UML-AD to be transformed to *Extends* between signatures. Figure 9 shows an example of a fork in UML-AD which is transformed into extends in Alloy.

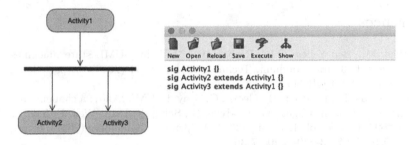

Fig. 9. Example of fork in UML-AD and extends between signatures in Alloy.

Alloy has a software component for model verification, Alloy Analyzer is known as the accurate semantic based tool designed for precise specifications, invariant, and operations are described by formulas that may involve conjunction. This feature is relevant for software modeling because it allows partial models to be analyzed. It uses an SAT solver to enable automatic model verification and to search for counterexamples that do not satisfy the predicates, i.e., falsify the original model. It converts verification queries to the satisfiability of Boolean logic formulas and calls an SAT solver to answer them. Alloy tool made the model checking easy since we use the command 'Check' to verify the properties and run to get examples in the Alloy tool. Once the model is created, it can be analyzed by searching for assertions or counterexamples. From the preference panel of Alloy Analyzer, we can choose the SAT solver that can be ZChaff and MiniSat for small problems or Berkmin that works better for larger problems. To check models in Alloy, we use the commands check and run to verify the properties and run to get examples. Based on the bounds declared in the check command, Alloy Analyzer translates the model and the negation of the assertion into a propositional formula.

5   Conclusion

In our paper, we propose a transformation from the basic UML-AD components to Alloy in the context of MDA. This transformation completes the missing part of verification in the UML-AD. First, it helped mainly in checking and verification of the new model with the Alloy analyzer. Then, it makes the semantics of UML-AD clearer. For future works, we plan to make the transformation reversible and the prototype executable to operationalize the models.

Acknowledgement. The project was supported by the European Union, co-financed by the European Social Fund (EFOP-3.6.3-VEKOP-16-2017-00002) and the project was partially supported by "Application Domain Specific Highly Reliable IT Solutions" project that has been implemented with the support provided from the National Research, Development and Innovation Fund of Hungary, financed under the Thematic Excellence Programme TKP2020-NKA-06 (National Challenges Subprogramme) funding scheme.

References

1. Abbas, M., Ben-Yelles, C.B., Rioboo, R.: Modelling UML state machines with focalize. Int. J. Inf. Commun. Technol. **13**(1), 34–54 (2018). https://doi.org/10.1504/ijict.2018.10010449
2. Anastasakis, K., Bordbar, B., Georg, G., Ray, I.: UML2Alloy: a challenging model transformation. In: Engels, G., Opdyke, B., Schmidt, D.C., Weil, F. (eds.) MODELS 2007. LNCS, vol. 4735, pp. 436–450. Springer, Heidelberg (2007). https://doi.org/10.1007/978-3-540-75209-7_30
3. Anastasakis, K., Bordbar, B., Georg, G., Ray, I.: On challenges of model transformation from UML to alloy. Softw. Syste. Model. **9**(1), 69 (2010). https://doi.org/10.1007/s10270-008-0110-3
4. Balaban, M., et al.: A comparison of textual modeling languages: OCL, alloy, FOMl. In: OCL@ MoDELS, pp. 57–72 (2016)
5. Cámara, J., Canal, C., Cubo, J., Vallecillo, A.: Formalizing WSBPEL business processes using process algebra. Electron. Notes Theor. Comput. Sci. **154**(1), 159–173 (2006). https://doi.org/10.1016/j.entcs.2005.12.038
6. Cunha, A., Garis, A., Riesco, D.: Translating between alloy specifications and UML class diagrams annotated with OCL. Softw. Syst. Model. **14**(1), 5–25 (2015). https://doi.org/10.1007/s10270-013-0353-5
7. Da Silva, A.R.: Model-driven engineering: a survey supported by the unified conceptual model. Comput. Lang. Syst. Struct. **43**, 139–155 (2015). https://doi.org/10.1016/j.cl.2015.06.001
8. Gammaitoni, L.: On the use of alloy in engineering domain specific modeling languages. Ph.D. thesis, University of Luxembourg, Luxembourg (2017)
9. Gammaitoni, L., Kelsen, P.: F-alloy: a relational model transformation language based on alloy. Softw. Syst. Model. **18**(1), 213–247 (2019). https://doi.org/10.1007/s10270-017-0630-9
10. Gammaitoni, L., Kelsen, P., Ma, Q.: Agile validation of model transformations using compound f-alloy specifications. Sci. Comput. Program. **162**, 55–75 (2018). https://doi.org/10.1016/j.scico.2017.07.001
11. Garis, A., Paiva, A.C.R., Cunha, A., Riesco, D.: Specifying UML protocol state machines in alloy. In: Derrick, J., Gnesi, S., Latella, D., Treharne, H. (eds.) IFM 2012. LNCS, vol. 7321, pp. 312–326. Springer, Heidelberg (2012). https://doi.org/10.1007/978-3-642-30729-4_22

12. Han, Z., Zhang, L., Ling, J., Huang, S.: Control-flow pattern based transformation from UML activity diagram to YAWL. In: van Sinderen, M., Johnson, P., Xu, X., Doumeingts, G. (eds.) IWEI 2012. LNBIP, vol. 122, pp. 129–145. Springer, Heidelberg (2012). https://doi.org/10.1007/978-3-642-33068-1_13
13. Huang, E., McGinnis, L.F., Mitchell, S.W.: Verifying SysML activity diagrams using formal transformation to petri nets. Syst. Eng. (2019). https://doi.org/10.1002/sys.21524
14. Jackson, D.: Alloy: a language and tool for exploring software designs. Commun. ACM **62**(9), 66–76 (2019). https://doi.org/10.1145/3338843
15. Karboos, M.H.: Integrating business process concepts into UML activity model. J. Eng. Comput. Sci. (JECS) **19**(1), 57–68 (2019)
16. Kautz, O., Maoz, S., Ringert, J.O., Rumpe, B.: Cd2alloy: a translation of class diagrams to alloy. Technical report. AIB-2017-06, RWTH Aachen University, July 2017 (2017)
17. Kherbouche, M., Bouafia, K., Molnar, B.: Transformation of UML state machine to YAWL. In: Ninth IEEE International Conference on Intelligent Computing and Information Systems (2019). https://doi.org/10.1109/icicis46948.2019.9014793
18. Khudori, A.N., Kurniawan, T.A.: Business process model transformation techniques: a comprehensive survey. Adv. Sci. Lett. **24**(11), 8606–8612 (2018). https://doi.org/10.1166/asl.2018.12311
19. Lano, K., Kolahdouz-Rahimi, S.: Model transformation specification and design. In: Advances in Computers, vol. 85, pp. 123–163. Elsevier (2012). https://doi.org/10.1016/b978-0-12-396526-4.00003-5
20. López-Campos, M.A., Márquez, A.C., Fernández, J.F.G.: Modelling using UML and BPMN the integration of open reliability, maintenance and condition monitoring management systems: an application in an electric transformer system. Comput. Industry **64**(5), 524–542 (2013). https://doi.org/10.1016/j.compind.2013.02.010
21. Maoz, S., Ringert, J.O., Rumpe, B.: CD2Alloy: class diagrams analysis using alloy revisited. In: Whittle, J., Clark, T., Kühne, T. (eds.) MODELS 2011. LNCS, vol. 6981, pp. 592–607. Springer, Heidelberg (2011). https://doi.org/10.1007/978-3-642-24485-8_44
22. Mazanek, S., Minas, M.: Transforming BPMN to BPEL using parsing and attribute evaluation with respect to a hypergraph grammar (2009). http://is.tm.tue.nl/staff/pvgorp/events/grabats2009/submissions/grabats2009_submission_8.Pdf. Accessed 14 Oct 2009
23. Molnár, B.: Applications of hypergraphs in informatics: a survey and opportunities for research. Ann. Univ. Scientiarum Budapestinensis de Rolando Eotvos Nominatae Sectio Computatorica **42**, 261–282 (2014)
24. Narayanan, A., Karsai, G.: Verifying model transformations by structural correspondence. Electron. Commun. EASST **10**, 1–14 (2008). https://doi.org/10.14279/tuj.eceasst.10.157
25. Recker, J., La Rosa, M.: Understanding user differences in open-source workflow management system usage intentions. Inf. Syst. **37**(3), 200–212 (2012). https://doi.org/10.1016/j.is.2011.10.002
26. Singh, M., Sharma, A.K., Saxena, R.: Formal transformation of UML diagram: use case, class, sequence diagram with Z notation for representing the static and dynamic perspectives of system. In: Satapathy, S.C., Joshi, A., Modi, N., Pathak, N. (eds.) Proceedings of International Conference on ICT for Sustainable Development. AISC, vol. 409, pp. 25–38. Springer, Singapore (2016). https://doi.org/10.1007/978-981-10-0135-2_3

27. Van Tendeloo, Y., Vangheluwe, H.: Discrete event system specification modeling and simulation. In: Proceedings of the 2018 Winter Simulation Conference, pp. 162–176. IEEE Press (2018). https://doi.org/10.1109/wsc.2018.8632372
28. Weidlich, M., Decker, G., Großkopf, A., Weske, M.: BPEL to BPMN: the myth of a straight-forward mapping. In: Meersman, R., Tari, Z. (eds.) OTM 2008, Part I. LNCS, vol. 5331, pp. 265–282. Springer, Heidelberg (2008). https://doi.org/10.1007/978-3-540-88871-0_19
29. Zarour, K., Benmerzoug, D., Guermouche, N., Drira, K.: A systematic literature review on BPMN extensions. Bus. Process Manage. J. (2019). https://doi.org/10.1108/bpmj-01-2019-0040

Structurally Recursive Patterns in Data Modeling and Their Resolution

András J. Molnár[1,2]([envelope]) [ID]

[1] Computer Science Institute, Christian-Albrechts-University Kiel,
24098 Kiel, Germany
ajm@informatik.uni-kiel.de
[2] SZTAKI Institute for Computer Science and Control, Budapest 1111, Hungary
modras@ilab.sztaki.hu

Abstract. By allowing relationship types defined on top of relationship types, the Higher-Order Entity Relationship Model (HERM) enables modeling of complex conceptual structures in a layered way, which usually results in a more compact design than the traditional Entity-Relationship model. Identification of data instances is achieved by composition of the (inherited) key attributes of the referenced instances (foreign keys becoming part of natural keys of higher-order relationships). Well-formedness excludes cycles in the structure. In this paper, we look at the possibility to relax this by allowing structural recursion in the conceptual model. Although it is formally represented as a cycle in the type structure, it will not allow any cycle on the instance (data) level. After looking at some motivating cases and conventional alternatives to this design, and conditions when such a modeling decision is reasonable, we will show how a structurally recursive HERM model can be transformed into an equivalent, conventionally well-formed HERM model, with the utilization of list type construction and complex, variable-length key domains. The analysis reveals some non-trivial aspects of the way of transformation, which may be easily overlooked, but are important to formulate a translation rule for the general case, where derived attributes and aggregation needs are present. The result can be used as a rule for conceptual schema translation for structuring, to obtain an intermediate schema ready for further optimization, and eventually, code generation.

Keywords: Conceptual modeling · HERM · Structural recursion · Schema translation

1 Introduction and Motivation

The process of designing the database structure of an information system involves modeling and schema design in different levels and stages. Ideally we start with a conceptual model which represents the application domain in an adequate and dependable way [13]. This is translated and optimized in further steps until a well-established logical and physical schema is reached. This process is supported by rules and practices such as schema translation or normalization

© Springer Nature Switzerland AG 2021
A. Dahanayake et al. (Eds.): M2P 2020, CCIS 1401, pp. 137–161, 2021.
https://doi.org/10.1007/978-3-030-72696-6_7

procedures [2,3,5–7]. While some of these can be applied without any user input, modeling usually has to involve manual design considerations in order to achieve an appropriate and effective schema, especially in complex systems.

The modeling-to-programming initiative aims to elaborate on methods and tools which can ease this process for schema designers by automatic schema translation, optimization and code generation, and eventually, making the models themselves executable [16]. One promising way to achieve this is to develop and define high-level concepts for enabling explicit user input on how a model should be compiled or interpreted (and run), which then can be specified as directives similarly to a program-code compiler. The model compiler or execution engine can take into account these user-specified guidelines or directives to guide schema translation where multiple options exist.

In this paper, we use the higher-order entity-relationship modeling language (HERM) [14,15] and look at the case of designing a conceptual schema with structural recursion. It occurs wherever a type is constructed so that its data instances may be built on or composed of other data instances of the same type (we assume a database instance in general containing all actual data elements for each type, and call the data elements of a type *data instances* of that type). It is formally represented as a cycle in the type structure, therefore, it is not considered to be a well-formed schema design and not supported by schema translation methods. However, it does not mean any cycle on the instance (data) level (although, in principle, that might also be allowed, but such cases are out of the scope of this paper). Our aim is to allow such structures by extending the modeling language and translate them into traditionally well-formed, recursion-free schemata, so that it can be further optimized and maganed in the standard way. While elaborating this special case has already its contributive value in itself, it can be treated as a case study allowing us to make in-depth considerations as well on what to look for when considering a general schema translation or model execution methodology.

Cyclic data types are not uncommon and appear in several design patterns. UML class diagrams allow to express them concisely. We are going to show how a sound HERM representation is possible, which extends the capability of the language. There are other alternatives to translate into, for example into a modeling language featuring reference semantics, but in this paper, we are aiming to show how we can handle such cases using the value semantics of HERM. We will see what issues we are facing when trying to translate such a schema into an equivalent conventional HERM schema, and how complex substructures may emerge or be needed for such a faithful translation, and what care needs to be taken in such cases. Although it seems to be complex in the general case, by keeping the equivalence and the possibly most general pattern, we allow a potential space for different real-life sub-cases where some of the parts are empty or some of the principles can be relaxed. But any of such possible cases will fit into the general pattern we are providing and can be used as a reference when evaluating real-life, simple-looking translations. And our general translation scheme can be further optimized, but keeping our translation as strict as possible, such optimizations will explicitly be separated from the schema translation (the resolution of the structural recursion).

The structure of the paper is as follows: Sect. 2 gives the foundations of the HERM modeling language with some motivating cases and concepts related to schema-translation and equivalence, considers structural object-oriented design patterns and their translatability to HERM, aspects and examples of structural recursion. The general pattern of structurally recursive schemata to be resolved by translation is presented in Sect. 3 with a generic definition of aggregation, whose proper translatability ensures the completeness of information and equivalence of the resulting schema for data instances composed by structural recursion. Section 4 gives the possible schema translations for various settings, briefly showing their development and equivalence with the original schema, along with general guidelines that may guide the translation process as directives. Application of these different translation patterns is summarized in Sect. 5 as an algorithm-like rule. Section 6 concludes with some open issues.

2   Foundations and Related Work

2.1   Conventional and Higher-Order Entity-Relationship Models and Our Notations

In conventional *Entity-Relationship (ER)* modeling, a conceptual schema is composed of *entity* and *relationship* types with their *attributes* [4]. Entities (data instances) are subsistent, i.e. they exist on their own without depending on other data instances. Relationships connect two or more entity classes and their data instances are dependant on the entities they connect. The connected entities can have named roles in the relationships, and even the same entity type can be connected by the same relationship multiple times, with different roles. In the relational paradigm, set semantics is assumed, however, tables function as multisets in real-life database systems.

Based on the ER model, Higher-Order Entity Relationship Model (HERM) [14,15] allows the schema designer to define higher-order relationship types, i.e. relationship types on top of other relationship types and entity types. This way, modeling of complex conceptual structures is possible in a layered way, which in many cases results in a more compact schema design than the traditional Entity-Relationship model.

Entities are uniquely identifiable by one or more designated *primary key* attributes. This key is also called a *natural key*, since it reflects how entities are identified in their real-life application domain. For technical reasons, a *surrogate key* without any specific semantics can be introduced in the schema design process, although it is not considered as best practice in the conceptual modeling phase [15]. Relationships usually inherit primary key attributes from the entities they connect. The primary key of a relationship is - by default - composed of these inherited key attributes of the participating entities, optionally extended by own primary key attributes. In the latter case, the same entities can be related to each other multiple times even with set semantics, with different values on the extending key attributes of the relationship. The ER or HERM schema can be translated and optimized to a logical database schema [15].

Identification of data instances of higher-order relationships is by design well-defined as the composition of the (inherited) key attributes of the referenced entity or relationship data instances. This way, a key attribute of an entity type is being inherited by the first-order relationship types directly referring to this entity type, and subsequently, every further higher-order relationship types built on top of them, unless the composed key is explicitly overriden by a relationship type definition.

We are going to use the following, simplified conventional notations when presenting and discussing schemata: entity or relationship types are denoted by capital letters, while attributes and relationship roles are referred by small caps, data instances (single tuples in database instances) by small greek letters. Assuming a particular database instance of a schema, type names denote actual relations as well and their elements are the single data instances (tuples) of the type in the actual relation, denoted by the $\in$ operator. For example, if R is a relationship type, then $\rho \in R$ is a data instance (tuple with attributes) of it. The dot operator is used to refer to an attribute, or, in a case of a relationship, a related member of the connected type with the specified relationship role. If R is defined to relate types P and Q with roles p and q, respectively, then $R.p$ means a function to be applied over any R-instance $\rho \in R$, resulting in the P-instance $\pi \in P$ identified by the foreign key referenced by ρ through its relationship role p. The latter function can be inverted using a superscript $^{-1}$, denoting the relationship instance which has the given data instance in its specified role. In this example, the function $P.(R.p)^{-1}$ over P-instances results in ρ for π. Furthermore, $\bowtie$ denotes a (natural) join of two relations (or types - as a function over their data instances) and Π denotes the projection of a relation to its specified attributes, e.g. $\Pi_p R$ is the (foreign) key of $R.p$, while $\Pi_{Attr(P)} R \bowtie P$ is the same as $R.p$ if $Attr(P)$ denotes the attributes of P.

Although multiple graphical ER representations exist, we will use the one which was taken and generalized by HERM: rectangles denote entities, diamonds denote relationships. If we use both a diamond and a rectangle for a type, it means it can be either one of them. In HERM, arrows do not represent cardinality or control, but dependence based on structural composition: a relationship depending on entities has arrows towards those entities, while a higher-order relationship depending on other relationships has arrows towards those lower-order relationships it depends on. Cardinality is expressed by number intervals with participation semantics [15], i.e. a number at an entity written towards a relationship shows how many times each data instance of the entity type should (and can) participate in that relationship (minimally and maximally). The default cardinality is $(0, n)$, meaning there is no restriction in the participation.

A special construction of HERM is the *cluster type*, which is a disjoint union of two different (sub)types, and acts as a generalization of these (sub)types [15]. The cluster type is a higher-order relationship, meaning that it is not subsistent on its own, but is dependant on the (sub)types it connects.[1] The cluster type is depicted with a cross in a circle on schema diagrams. We assume a default cardinality of the cluster type as $(0, 1)$, so a specific subtype instance takes part of the cluster type at most once.

HERM defines *type constructors*, by which complex attribute domains or relationship roles can be constructed [15]. For our case, the *list constructor* is relevant, meaning that an attribute of a single data instance of a type can take multiple values in an ordered (indexed) way. It can be applied to relationships as well, resulting in a relationship having a list of related data instances of one type or role instead of one single data instance. It is denoted by square brackets on schema diagrams. Key inheritance extends to type constructors in a natural way, when a list-constructed attribute is part of a key, or key attributes are inherited to relationships via list-constructed roles, the list itself is becoming (part of) the (natural) key, resulting in a key with a complex domain.

The classical definition of well-formedness of such a schema includes a strict layering requirement, where no cycles are allowed in the structure of these type definitions. We will look at the possibility to relax this by allowing a special case of structural recursion in the conceptual model, using the cluster type construct. Specific cases of its schema translation will use the list type constructor, including inheritance of key attributes, thus resulting in a complex key domain for the data instances composed by structural recursion.

2.2 Modeling and Design. Schema Translation and Optimization

Modeling and schema design is a complex process when done systematically, involving different ascpects and levels. A common method is to start with a conceptual model of the application domain, which is then refined and adapted to the system needs, translated to a logical schema (relational or other) and implemented in a specific way (physical schema). Optimizations and variations can be done in any of the stages [7]. Modeling-to-programming tries to automate this process as much as possible, while modeling-as-programming aims to make the models themselves executable. Both cases require intermediate schemata and inner optimizations, which can have various influential factors. For instance, although the theory of normalization [5] may be used for automatic schema optimization, there are specific aspects causing an opposite effect at the end (denormalization, [6]), and the schema designer must make considerations towards the optimal schema in each specific case. Some of these can already take effect at the conceptual level, not in the logical schema for which normalization is usually defined [7].

In each of the schema translation steps, it is important to ensure an equivalence of the resulting schema with the original. In most cases it is a simple correspondance between types and attributes, in more complex cases types can be

---

[1] Specialization is considered in HERM as a different case where the general type is subsistent, and its subtypes depend on it. To model this, the so-called *unary relationships* are used, which is not directly relevant for this paper.

split or merged, rearranged, etc. A bi-directional mapping has to be given which ensures information equivalence, so both schemata have the same expressivity. We will consider information equivalence between the original and translated schemata similarly to the concept of infomorphisms [9,10], but in most cases the mappings will be obvious.

2.3   Structural Design Patterns and Their Translatability

Design patterns are investigated in conceptual and relational modeling [1,7], but they are mostly well-known in object-oriented modeling and design [8]. Structural patterns include the *adapter, facade, bridge, flyweight, proxy, composite and decorator*. They are mostly expressed in UML class diagrams. Expressing most of them in HERM looks straightforward, however, the proxy, composite and decorator patterns feature non-trivial composition relations.

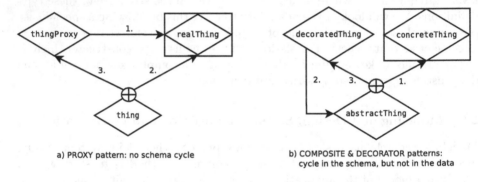

a) PROXY pattern: no schema cycle   b) COMPOSITE & DECORATOR patterns:
                                                  cycle in the schema, but not in the data

Fig. 1. Two non-trivial structural design patterns expressed in HERM.

The *proxy* is a type whose data instances contain instances of another type ('real type') and both of them are generalized to a third type (the general type). A natural way of modeling it by HERM is using a cluster type whose subtypes are the proxy and the real type, and the former builds on the latter. Figure 1/a) shows this setting. Numbers denote a possible order of schema construction. Although it is non-trivial, it is a well-formed schema in conventional HERM.

The *composite and decorator* patterns, however, have a self-referencing property, i.e. a data instance of a composite or decorated version of a type may contain another data instance(s) of the same type, which again may either be composites or decorated instances, or pure (concrete) instances. This can be expressed again by a cluster type, but here, a decorated or composite instance will depend not directly on a concrete instance but on a general (abstract) instance, which is the cluster type. This results in a directed cycle in the HERM schema structure, and therefore, cannot be considered as conventionally well-formed. See Fig. 1/b). However, there is no cycle in the data, if the composition has a proper layering on the instance level, for example, a concrete data instance becomes abstract so that it can be decorated, but a decorated instance is becoming abstract too, so that it can be further decorated. This composition results in an iterative data construction, and not actually a cycle.

Note that UML uses a reference semantics, while ER and HERM use value semantics. As we will see later in the paper, this adds an extra complexity to the resolution of the structural recursion. One of the points of this papeer is to reveal this complexity and the care need to be taken when one faces such type of schemata. Despite of this - sometimes unexpected - complexity, we are to show that this is doable and HERM is capable of handling such cases without a need to change its semantics or use a different target modeling language. The source schema is given in HERM (extended with the notation of the structural cycle expressing the structural recursion) and the resulting schema is still in (conventional) HERM, proving that HERM remains a full-fledged schema language with a sound management capacity of structurally recursive schemata with its value semantics, using the special key construct as we will see.

2.4 Structural Recursion in Schemata

Structural recursion occures wherever a type is constructed so that its data instances may be built on other instances of the same type. Examples of stucturally recursive relationships - or relationships that can be modeled using structural recursion - include part-of or nested-into relationships such as departments of organizations, or a hierarchy of heterogenous administrative regions (esp. if data is from multiple sources without a common prescribed layering - e.g. the disjoint union of regions of different countries on multiple administrative levels), or when data is organized into a linked list or other structure where the depth of the hierarchy is not bounded.

Note that structural recursion may not be the single valid way of modeling a phenomenon. It is especially useful if the nature of the domain is so that the composite objects have no subsistence on their own, but they are dependent on other composite objects of the same type, which is in some cases even reflected in the identification (key attribute inheritance) as well. A region, for instance, does not have its global worldwide unique identifier on its own by nature, but its identification assumes the country which it is part of, so its own identifier becomes a global key only with the inherited country identifier. A street in a city is on an even lower level, and inherits the country, region, city key attributes as part of its identification.

Another typical case of structural recursion is when the items are purely logical, they can be composed in various ways and their natural identification is based on the entire structure. An example is given in [11] where semi-automatic generation of trail signpost items is considered, where in the planning phase only the content is given, but is not assigned to any physical sign yet, so their whole semantical construct is inherently part of their natural key. A more common example is when formulae are the data instances and they are composed of atoms and operator symbols by structural recursion, and have no other natural key than their whole content with their structural composition. It can be specifically relevant to active databases with logical data implications [12]. Although a simplified derived representation of the key as identifier can be introduced into the schema later, this phenomena results in possibly complex keys when modeling the nature of the domain.

3   General Formulation and Proposed Extension

3.1   A General Example of a Structurally Recursive Schema

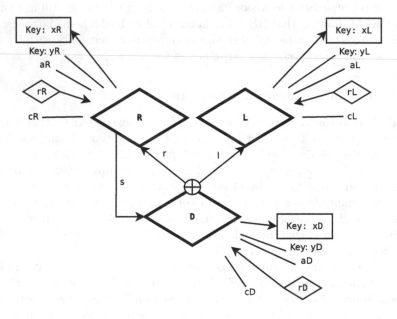

Fig. 2. General HERM schema pattern with unary structural recursion.

Let us consider the schema on Fig. 2 as a general pattern for unary structural recursion. This is a direct generalization of the logical trail signpost structure model presented in [11]. Its semantics is obtained by a straightforward extension of the usual HERM semantics in the following way.

Type L is called the *initial type* (a.k.a. *leaf type or base type*), which can be either an entity (0th order) or a relationship (1st or higher order) type. We represent it as a relationship type which is the more general case. If it is an entity, its primary key is formed by one or more of its attributes. If it is a relationship type, it inherits the key attributes from the entity types it is based on, and the key is formed by these attributes, optionally extended by own attributes. The modeler may decide to override the inherited key attributes and compose a primary key for a relationship type based on one or more own attributes only.

The initial type L is generalized to a cluster type D, called the *domain union type or common type* which may add its own key or non-key attributes, entities or lower-order relationships it is based on, and may participate in relationships of higher order.

The structural recursion is realized by a relationship type R, called the *recursive type (or composite type)*, each of whose data instances is based on either an instance of the initial type L or another instance of the composite type R. It can be modeled by a relationship type, which is based on D and is generalized by D at the same time.

Although the model graph becomes cyclic, there should be no cycles in the data instances of any valid database instance. A special constraint is required to avoid cycles in the data: an assignment of a positive integer *rank* must be possible to each data instance r of R so that it must be higher than the rank of the data instance of R on which r is directly based (if r is not directly based on a data instance of L). Certainly, R may have its own attributes including key attributes, connected entities which it is based on and inherits key attributes from, as well as higher-order relationship types that are based on it.

Note that R inherits the key attribute(s) from D. Due to the structural recursion, this inheritance may be of an arbitrary depth, so the length of the key of R (and D) may be variable. This results in a key with a complex domain, which follows the data instance composition by structural recursion. To avoid this, the schema designer can override the inherited key attributes by declaring an explicit primary key of R or D based only on its (local) attributes, but there are cases where it is not possible, and identification must be based on the entire sequence of the D-instances an instance of R is based on.

The notations of Fig. 2 are the following. Each element represents an attribute or relationship type set (i.e. stands for one or more items) with a specific characteristic to its respective type.

- xL, xR, xD denote inherited key attributes from entity types the respective relationship type is based on (xL is considered to be empty if L is an entity type);
- yL, yR, yD denote own attributes of the respective type which are part of the primary key (additionally to any inherited key attributes);
- aL, aR, aD are non-(primary-)key attributes of the respective type;
- rL, rR, rD are (higher-order) relationship types built on the respective types;
- cL, cR, cD are computed (derived) attributes of the respective types. We assume for the sake of simplicity that they denote single attributes, but the results can be trivially extended to a vector or derived attributes.

Note that $xR \cup xD \cup yR \cup yD$ must not be empty in order to have proper identification for the composite data instances of R.

3.2 Aggregation as an Example of Structurally Recursive Derived Attributes

Aggregation may be defined for types R and/or D, resulting in a derived attribute value based on the values taken from the structurally recursive composition of data instances. Similarly, any function or operation may be defined over the data instances of these types which take such values. In order not to lose the ability to reference any of these values in a translated schema in a way corresponding to the composition structure, we must take extra care of keeping the translatability of such functions. We will thus define general aggregation functions for computing the derived attributes cL, cR, cD as an example and will consider their proper translatability.

To define a general aggregation, we assume two aggregative functions f_R and f_D defined for data instances of types R and D. These compute a value recursively, based on own attribute values of the respective instance i (and/or values taken from its connected relationships), and the respective aggregative function value of the instance on which i is directly based by the model structure. The zero-level aggregation is defined by a simple function f_L over data instances of L. Our aggregation functions F_L, F_R, F_D for each type and thus the values of the derived attributes cL, cR, cD are then being defined as follows:

- $\lambda.cL ::= F_L(\lambda) = f_L(\lambda.xL, \lambda.yL, \lambda.aL, \lambda.rL)$ if $\lambda \in L$,
- $\delta_l.cD ::= F_D(\delta_l) = f_D(F_L(\delta_l.l), \delta_l.xD, \delta_l.yD, \delta_l.aD, \delta_l.rD)$ if $\delta_l \in D$ a data instance based on L,
- $\delta_r.cD ::= F_D(\delta_r) = f_D(F_R(\delta_r.r), \delta_r.xD, \delta_r.yD, \delta_r.aD, \delta_r.rD)$ if $\delta_r \in D$ a data instance based on R,
- $\rho.cR ::= F_R(\rho) = f_R(F_D(\rho.s), \rho.xR, \rho.yR, \rho.aR, \rho.rR)$ if $\rho \in R$.

To define a unified aggregation function F for all the types, we may simply take their union:

$F(\iota) = F_L(\iota)$ if $\iota \in L$, $F_D(\iota)$ if $\iota \in D$ and $F_R(\iota)$ if $\iota \in R$.

Since the types are disjoint, and the above computation can be uniquely evaluated for each data instance composed by structural recursion, we can state the following:

Proposition 1. *The aggregate function F and the computation of the derived attributes cL, cR, cD are well-defined.*

4   Schema Translation to Non-recursive Schemata

4.1   Translation Guidelines

Taking the above example as a basis, we want to give an equivalent alternative schema without the formal cycle of structural recursion, using the list type constructor [15] denoted by [], as necessary.

Considering schema translation, we have identified the following guidelines as proposals for guiding automatic schema translation, keeping the interpretability and integrity of the original types as much as possible. The schema designer may choose and select some or all of them as relevant for an actual case, and this selection, acting as a directive, should determine the way of schema translation in an envisioned model-to-program framework.

The reason for these guidelines is to provide a basis for an automatic translation (being introduced in the next sections) which harmonizes general common-sense schema design principles and preserves the structure as well as the properties of the original schema and each of its parts as much as possible. This way no 'hidden' simplification or transformation will occur during this transformation step. The guidelines are informally described here, but definitions of the automatic translations will build on them in a formally well-specified way. However, the resolution of the structurally recursive schema to a non-recursive schema is considered to be an intermediate schema only, possibly ready for any further schema optimizations and (de)normalization procedures, either automatically or user-involved. These further optimizations can be separated explicitly from the resolution of the recursion cycle in the schema, and therefore, having the broadest possible opportunity space. That's one main reason why we aim equivalence and not only a one-directional schema conformity. In practice, schema transformation and optimization patterns can be defined for different special cases, resulting simpler-looking resulting schemata (as some of the parts will, for instance, be empty), but each of them can be put in correspondance with our, possibly most general schema translations and their soundness evaluated based on these.

Information Equivalence. The translated schema must have the same expressivity as the original schema. Any valid database instance of one of the schemata must be mappable to the other schema so that one can tell for each type and attribute its correspondant(s) and they must preserve the structure of the information, i.e. the relational connections in the data. We can define an equivalence mapping (denoted by $\equiv$) from the original schema to the translated schema where each entity or relationship of the original schema with its attributes and connections has a structurally analogous counterpart in the translated schema, and vica versa. In most cases it will be trivial, and it will be shown for the non-trivial settings only. We will assume a valid database instance each time and will refer to its relations by the type names with capital letters as sets (relations), and their members by small greek letters as the data instances (tuples). The instance will not be named explicitly, and as the equivalence is shown for the generic case, it must be valid for all valid instances.

Self-containment Principle. During the schema translation, we want to preserve the compositionality of the schema for the aggreations. It means, each attribute value or connected relationship intsance belonging to a data instance of a type, or being reachable from it along a directed path of the instance graph along the arrows defined by the schema, should remain reachable from the corresponding data instance in the translated schema, if it contributes to the specified aggregation computation of a derived attribute of it. For example, if an attribute in aL is referenced by the computation function of cR, then it must be reachable from the type in the translated schema to which cR belongs, using only the arrows in the HERM graph of the instance graph in terms of the translated schema. It also means, for example, that any of the attribute values of a data instance ρ of R contributing to the aggregation of cR of another data instance $\rho' \in R$ or of cD of a data instance $\delta \in D$ must remain reachable from ρ' or δ, respectively, if they are - even indirectly - based on ρ by structural recursion.

Inverse Self-containment Principle. This principle states validity of the above self-contaninment principle for the inverse translation of the resulting schema to the original one. It means no attributes or any other parts of a type can be subordinated to a relationship in the translated schema which was not subordinated to its counterpart in the original schema. Subordinated means it is put 'under' the relationship, so that the relationship is directly or indirectly built on top of it.

Natural Key Principle. Closely related to the self-containment principle, during the schema translation, we want to preserve the key composition of the types by the standard inheritance of HERM, introducing possibly complex key structures such as by list type construction so to give natural self-identification to the data instances. It is then up to the schema designer or database imlementer at a later phase if (s)he wants to introduce surrogate keys inside the database schema for effectivity. However, these surrogate keys will not be visible to the users normally and they will still need a natural unique key for each type to be able to identify its data instances, and this should be based on the natural key set in the conceptual schema.

Duplication Avoidance. Another principle is we do not want to duplicate attributes or relationship types in the schema. For instance, if a cluster type has to be split so that some of its attributes will become part of another relationship type, there must be an exact unique location in the schema where such an attribute is connected, without declaring the attribute twice, for two different types.

Mixture Avoidance. Moreover, we want to keep the integrity and clear separation of the types in a way that although a type may be split into two or more types, but we do not want to mix attributes of formerly different types into one type in the translated schema.

Semantic Unit Encapsulation. Lastly, by the principle of semantic unit encapsulation we try to avoid repetitive reference patterns, which means, if two or more relationship types is connected to two or more other relationship types in a similar way, and for the similar reason, because the combination of these other types form a semantic unit, than we make this semantic unit explicit by forming a relationship type which connects them, and the multiple relationship types which referenced them in a similar way will reference only this new, "encapsulated" relationship type. It helps to define a clearer, more understandable and overseeable schema, takes advantage of the structural expressivity of HERM and eliminates some arrow crossings.

Depending on these guidelines, we will give properly translated variants of the structurally recursive schema of Fig. 2 in the following. Information equivalence will be shown or explained where non-trivial. Self-containment and its inverse will be partially relaxed (Sect. 4.2) as well as semantic unit encapsulation (Sect. 4.5). Natural key, duplication and mixture avoidance will be kept throughout all given translation patterns.

4.2   Translation by Introducing a Relationship Type

Introducing an extra relation in the conceptual schema instead of the connection denoted by role s seems to be the most straightforward resolution as it is used in classical examples ([15] and others). However, it is worth to note that when coming to the logical schema obtained by classical schema implementation, it is likely to be eliminated and transformed into a foreign key in the table of R, referencing D, which looks visually closer to the original schema with structural recursion.

Figure 3 shows variants of this method (attributes and further relationship connections omitted). Depending on the role and content of D, it may be included or omitted, or even left out of the whole schema (if D has substantial content, also contributing to the aggregation, then variant a) is to be chosen). Choosing any of these patterns, however, breaks the self-containment principle for R, since a data instance of R will structurally not 'contain' (i.e. entail or reference by itself) those D-instances on which it is built by structural recursion, and are therefore integral parts of it. Any aggregation along the structurally recursive construct must be defined through S, which is a higher-order type, formally became external to R.

Considering key inheritance paths, the potential problem becomes more obvious: if identification (i.e. the key) of R is based on the data instances involved in its structurally recursive composition, then the desired key inheritance is not achieved by any of these schemata. Relation S (or SL, SR) inherits the key attributes from D and R, but R does not inherit any key through it. In variant b), R inherits the key of L, with its initial component instance, but does not inherit any key from other R data instances. Therefore, it can be used when this is allowed. The other variants a), c) and d) do not even inherit the key of L towards R.

Information-equivalence of these schemata with the original one is obvious, if data acyclicity can be ensured w.r.t. S (or SR). If the self-containment guideline is not strictly applied and key inheritance in R is overridden, these are simple options to choose from.

As an example, the information equivalence mapping of R for variant a) is: $R_{orig}.s \equiv R.(S.r)^{-1}.d$, or simply expressed by the relation S.

Similar equivalences can be given for the other variants, while equivalence for all other types and attributes is the identity function.

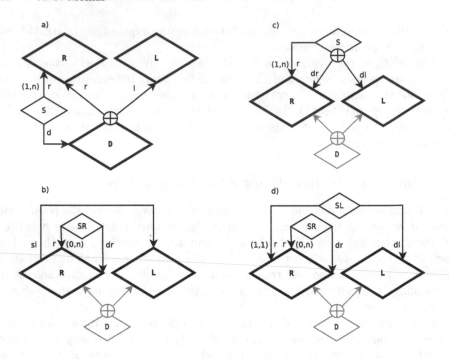

Fig. 3. Translation of the recursive model: adding a relationship type.

However, complex integrity constraints are potentially required for ensuring the acyclicity of the data [15], as the transitive closure of S (or SR) must be irreflexive.

If identification of an R-instance is inherently based on the data instances appearing in its structurally recursive composition, then we must seek a different solution.

4.3   Translation by Splitting the Composite Type

To go beyond the above solutions, when keeping the self-containment of type R is necessary, especially if identification is based on the structurally recursive construct, and the aggregation of cR must be kept insde type R, we discuss two cases, a simpler and a more general.

The Simple-Case Condition. For the simpler case, we assume D has no own key attributes, its own attributes or connected relationships (if there is any) do not contribute to the aggregation of cR, and has no specific aggregation function (cD is either nonexistent or is equal to cR or cL, depending on the actual instance of the cluster type). Put simply, D may have generally no effect on the aggregations and the structural recursive composition, it acts only as a generalizer façade over L and R and may add some simple higher-level, non-aggregative attributes and may participate in higher-order relationships on behalf of the whole structurally recursive part of the schema.

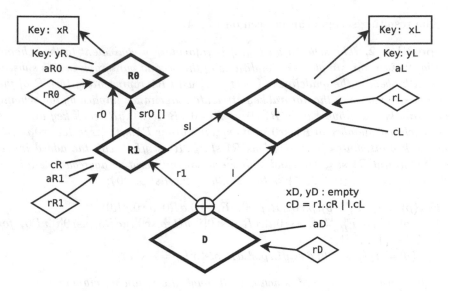

Fig. 4. Translation of the recursive model: mid complexity case.

We have to consider possible attributes and connected relationships of R, which of them do contribute to the aggregation of cR and which do not. We denote by $aR0$ those attributes of the attribute set aR which contribute to the aggregation, and by $aR1$ those which do not contribute to the aggreation. We use a similar notation $rR0$ and $rR1$ for the relationships rR as well.

To eliminate the formal cycle in the schema graph, we use the list (or array) constructor, which means a relationship type can be defined so that its component type has multiple (zero or more) data instances assigned to the same instance of that component type, in an ordered (indexed) way. This is denoted by a [] in the HERM schema graph.

Anything that contributes to the aggregation must be defined as part of a base type, of which a list is formed and another, higher-order relationship type is defined over it, where the actual aggregation is taking place. This implies the type R to be split into two relationship types $R0$ and $R1$, where $R1$ contains cR and everything else not contributing to the aggregation, and builds on a list of $R0$, which then contains the original key of R and everything contributin to the aggregation. $R0$ must also build on the initial type L of the structural recursion, since every data instance of R references a data instance of L at the end. For each instance of $R1$ we will have a specific instance of $R0$ which contains the rest of its own attributes, and zero or more other instances of $R0$ in an order corresponding the structurally recursive composition of "previous" instances of R on which the original instance R is built on. Although this can be merged into one list with an obligatory first instance, it is more expressive to model it separately, so $R1$ will have a duplicate (a non-list and a list) schema connection to $R0$.

The resulting schema can be seen on Fig. 4.

Proposition 2. *The schema on Fig. 4 is information-equivalent to the schema on Fig. 2 given the simple-case conditions of the second paragraph in this subsection, with obeying the guidelines of Sect. 4.1, with $R1$ representing type R of the original schema, with the natural key attribute inheritance implied by the schema (including key attributes from $R1.r0$ as $R1.r0.xR, R1.r0.yR$, each key attribute from each list member of $R1.sr0$ in its specific order $R1.sr0[i].xR, R1.sr0[i].yR$, and the key attributes from $R1.sl$ as $R1.sl.xL, R1.sl.yL$), with the added inclusion constraint $R1.sl \subseteq D.l$, and with the following iterative aggregate definition (where $\rho \in R$, $n \in \{0, 1, 2, ...\}$ is the length of the list $\rho.sr0$):*

- $F_{R1}(\rho) = f_R(F_{RL}^n(\rho), \rho.r0.xR, \rho.r0.yR, \rho.r0.aR0, \rho.r0.rR0)$;
- $F_{RL}^i(\rho) = f_R(F_{RL}^{i-1}(\rho), \rho.sr0[i].xR, \rho.sr0[i].yR, \rho.sr0[i].aR0, \rho.sr0[i].rR0)$ *for each $i \in \{1, ..., n\}$;*
- $F_{RL}^0(\rho) = f_L(\rho.sl.xL, \rho.sl.yL, \rho.sl.aL, \rho.sl.rL)[= \rho.sl.cL]$.

Information-equivalence is achieved through the following mappings:

- *For type L and D : identity in both directions (see conditions for D).*
- *Type R is mapped to $R1$ with correspondances*
  - $\Pi_{aR1,rR1,cR}(R_{orig}) \equiv R1$
  - $\Pi_{xR,yR,aR0,rR0}(R_{orig}) \equiv R1.r0$
  - $R_{orig}.s.l \equiv R1.sl$ *and* $R.s \equiv R1.sl.(D.l)^{-1}$ *if $R.s$ is an L-based D-instance*
  - $R_{orig}.s.r \equiv R1.sr0[1]$ *and* $R.s \equiv R1.sr0[1].(D.r1.r0)^{-1}$ *if $R.s$ is an R-based D-instance*
  - *Furthermore, $(R1.sr0[], R1.sl)$ is generally equivalent with the sequence of the structurally recursive composition of the corresponding R-instance in the original schema, with R-instances projected as $\Pi_{xR,yR,aR0,rR0}R$.*

Remark. The recursive definition of F_{R1} in the translated schema is usually rewritable to closed form, making the aggregation more effective. This is beneficial (if the array is stored compactly), since the schema translation implies multiple computations of the same function values, due to multiple references of $R0$ data instances or sequences in $R1$ data instances.

4.4   Translation by Splitting both the Composite and the Domain Types

The Complex-Case Condition. In the most general case, when type D has its own key attributes, aggregate function(s) for cD and/or its attributes or relationships contribute to the aggregation of cR or cD, the situation becomes far more non-trivial. This is due to the effect that an arbitrary data instance of D or R is built on other instances of D and R (and eventually, an instance of L) by structural recursion, and the key attributes must be properly reachable - along a directed path in the structure - and inherited for each data instance, as well as the other aggregation-contributing attributes must be reachable and correctly referenced.

Besides keeping the separation of type R into $R0, R1$ as in the previous section, we will have to use the same separation technique for D to organize key and aggregation-contributing attributes (and possible aggregation-contributing relationships) into a base type $D0$, and keep the rest of the attributes and relationships together with the aggregate attribute cD in a type $D1$ which will build on $D0$ and substitute the original type D.

But where to put type $D0$ in the translated schema, so that the reachabilities are ensured and the identification as well as the aggregation will not break, and the general guidelines (see Sect. 4.1) set for the translation are obeyed?

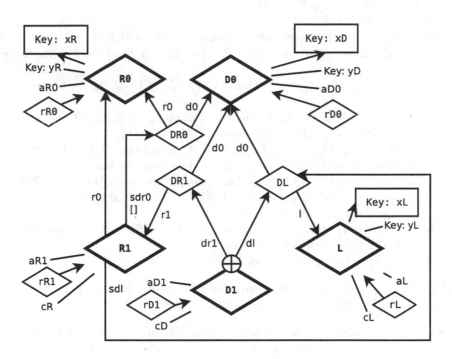

Fig. 5. Translation of the recursive model: complex, general case.

Constructing a properly translated schema turns out to be more difficult than expected, as there are several points where one may go wrong, but Fig. 5 shows a possible way. The reasoning below makes the following statement clear:

Proposition 3. *The schema on Fig. 5 is information-equivalent to the schema on Fig. 2, given the general guidelines of schema translation as introduced in Sect. 4.1 and the following conditions:*

- *Attribute sets aR and aD are decomposed to $aR0 \cup aR1$ and $aD0 \cup aD1$, respectively, where $aR0$ and $aD0$ contribute to the aggregations cR and cD.*
- *Similarly, relationship sets rR and rD are decomposed to $rR0 \cup rR1$ and $rD0 \cup rD1$, respectively, where $rR0$ and $rD0$ contribute to the aggregations cR and cD.*

- *D1 represents original type D, R1 represents original type R in the translated schema.*
- *Identification is done by the natural key attribute inheritance implied by the schema (including key attributes from R1.r0 as R1.r0.xR, R1.r0.yR, each key attribute from each list member of R1.sr0 in its specific order R1.sr0[i].xR, R1.sr0[i].yR, and the key attributes from R1.sl as R1.sl.xL, R1.sl.yL).*
- *The following integrity constraints must hold:*
  - $D0 \subseteq DR1 \cup DL \subseteq D1$
  - $DR0 \subseteq \Pi_{r1.r0,d0}(DR1 \bowtie R1)$
  - $D1 \subseteq DR1 \cup DL$
- *The following iterative aggregate definition is given which is equivalent to F in original schema (where $n \in \{0, 1, 2, ...\}$ is the length of the list $\rho.sdr0$ for $\rho \in R1$):*
  - $\lambda.cL ::= F_L(\lambda) = f_L(\lambda.xL, \lambda.yL, \lambda.aL, \lambda.rL)$ *if $\lambda \in L$ (as in the original schema),*
  - $\delta_l.cD ::= F_{D1}(\delta_l) = f_D(F_L(\delta_l.dl.l), \delta_l.dl.d0.xD, \delta_l.dl.d0.yD, \delta_l.dl.d0.aD, \delta_l.dl.d0.rD)$ *if $\delta_l \in D1$ a data instance based on DL,*
  - $\delta_r.cD ::= F_{D1}(\delta_r) = f_D(F_{R1}(\delta_r.dr1.r1), \delta_r.dr1.d0.xD, \delta_r.dr1.d0.yD, \delta_r.dr1.d0.aD, \delta_r.dr1.d0.rD)$ *if $\delta_r \in D1$ a data instance based on DR1,*
  - $\rho.cR ::= F_{R1}(\rho) = f_R(F_{DRL}^n(\rho), \rho.r0.xR, \rho.r0.yR, \rho.r0.aR0, \rho.r0.rR0);$
  - $F_{DRL}^i(\rho) = f_D(F_{RDL}^i(\rho), \rho.sdr0[i].d0.xD, \rho.sdr0[i].d0.yD, \rho.sdr0[i].d0.aD0, \rho.sdr0[i].d0.rD0)$ *for each $i \in \{1, ..., n\}$;*
  - $F_{RDL}^i(\rho) = f_R(F_{DRL}^{i-1}(\rho), \rho.sdr0[i].r0.xR, \rho.sdr0[i].r0.yR, \rho.sdr0[i].r0.aR0, \rho.sdr0[i].r0.rR0)$ *for each $i \in \{1, ..., n\}$;*
  - $F_{DRL}^0(\rho) = f_{D1}(\rho.sdl)[= \rho.sdl.l.cL].$

Information equivalence can be constructed in a similar way as in the previous section, extending it for type D analogously to type R.

Explanation. In order to make any aggregation (iterative computation) possible, under the reachability condition, having an acyclic schema, we have to separate the types with aggregation into (at least) two types, where one is based on a list of the other (directly or indirectly). It must be applied to R and D. Type L does not have to be decomposed. However, the higher-order part of R with the aggregated attributes and those not participating in the aggregation must reference the base type part of D with its attributes participating in the aggregation cR so that the aggregation can take all the relevant attribute values along the structural recursive composition of any data instance r. Therefore, the type $R1$ which becomes the correspondant of R in the translated schema must build on $R0$ and $D0$, and L somehow directly or indirectly.

Since attributes are not allowed to be merged from different types of the original schema to the translated schema, these separations must be disjoint, resulting in 5 different types: $L, R0, R1, D0, D1$. Based on which attributes or relationships are keys or contribute to the aggregation, the separation of these among the above types becomes straightforward.

In order to have proper identification (making a variable-length keys in this case for $R1, D1$), key attributes must be put into the base types $R0, D0$, so that the primary key of $R1, D1$ (respectively) can be composed similarly to the aggregation, as a list of the inherited key attributes. The key of $D0$ is inherited by $R1$ only for the structurally recursive part, not for the data instance $\delta \in D$ for which $\delta.r = \rho$.

Consider the initial step of the structural recursion, given a data instance $\lambda \in L$. If it takes part of any structural recursion, it has to be referenced by an instance $\delta_l \in D$, so that $\delta_l.l = \lambda$ in the original schema. If an instance $\rho \in R$ is based on this, then $\rho.s = \delta_l$ so that not only the own attributes of L must be reachable in the instance graph of the translated schema along the structural arrows, but also all attributes of D which do contribute to the aggregation. Therefore, $R1$ has to be based on - directly or indirectly - L and $D0$ (additionally to $\lambda \in L$, there must be a data instance $\delta_0 \in D0$ which is referenced by $\rho_1 \in R1$, the translated correspondant of ρ). On the other hand, because δ_l is a full-fledged data instance of D in the original schema, and has an aggregated value cD, it must correspond to an instance $\delta_1 \in D1$ in the translated schema with all the other attributes of D not contributing to the aggregation. So the pair (λ, δ_0) becomes a semantic unit referenced by both $R1$ and $D1$, and therefore, it is modeled as a new relationship type DL by the semantic encapsulation principle, representing the "internal" manifestation of the type of L-based D-instances (which participates in the structural recursion), while the "external" manifestation of the cluster type D becomes the cluster type $D1$.

Analogously, $R0, D0$ can be observed a semantic unit as the internal manifestation of R-based D-instances contributing to the composition of a data instance $\rho \in R$ by structural recursion. It becomes the intermediate type $DR0$ which is referenced as the list of translated R-based D-instances building up ρ by structural recursion (role $sdr0[]$). Altough not referenced more than once in the schema, its convenience is being the list member type (otherwise we would need two separate array-type references). At the depth of the recursive composition path stands an L-based D-instance in the original schema, which is mapped to a DL-instance in the translated schema and is referenced by $R1$ (role sdl). The translation of the role s with its all iterations through roles $D.r$ and $D.l$ in the original schema becomes the role pair $sdr0[], sdl$. The "own" attributes and relationships of ρ contributing to the aggregation are referenced directly as another role $r0$ towards the type $R0$.

The intermediate types $DR0$ and DL and their references make clear the different roles of referenced $D0$-instances from the various directions (whether it is a translation of an L-based or an R-based D-instance and on which level in the structural recursion from the point of a translation of a particular R-instance).

The internal manifestation of the R-based part of cluster type D in the translated schema is the $DR1, DR0$ type pair, and at the same time the external manifestation of the original type R becomes $R1$. The external manifestation of the full original cluster type D becomes $D1$ which is composed of DL and $DR1$, adding its own aggregate attribute cD and the other related items not contributing to the aggregation.

Therefore, the required attributes and relationships can be properly reached in the translated schema in Fig. 5 for the aggregation of cR from type $R1$, and the same is true for cD from $D1$. Moreover, all the guidelines of Sect. 4.1 hold.

Furthermore, Fig. 6 shows a refinement of this schema with the relaxation of the guidelines, by abolishing the inverse self-containment principle. R must be fully covered by D, so parts of D (here, $D0$) can be subordinated to $R1$. If this constraint holds in the original schema, this translation pattern can also be applied.

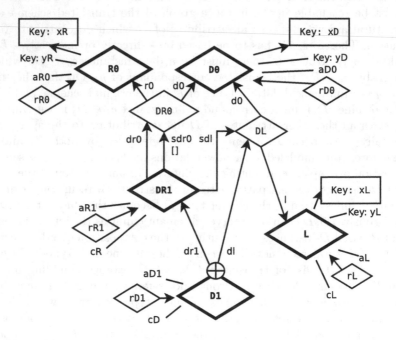

Fig. 6. Refined translation of the recursive model in the complex, general case, when D0 is subordinated to R.

4.5   Flattening the Split Schemata

If the guideline of semantic unit encapsulation is not in effect, the intermediate relationship types DL and $DR1$ can be eliminated from the schemata of Fig. 5 and Fig. 6 by linking the higher-order relationships built on them directly to the entities or relationships they connect. This results in the 'flattened' schemata depicted in Fig. 7 and Fig. 8, respectively. For the latter case, a full covering of both L and R is assumed by D (so each data instance of L and R must participate in D). This constraint must hold in the original schema for information equivalence. The main difference is the reachability of $D0$ via $R0$ and L, whether $D0$ is part of the composition of the latter relationships or only directly of $D0$. The latter case assumes the inverse self-containment guideline is not in effect.

The information equivalence of these schemata under the above conditions is obvious, and similar propositions may be formulated for these flattened schemata as for the ones in the previous section.

Note that we have kept the other principles (mixture or duplication avoidance, natural key principle) strictly in effect for all of the translation patterns. If one or more of these are put aside, new patterns can be constructed. However, a reasonable method is to keep these principles for the resolution of the structural recursion, and relax them only if the schema needs further optimization. This way, a clear separation is achieved in the method: we keep the resolution of the structurally recursive schema separated from further schema optimizations.

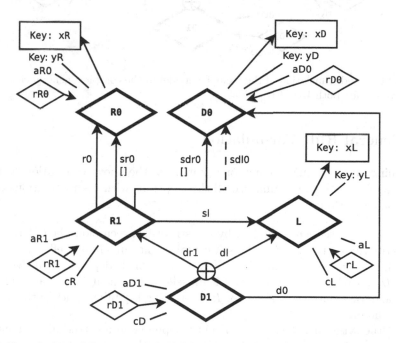

Fig. 7. Translation of the recursive model: complex, general case - flat variant (note: *sdl0* is optional, as it can be merged with sdr0[] to form a common sd0[]).

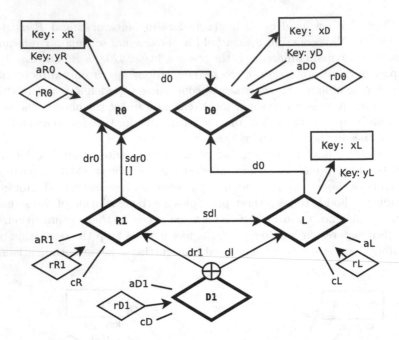

Fig. 8. Flattened translation of the recursive model in the complex, general case, when D is covering for both L and R.

5   General Rule Formulation

Depending on the actual setting, one or more of the above translation patterns can be applied. We can summarize all these options with their conditions in the following algorithm:

- Does the key sequence implied by the structural recursion via D have to be inherited via s to R and is the self-containment guideline in effect?
    - If not: choose a schema from Fig. 3/a), c) or d) depending on the role of D (based on its content and if its self-containment is relevant w.r.t. S) and formulate an own key for R (overriding key inheritance in the original schema).
    - Otherwise, identification of R must depends on its structurally recursive composition (partly or fully). Continue with the next step.
- Is the key of L the only key implied by the structural recursion via D contributing to the identification of R (i.e. a data instance of R does not inherit any key attributes from the sequence of R-instances it is built on by structural recursion) and is the self-containment guideline not in effect?
    - If yes: take schema in Fig. 3/b) and make the key of L part of the key of R.
    - Otherwise, identification of R depends on the full key chain of its structurally recursive composition. Continue with the next step.

- Are the simple-case conditions described in the second paragraph of Sect. 4.3 hold for D?
  - If yes: choose schema in Fig. 4, otherwise continune with the next step.
- Is D covering for both R and L (i.e. each data instance of R and L must participate in D) and can the inverse self-containment guideline be put aside?
  - If yes: you may choose schema in Fig. 8, otherwise continue with the next step.
- Is D covering for R (i.e. each data instance of R must participate in D) and can the inverse self-containent guideline be put aside?
  - If yes: you may choose schema in Fig. 6, otherwise continue with the next step.
- If none of the previous conditions hold, or the offered schema is otherwise inconvenient, the schema of the most general case as in Fig. 5 or its flattened variant in Fig. 7 must be taken, based on whether the semantic unit encapsulation guideline is in effect.
- The schema is well-formed without a formal directed cycle in its structure. Considering it as an intermediate schema, make further optimizations on the schema as usual, based on the modeling methodology on conventional schemata being applied. This should be guided by the other translation principles in effect (mixture or duplication avoidance, natural key principle, or even the information equivalence may be relaxed in specific cases).

6   Conclusion and Future Work

In this paper, we have shown how the Higher-Order Entity-Relationship model (HERM) can be extended to allow unary structural recursion to be expressed, which formally contains a cycle in the model graph (thus not considered well-formed as a conventional schema), but without actual cycles on the instance (data) level. Several variants of reasonable translation patterns have been developed and presented in order to achieve an equivalent, conventionally well-formed schema. An algorithm-like rule summarises their applicability, which is based on the specific properties of the original schema, as well as some general guidelines determining the actual methodology of schema translation. The result is an intermediate schema possibly involving complex key domains by list type construction, and is ready for further optimization in the most general sense.

Future issues and open questions include further generalization towards more complex structures, including recursivity on the instance level, investigation on the effect on database constraints and constraint management of structurally recursive schemata, and further discussion on the translation variants, for example, regarding usage patterns and query efficiency.

Considering the modeling-to-programming initiative, this case study gives an example of a relatively simple-looking but complex scenario, where model translation is achieved by choosing from pre-designed schema patterns, and the choice is determined by explicit guidelines and inherent model properties as well. In can be directly built into a model-to-schema translator engine or similar software tool, and used as a scenario for more considerations related to the nature of model translation and structural recursion. A more general contribution of this paper is the collection of translation guidelines which can be used as possible directives set on or off by the modeler or schema designer for model translations.

References

1. AlBdaiwi, B., Noack, R., Thalheim, B.: Pattern-based conceptual data modelling. Front. Artif. Intell. Appl. **272**, 1–20 (2014). https://doi.org/10.3233/978-1-61499-472-5-1
2. Arenas, M., Libkin, L.: An information-theoretic approach to normal forms for relational and xml data. J. ACM (JACM) **52**(2), 246–283 (2005)
3. Bahmani, A., Naghibzadeh, M., Bahmani, B.: Automatic database normalization and primary key generation. In: 2008 Canadian Conference on Electrical and Computer Engineering, pp. 000011–000016, June 2008. https://doi.org/10.1109/CCECE.2008.4564486
4. Chen, P.: Entity-relationship modeling: historical events, future trends, and lessons learned. In: Broy, M., Denert, E. (eds.) Software Pioneers, pp. 296–310. Springer, Heidelberg (2002). https://doi.org/10.1007/978-3-642-59412-0_17
5. Codd, E.F.: A relational model of data for large shared data banks. Commun. ACM **13**(6), 377–387 (1970). https://doi.org/10.1145/362384.362685
6. Date, C.: Logic and Databases: The Roots of Relational Theory. Trafford Publishing (2007). https://books.google.de/books?id=2egNzTk871wC
7. Embley, D., Thalheim, B.: Handbook of Conceptual Modeling: Theory, Practice, and Research Challenges. Springer, Heidelberg (2012). https://books.google.de/books?id=oWmp10vBI7cC
8. Gamma, E., Helm, R., Johnson, R., Vlissides, J.M.: Design Patterns: Elements of Reusable Object-Oriented Software, 1st edn. Addison-Wesley Professional, United States (1994)
9. Klettke, M., Thalheim, B.: Evolution and migration of information systems. In: Embley, D., Thalheim, B. (eds.) Handbook of Conceptual Modeling, pp. 381–420. Springer, Berlin, Heidelberg (2011). https://doi.org/10.1007/978-3-642-15865-0_12
10. Krtzsch, M., Hitzler, P., Zhang, G.: Morphisms in context (2005). www.aifb.uni-karlsruhe.de/WBS/phi/pub/KHZ05tr.pdf
11. Molnár, A.J.: Conceptual modeling of hiking trail networks with logical rules for consistent signage planning and management. In: Thalheim, B., Tropmann-Frick, M., Jaakkola, H., Kiyoki, Y. (eds.) Proceedings of the International Conference on Information Modelling and Knowledge Bases (EJC 2020). KCSS, vol. 2020/1, pp. 1–25. Department of Computer Science, Faculty of Engineering, Kiel University, June 2020. https://doi.org/10.21941/kcss/2020/1
12. Paton, N.W., Díaz, O.: Active database systems. ACM Comput. Surv. **31**(1), 63–103 (1999)
13. Thalheim, B.: The conceptual model = an adequate and dependable artifact enhanced by concepts. Front. Artif. Intell. Appl. **260**, 241–254 (2014)
14. Thalheim, B.: Foundations of entity-relationship modeling. Ann. Math. Artif. Intell. **7**, 197–256 (1993). https://doi.org/10.1007/BF01556354

15. Thalheim, B.: Entity-Relationship Modeling: Foundations of Database Technology. Springer, Berlin (2000)
16. Thalheim, B., Jaakkola, H.: Model-based fifth generation programming. In: Dahanayake, A., Huiskonen, J., Kiyoki, Y., Thalheim, B., Jaakkola, H., Yoshida, N. (eds.) Information Modelling and Knowledge Bases XXXI - Proceedings of the 29th International Conference on Information Modelling and Knowledge Bases, EJC 2019, Lappeenranta, Finland, 3–7 June 2019. Frontiers in Artificial Intelligence and Applications, vol. 321, pp. 381–400. IOS Press (2019). https://doi.org/10.3233/FAIA200026

A Models-to-Program Information Systems Engineering Method

Rene Noel[1,2]([✉])[iD], Ignacio Panach[3][iD], and Oscar Pastor[1][iD]

[1] Centro de Investigación en Métodos de Producción de Software,
Universitat Politècnica de València, Valencia, Spain
{rnoel,opastor}@pros.upv.es

[2] Escuela de Ingeniería Informática, Universidad de Valparaíso, Valparaíso, Chile
rene.noel@uv.cl

[3] Escola Tècnica Superior d'Enginyeria, Departament d'Informàtica,
Universitat de València, Valencia, Spain
joigpana@uv.es

Abstract. The Model-Driven Development paradigm aims to represent all the information system features through models. Conceptual-Model Programming offers a similar approach, but with a focus on automatic code generation. Both approaches consider modeling and traceability of different abstraction levels, where each level can be tackled with different modeling methods. This heterogeneity introduces a challenge for the quality of the traceability and transformations among models, especially when aiming for automatic code generation. In this paper, we introduce a holistic conceptual-model programming method to generate code from different abstraction levels (from the problem space to the solution space), through three modeling languages whose consistency has been ontologically ensured by two transformation techniques. Particularly, we focus on transformations from the strategic layer using i*, to business process layer using Communication Analysis (CA), and to the system conceptual model layer with OO-Method, which can automatically generate fully functional systems. Even though there are previous works that have proposed partial transformations among these modeling methods, this paper is the first one that deals with the perspective of putting together all the models in a single development method. For each transformation, we discuss what parts can be automatically performed and what parts need human intervention.

Keywords: Modeling methods combination · Model-driven interoperability · Conceptual model programming

This project has the support of the Spanish Ministry of Science and Innovation through the DATAME project (ref: TIN2016-80811-P) and PROMETEO/2018/176 and co-financed with ERDF and the National Agency for Research and Development (ANID)/Scholarship Program/Doctorado Becas Chile/2020-72210494.

A. Dahanayake et al. (Eds.): M2P 2020, CCIS 1401, pp. 162–176, 2021.
https://doi.org/10.1007/978-3-030-72696-6_8

1   Introduction

The use of modeling languages for different information systems abstraction levels and the transformation between them, are key characteristics of model-driven approaches [13]. Most of the claims of these approaches, regarding improvements on product quality, process efficiency, and developer's satisfaction [18] are based on the suitability of the modeling methods and the quality of the transformations. However, combining modeling methods from different abstraction levels with different languages, semantics, and theoretical foundations is an open challenge: it is necessary to precisely define their connection to ensure the internal quality of the transformations, the quality of the models generated by the transformations, and the overall method quality, besides the quality of the independent methods [12].

This article presents a Models-to-Program Information Systems Engineering Method (M2PM), which combines three modeling methods for different abstraction levels, going from organizational modeling of strategic dependencies with i* [23], to business process modeling with Communication Analysis [6], and to an executable conceptual model of the system with OO-Method [19]. As its main contribution, this paper reinforces the feasibility of Conceptual-Model Programming paradigm [5] in practice, by showing that it is possible to design a holistic software production method that connects -with a sound methodological background- stakeholder's goals and requirements with their associated code. This is achieved by connecting in a precise way scientifically (but individually) validated methods and transformation techniques, ensuring traceability throughout the process and providing as much automation as possible.

The rest of the article continues with Sect. 2, where the related work is presented. An overview of the holistic modeling method and a detailed working example showing the model-to-program process is presented in Sect. 3. Finally, Sect. 4 details the conclusions and future work for the method.

2   Related Work

2.1   Connection of Modeling Methods

The model-driven community has widely studied the connection of models of different abstraction levels for developing information systems in the last decade. In a systematic literature review about interoperability [10], the authors identified several approaches for model-driven interoperability, i.e., the exchange of information among models. Model weaving regards the identification of semantic equivalences between the metamodels of the models to integrate, to generate specific maps between the concepts of the models. The pivotal metamodel approach is the equivalencies between metamodels identification using a reference metamodel to compare them; Pivotal ontology follows a similar approach. Meta-extensions are the transformations semantics additions to models to improve interoperability. Despite the early recognition of the interoperability approaches, the traceability among models is still an open challenge. In another literature review [17], authors studied the state of traceability among models, identifying challenges related to the semantics of traceability and its generality. Most of the reviewed studies described problem-specific semantics for the transformations, which might be domain, organization, or project dependent.

With regard to the quality definition for the combination of modeling languages in a single method, Giraldo et al's. [13] report issues both in the criteria for choosing the languages to be combined and in the overall quality assessment of the combined methods. The literature review concludes that there is a predominant subjectivity in selecting modeling languages, and raises questions about how it is assessed the suitability, coverage, pertinence, and utility of the languages to be combined. It also reports that most of the existing quality evaluation frameworks have definitions of a high level of abstraction, lacking implementation details, and are specific for a unique language combination. Authors continue this work in [11], presenting a method and a tool for a general quality evaluation framework, which helps to better define the quality concepts and the metrics for language comparison. One of the quality metrics supported by the framework regarding information loss is the preservation of constructs through the model transformations. Another quality metric regarding the suitability of a modeling language is the number of integration points that it provides for its connection with the other languages.

In summary, modeling language connection is still a challenge, although recent proposals approach systematically its quality evaluation. These additions offer insights about the desired characteristic for a new combination of methods, such as problem-independent traceability, transformations with a clear and defined interoperability approach, and focus on key quality attributes such as constructs preservation and the suitability of each modeling language.

2.2   Background

I* is an agent-oriented and goal-oriented modeling framework for the description and reflection of the intentionality of the actors of an organization. I* considers two modeling levels: the Strategic Dependency Model and the Strategic Rationale Model. In the Strategic Dependency Model (SDM), the actors are presented as nodes, and their intentions are represented by directed relationships from the actor that wants to achieve a goal to the actor that enables the achievement of the goal. These relationships are called dependencies, and there are four types of them: goal, soft-goal, task, and resource dependency. The Strategic Rationale Model (SRM) aims to detail the way that those dependencies are satisfied, linking the SDM dependencies to specific goals, soft-goals, tasks, and resources inside the boundaries of each actor. Those elements can be linked to represent task decomposition, means to an end, and contribution to soft-goals. The framework is implemented in OpenOME Requirements Engineering Tool [15]. The version 2.0 of the modeling language [3] is supported by the piStar Tool [20].

Communication Analysis (CA) [6] is an information system's requirements specification method, which allows business process modeling from a communication perspective. The model support three specification artifacts: the

Communicative Event Diagram, the Communicative Event Specification, and the Message Structures specification. The Communicative Event Diagram graphically depicts the sequence of interactions between a Primary Actor (who starts the communication), a Support Actor (who is the organization's interface in the communication), and the Receiver actor (who is notified of the results of the event). The Communicative Event Specification allows the textual specification of requirements, through a template that considers contact requirements, the content of the communication, and the reactions produced after the communicative event. The Message Structure Specification allows to represent the information that is inputted, derived, or generated in the communication by defining one or more data fields, aggregations of data fields, and substructures. Aggregations are structures valuable to business logic, so they are also called Business Objects. The supporting tool for CA is a functional prototype based on Eclipse modeling Framework, the GREAT Process Modeler, described in [21].

The OO-Method (OOM) [19] is an automatic software production method from platform-independent conceptual schemes. It considers four views to model the information system: the structural view (Object Model), the behavioral view (Dynamic model), the logic (Functional Model), and the user interfaces (Presentation Model). OOM is based on the OASIS language [16] and considers a Conceptual Schema Compiler for the generation of platform-specific models and code. The supporting tool for OOM is INTEGRANOVA [2], that can generate fully functional web or desktop systems in many programming languages.

GoBIS [22] technique proposes nine guidelines for the derivation of CA models from i* models. The guidelines propose to derive a Communicative Event in CA for each dependency between i* actors, as well as to derive precedence of the events, although there is no temporal dimension in i*. Also, it promotes the generation of communication events for the registry of information of relevant actors. GoBIS guidelines are implemented in the tool GREAT Process Modeler, described in [21].

España proposes in [7,14] the integration of CA models with OOM models, presenting a set of rules to derive OOM's object, functional, and dynamic models. The proposal considers rules that are fully automatable, as well as semi-automatic transformations that require manual modeling tasks from the analyst. This transformation technique is also implemented in the GREAT Process Modeler [21].

3 The M2P Information Systems Engineering Method

3.1 Method Overview

We introduce the Models-to-Program Information Systems Engineering Method (M2PM), as a connection of existing modeling methods and model transformation techniques. The goal of the method is to support the following claims:

- Improve the maintainability of the software product through traceability between the organizational level, business processes level, and the conceptual model of the system level.

– Improve the efficiency of the development process by providing as much automation as possible between the abstraction levels.

This is achieved by connecting in a precise way scientifically (but individually) validated methods and model transformation techniques. In Fig. 1 we present the connection of methods proposed: organizational modeling with i* [23], business process modeling with Communication Analysis (CA) [6], and Systems modeling with OO-Method (OOM) [19].

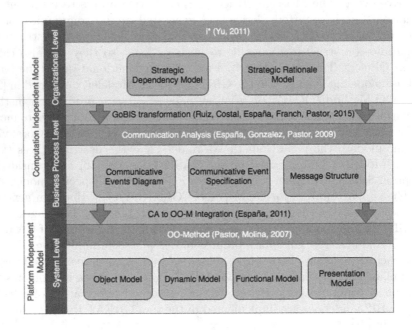

Fig. 1. Proposed connection of modeling methods.

As commented in Sect. 2, one of the key quality elements for method integration is its semantic consistency. We choose i*, CA, and OOM because of the ontological alignment of the existing transformation techniques [7,22]. The transformation techniques use FRISCO [8] as a pivotal ontology to ensure the consistency of i* concepts with CA concepts, and of the CA concepts with the OOM concepts.

In the following subsections, we will present the models and transformations of the proposed method following an example. For each stage modeling level, we will provide the semantic justification for the transformations, as well as the rationale for mapping concepts from different abstraction levels, which are the basis for the successful combination of modeling languages [11,17]. This ontological alignment led us to choose CA over other similar business process modeling methods, such as BPMN Collaboration Diagrams [1] and S-BPMN [9].

3.2   Working Example

For presenting the key elements of the method, we introduce the Custom Bicycle Company. The customers can order a custom bicycle, that is composed of a basic structure (that includes the frame, rims, grips, and chain) and one or many additional components, such as custom handlebars, tires, and pedals. Customers can choose a model for the basic structure (for example, a sports bicycle), its color, and size. For each of the components, customers can choose the color. The company must request the additional components to an external company. Once all the components are provided, the company delivers the bicycle to the customer.

3.3   Organizational Level Modeling with i*

The Strategic Dependency Model depicted in Fig. 2 represents the actors and their strategic dependencies. Circles represent the actors of the domain example: the customers, the clerk (who represents the organization before the external actors), and the provider of the components. The goals of the actors are pictured as an ellipse, and the direction of the relationship indicates that the source actors depend on the target actor to satisfy the goal. Resources dependencies are pictured as rectangles and represent that the source actor needs the resource from the target actor. Although i* provides a rich language to specify other types of dependency as well as how the goals are achieved, the example does not cover these aspects for the sake of simplicity.

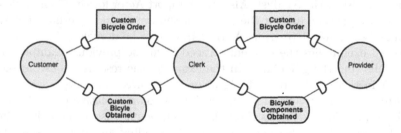

Fig. 2. Strategic Dependency Model.

3.4   Business Process Level Modeling with Communication Analysis

Transformation from i* Model to Communication Analysis Model. The guidelines presented in [22] provide support for the transformation of i* models into Communication Analysis (CA) models. The transformation is not problem specific. The central idea of the transformation is that a strategic dependency of any type in i*, generates a communicative interaction between the same actors in CA. In model transformation terms, organizational goals (represented in a source istar model) are materialized by business processes (represented in a target CA model). Resource dependencies that relate to information are transformed into a Communicative Event in CA, with all its associate concepts. The semantic of this transformation is as follows: for an Actor A to satisfy the need of an informational resource of an Actor B , the Actor A must communicate with Actor B to deliver the informational resource. Other types of dependencies also transform into communicative events with all their associated concepts, as previously detailed. It is noticeable that the semantic for each type of dependency is different. For instance, for goal dependencies the semantic can be expressed as: if an actor A depends on Actor B for achieving a goal, Actor B must communicate to Actor A the information that is relevant for Actor A to verify that the goal has been achieved.

The guidelines also support the transformation of actors from i* whose information is relevant for the business model, into a communicative event for the registry of its information. Other transformation supported by the guidelines deals with actors which satisfy the same dependency for two or more actors, which transform into a single communicative with a primary actor and many receiver actors. Also, subsequent dependencies between three or more actors are transformed into precedence relationships between the communicative events. The semantic of this transformation is: before Actor A can satisfy the need for the resource of Actor B, Actor C must satisfy the need of Actor A. This provides a sense of temporal precedence which is not explicitly modelled in i*.

It is important to note that some Communication Analysis Concepts cannot be generated following the guidelines. The structure of the input and output messages (that will be explained in the following subsections) must be elicited and documented by the Analyst. Also, the Support Actor for the Communicative Event must be chosen among the actors of the event, and alternate behaviors (known as Communicative Event Variants), cannot be derived.

Figure 3 exemplifies the elements traced from the previous example to CA models, following the guidelines. In the example, the resource "custom bicycle order" (A in the left diagram of Fig. 3) and its source and target actors, clerk and customer, respectively, are mapped into a communicative event (A in the right diagram). This event has the following elements: customer as the primary actor (A.1) who starts the communication by sending an input message (A.2) to the clerk, who is the receiver actor (A.3) of the output message (A.4). The details of the communication are meant to be specified in the communicative event "customer places a bicycle order" (A.5).

The same transformation described above also applies to the dependency B in the diagram in the left of Fig. 3, which is transformed in the elements of the communicative event marked as B in the right. It is important to note that the Analyst can choose a more appropriate name for the message: although the content of the communication between the clerk and the provider can be the same "bicycle order", the aim of the communication of the clerk with the provider is to request the additional components, so the input and output messages are named as "components order" (B.1 and B.2 in Fig. 3). This is the same case of the dependencies D and E in the diagram at the left in Fig. 3, which transforms into the communicative events D and E in the right of the diagram in the same figure.

The subsequent dependency of the resource "custom bicycle order" (C at the left) is transformed into the precedence relationship between the events "customer places a bicycle order" and "clerk places a component order" (C at the right of Fig. 3). Finally, regarding the registry of data of relevant actors, customer data would be valuable to represent in this way, but it is not depicted in Fig. 3 for simplicity.

As has been shown, almost all of the i* constructs are preserved in the CA model. Table 1 summarizes the elements that can be traced from i* to Communication Analysis, and what must be manually addressed by the Analyst.

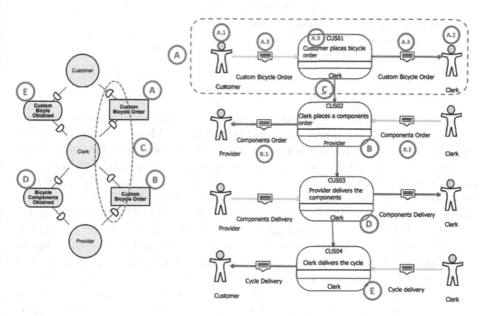

Fig. 3. Transformation from i* Strategic Dependency Model to a Communicative Event Diagram.

Additional Business Modeling Activities. Communication Analysis (CA) supports the specification of the communicative events, allowing the Analyst to specify requirements regarding the goal of the communicative event, the description, and a more detailed specification of contact, content, and reaction requirements. These elements are exemplified in Fig. 4 for the communicative event "customer places a bicycle order".

Table 1. Traceability of concepts between i* and Communication Analysis.

CA concept	I* Concept	Comment
Communicative Event	Goal, soft-goal, task, resource dependums	Traceable and semiautomatic
Actors	Actors	Primary and receiver actors are derivable. Support actors cannot be derived
Messages	Goal, soft-goal, task, resource dependums	Traceable. No details for message structure can be derived
Precedence	Subsequent dependencies of the same dependum	
Communicative Event Specification	Not supported	–
Communicative Event Variant	Not supported	–

In the communicative event specification, the content requirements detail the information of the communication, in the form of a Message Structure (MS). The MS specifies the data elements in the communication, as well as other more complex structures, such as aggregations (structures containing one or more data fields or other structures), and iterations (several repetitions of the same field or structure). In the example, the MS "Bicycle Order" (colored in orange in Fig. 4) is composed of an initial aggregation (BICYCLEORDER, in red), which is composed of six data fields (number, date, and price of the order; model, size or color of the basic bicycle structure), and an iteration of several components (in violet). "Component" is also an aggregation, with two data fields (type and color). A special case of data field is customer (colored in brown): this is a reference field for other aggregations already defined in other communicative events. In the same way, the aggregations defined in this structure can be referenced in other communicative events. These aggregations are also known as Business Objects, given its value for the business process.

Finally, it is important to identify the supporting actor of a communicative event. Although GoBIS rules do not provide support for its automatic generation, the Analyst has the information to identify which of the two actors in the event belongs to the organization and set it as the supporting actor.

3.5   Conceptual Modeling of the System with OO-Method

Transformation from Communication Analysis Model to OO-Method Model. The rules in [7] allow the transformation of communicative events and message structures of CA into elements of the object model, functional model, and dynamic model of OO-Method (OOM). The transformation is not

CUS01 Customer places a bicycle order
Goals: Customer orders a custom bicycle.
Description: Customer selects a basic structure and one or more additional components. Customer can select the color and size of the basic structure, and the color of each additional component.
Contact Requirements
Communication Channel: In person, by phone, by e-mail.
Temporal Restrictions: Only working days (09:00-18:00)
Frequency: 50 orders per week.
Required supports: Customer information.
Communication Content Requirements

Message Structure: Bicycle Order

Field	OP	Domain	Example
`<BICYCLEORDER =`			
`{number +`	g	number	43211
`date +`	i	date	01-05-2020
`price +`	i	money	250.5
`customer +`	i	customer	C0122,F.Miler
`model +`	i	text	Sport
`size +`	i	number	53
`color +`	i	text	silver
`{COMPONENTS`			
`<COMPONENT=`			
`{type +`	i	text	handlebar
`color`	i	text	black
`}>}}>`			

Structural constraints: Custom cycles must contain at least one cycle. **Contextual constraints:** Order Number is correlatively assigned and is unique.
Reaction Requirements
Treatments: The order is stored. **Linked Communications:** The Clerk is notified of the new order. **Linked behavior:** no exceptional behaviors are considered.

Fig. 4. Communicative Event Specification example. (Color figure online)

problem-specific. The presentation model of OOM is out of the scope of the transformation. In these rules, the Message Structures (as presented in Table 1) provide information for OOM's object model. The aggregations in the MSs (hereinafter namely Business Objects or BOs) transform into Classes in OOM's object model. The semantic of this transformation can be understood as: If the contents of the communication between two actors in the business process level are valuable, they must persist in the information system that supports the process.

Regarding the Communicative Events (CE), the primary receiver and support actor are transformed into Agents of the object model of OO-Method. Agents are classes that have execution permissions for the services of the classes. The services of the classes are derived from CEs, to allow the actors to create, edit, delete, and make complex operations with the objects, according to the behavior described in the communicative events. The semantics of these transformations can be interpreted as: If an actor has behavior associated with the content of the communication at the business process level, the actor must be able to execute the services that encapsulate that behavior at the system level. If the same BO is referenced in several communicative events, the transformation rules guide the generation of edit service; also, the rules support the generation of the logic to update the class, by introducing a valuation rule in OOM's functional model. For BOs that are referenced in several events, the transformation rules support the generation of OOM's dynamic model, where the states and transitions of each class are defined.

A special case are the BOs that change of state through the business process, which is also supported by the rules by generating the attributes, services, and functionality to implement the state machine for the class. Finally, for communicative events in which the messages introduce changes for several BOs at the same time, the transformation rules support the generation of a transaction service in the object model, and a transaction formula in the functional model to specify all the services that must be connected in the transaction.

There are OOM's model elements that cannot be automatically generated following the rules and require manual modeling by the Analyst. For instance, the cardinality of some structural relationships in OOM's object model, the selection of data fields as unique identifiers of objects, as well as the null allowance and variability of attributes.

Figure 5 presents examples for the most powerful transformations, that are commented below. Dealing with the generation of classes from Message Structures, the business object BICYCLEORDER (Fig. 5A in the left) transforms into the class BicycleOrder (A in the diagram at the right). Data fields of the BO transform into attributes of the class. The referenced BOs, such as customer (left B), are transformed into structural relationships (right B). In this case, the customer is referenced but not defined, but, as was presented in the previous section, the guidelines provided support to generate a BO for the customer's relevant data. Regarding the nested aggregations defined in the MS, such as Component (left C), they are also transformed into structural relationships, and in this case, into a new class, with a cardinality given by the iteration (right C). Regarding the generation of services, when an actor introduces a new BO in the business process, i.e., the customer places a new bicycle order (left D in Fig. 5), it generates a creation service for the corresponding class (BicycleOrder), and the clerk, which is the supporting actor of the organization, gets access to this service as an agent (right D). If the bicycle order is referenced in several communicative events through the process (left E in Fig. 5), then an editing service is generated for the BicycleOrder class, and the valuation rules for registering the change of states of the object, in OOM's functional model (bottom right in Fig. 5).

As an example of a transaction service, if for the final delivery of the bicycle it is needed to register the "delivery date· in the BicycleOrder, and set the "last delivery date" attribute in the Customer (left F in Fig. 5), this would produce a transaction service in the BicicyleOrder class (right F).

Table 2 summarizes the elements that can be traced from i* to Communication Analysis, and what must be manually addressed by the Analyst. Most of the constructs of CA are preserved to OOM's models, including constructs originated in i* concepts. For example, the class BicycleOrder is traceable to a resource dependency in i*, offering strategic and business process context for the Analyst. This is a key contribution of the method combination proposal: the modeling methods and transformation techniques combination preserve most of the high abstraction level constructs, which gives strategic and business context to the system modeling, providing traceability and automation in the generation of the most important concepts in each level.

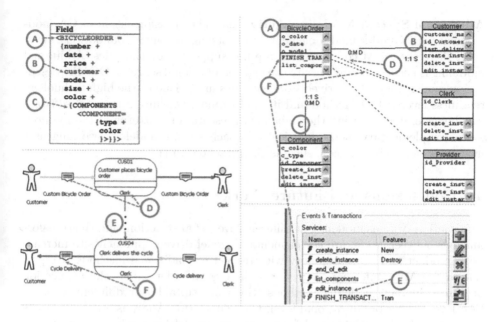

Fig. 5. Communicative Event Specification example.

Table 2. Traceability of concepts between Communication Analysis and OO-Method.

OOM Concept	CA concept	Comment
Classes, attributes and relationships	Message structures	Traceable and automatic
Services definition	Communicative events	Traceable and semi-automatic. Require some manual modeling and interpretation of text requirements
Classes structural relationships	Message Structures, Communicative Events	Traceable and semiautomatic. Require some manual modeling and interpretation of text requirements
Agents	Actors	Traceable and automatic
States and transitions	Communicative Events and precedence	Traceable and automatic
Services logic (functional model)	Communicative events	Semi traceable and semiautomatic. Require some manual modeling and interpretation of text requirements
Presentation model	Not supported	–

Additional System Modeling Activities. The transformation of CA models generates OOM's model elements with strong semantic foundations, however, there are OOM concepts that are not supported by the rules. Additional modeling is needed to fully specify the logic of additional services. OOM's presentation model cannot be derived from the rules in [7]. Due to the high technology readiness level of OO-Method and its tool support [2], fully functional software can be generated by using the embedded presentation patterns of the method. Also, complementary methodological approaches from models to working user interfaces can be introduced, such as the presented in [4].

4   Conclusions and Future Work

Information systems modeling at different levels of abstraction, and the transformations between them, are key elements of model-driven approaches to increase both product and process quality with respect to traditional methods. We presented the M2P Information Systems Engineering Method as the connection of three different modeling methods which are suitable for different abstraction levels: i* for organizational level, Communication Analysis for the business process level, and OO-Method for the system model level, which supports the generation of working code of the information system. The connection among these methods is supported by well-defined and empirically validated transformation techniques, that have been developed separately, and have never been put together in a holistic method. With an example, we showed the feasibility of conceptual model programming in practice, emphasizing the semantics of the transformations, and the support provided by the method for the Analyst to complete the models of each abstraction level.

Regarding the limitations of the example, certainly many special cases are not covered (for instance, exception handling in business process models), and the scalability of methods that work in small examples is a matter of concern. However, the example goal is to demonstrate the feasibility of the method and identify traceability and automation issues that are also present in more complex problems. Further work aims for analyzing improvement opportunities to connect concepts that could be not currently considered by the transformation techniques, to enhance traceability and provide as much automation as possible. Also, modeling challenges for improving the overall quality of the modeling method, such as overlapping of modeling activities, must be identified.

References

1. Business Process Model and Notation (BPMN), Version 2.0, p. 532 (2015)
2. Integranova Software Solutions. http://www.integranova.com/es/
3. Dalpiaz, F., Franch, X., Horkoff, J.: iStar 2.0 language guide. arXiv preprint arXiv:1605.07767 (2016)

4. Díaz, J.S., López, O.P., Fons, J.J.: From user requirements to user interfaces: a methodological approach. In: Dittrich, K.R., Geppert, A., Norrie, M.C. (eds.) CAiSE 2001. LNCS, vol. 2068, pp. 60–75. Springer, Heidelberg (2001). https://doi.org/10.1007/3-540-45341-5_5

5. Embley, D.W., Liddle, S.W., Pastor, O.: Conceptual-model programming: a manifesto. In: Embley, D., Thalheim, B. (eds.) Handbook of Conceptual Modeling, pp. 3–16. Springer, Heidelberg (2011). https://doi.org/10.1007/978-3-642-15865-0_1

6. España, S., González, A., Pastor, Ó.: Communication analysis: a requirements engineering method for information systems. In: van Eck, P., Gordijn, J., Wieringa, R. (eds.) CAiSE 2009. LNCS, vol. 5565, pp. 530–545. Springer, Heidelberg (2009). https://doi.org/10.1007/978-3-642-02144-2_41

7. España Cubillo, S.: Methodological integration of Communication Analysis into a model-driven software development framework. Ph.D. thesis (2012)

8. Falkenberg, E.D.: A framework of information system concepts: the FRISCo report. Department of Computer Science, University of Leiden, Leiden (1998)

9. Fernández, H.F., Palacios-González, E., García-Díaz, V., G-Bustelo, B.C.P., Martínez, O.S., Lovelle, J.M.C.: SBPMN–an easier business process modeling notation for business users. Comput. Stand. Interfaces 32(1–2), 18–28 (2010)

10. Giachetti, G., Valverde, F., Marín, B.: Interoperability for model-driven development: current state and future challenges. In: 2012 Sixth International Conference on Research Challenges in Information Science (RCIS), pp. 1–10. IEEE (2012)

11. Giraldo, F.D., España, S., Giraldo, W.J., Pastor, O.: Evaluating the quality of a set of modelling languages used in combination: a method and a tool. Inf. Syst. 77, 48–70 (2018)

12. Giraldo, F.D., España, S., Pastor, O.: Analysing the concept of quality in model-driven engineering literature: a systematic review. In: 2014 IEEE Eighth International Conference on Research Challenges in Information Science (RCIS), pp. 1–12. IEEE (2014)

13. Giraldo, F.D., España, S., Pastor, Ó., Giraldo, W.J.: Considerations about quality in model-driven engineering. Softw. Qual. J. 26(2), 685–750 (2016). https://doi.org/10.1007/s11219-016-9350-6

14. González, A., España, S., Ruiz, M., Pastor, Ó.: Systematic derivation of class diagrams from communication-oriented business process models. In: Halpin, T., et al. (eds.) BPMDS/EMMSAD -2011. LNBIP, vol. 81, pp. 246–260. Springer, Heidelberg (2011). https://doi.org/10.1007/978-3-642-21759-3_18

15. Horkoff, J., Yu, Y., Eric, S.: OpenOME: an open-source goal and agent-oriented model drawing and analysis tool. iStar 766, 154–156 (2011)

16. Lopez, O.P., Hayes, F., Bear, S.: Oasis: an object-oriented specification language. In: Loucopoulos, P. (ed.) CAiSE 1992. LNCS, vol. 593, pp. 348–363. Springer, Heidelberg (1992). https://doi.org/10.1007/BFb0035141

17. Mustafa, N., Labiche, Y.: The need for traceability in heterogeneous systems: a systematic literature review. In: 2017 IEEE 41st Annual Computer Software and Applications Conference (COMPSAC), vol. 1, pp. 305–310. IEEE (2017)

18. Panach, J.I., España, S., Dieste, O., Pastor, O., Juristo, N.: In search of evidence for model-driven development claims: an experiment on quality, effort, productivity and satisfaction. Inf. Softw. Technol. 62, 164–186 (2015)

19. Pastor, O., Molina, J.C.: Model-Driven Architecture in Practice: A Software Production Environment Based on Conceptual Modeling. Springer, Heidelberg (2007). https://doi.org/10.1007/978-3-540-71868-0

20. Pimentel, J., Castro, J.: piStar tool-a pluggable online tool for goal modeling. In: 2018 IEEE 26th International Requirements Engineering Conference (RE), pp. 498–499. IEEE (2018)
21. Ruiz, M.: TraceME: A Traceability-Based Method for Conceptual Model Evolution. Springer, Cham (2018). https://doi.org/10.1007/978-3-319-89716-5
22. Ruiz, M., Costal, D., España, S., Franch, X., Pastor, O.: GoBIS: an integrated framework to analyse the goal and business process perspectives in information systems. Inf. Syst. **53**, 330–345 (2015)
23. Yu, E.: Modeling strategic relationships for process reengineering. Soc. Model. Requir. Eng. **11**(2011), 66–87 (2011)

Automating Implementation of Business Logic of Multi Subject-Domain IS on the Base of Machine Learning, Data Programming and Ontology-Based Generation of Labeling Functions

Maksim Shishaev[✉] [iD] and Pavel Lomov[iD]

Institute for Informatics and Mathematical Modeling – Subdivision of the Federal Research Centre, "Kola Science Centre of the Russian Academy of Science", 24A, Fersmanst., Apatity, Murmansk Region 184209, Russia
{shishaev,lomov}@iimm.ru

Abstract. The article analyzes the possibility of using machine learning (ML) models built with the use of a data programming approach for the implementation of the business logic of multi subject-domain information systems (MSIS). MSIS characterized by the heterogeneity and variability of users, data and functions. ML considered as a promising approach to the implementation of business logic in conditions of variability and heterogeneity of MSIS. To effectively use ML models within MSIS the model-centric architecture on the base of data programming approach is proposed. To quickly obtain high-quality sets of labelled training data, it is proposed to use the data programming approach which based on simple code snippets named labelling functions. To ensure the reuse of knowledge and accelerate the implementation of business logic based on ML models, a technology for automated generation of labelling functions based on domain ontologies has been proposed. The performed experiments confirmed the efficiency and potential effectiveness of the proposed technology.

Keywords: Multi subject-domain information system · Model-centric architecture · Machine learning · Data programming · Labeling function · Ontology

1 Introduction

The article discusses issues concerning the use of machine learning within the special kind of information systems (IS) characterized by the following key features: heterogeneity, large scale, variability. We call such systems multi subject-domain information system (MSIS). The need to create and maintain such systems arises in many areas of regional management. A difference of the management tasks drives differences in criteria used, constraints and management methods. All these factors determine the heterogeneity of users and the functionality of the information system. The common 'glue'

A. Dahanayake et al. (Eds.): M2P 2020, CCIS 1401, pp. 177–190, 2021.
https://doi.org/10.1007/978-3-030-72696-6_9

of such systems is the territory (region), characterized by some set of significant inter-dependent properties. Complex territorial systems are managed both at the strategic and operational levels, this makes advisable both to operationally collect and to accumulate information, that leads to the emergence of big data. Besides, the structural complexity and large scale of the object under control (a region) determine the corresponding scale of the information system. That is, such an IS has a large scale in every sense - the amount of processed data, the number of users, the number of supported applications. Another important property of such ISs is the variability of external conditions and relevant applied tasks to be solved, which leads to variability of user types (in the sense of the difference of information tasks they solve), data and system functionality.

At the same time, within the framework of many tasks of regional management, priority is given to the promptness of decisions made by reducing accuracy and reliability. This fundamentally opens up the possibilities of using machine learning (black-box approach) to implement business logic quickly adaptable to the changing requirements.

Substantially, the article consists of two parts. In the first part, we discuss the concept of using machine learning for the automated implementation of the business logic of information systems, give a brief description of weak supervising (specifically, the data programming technique) as a promising approach to solve this task and propose a model-centric architecture that provides a flexible and universal implementation of the MPIS's business logic on the base of multi-level model of subject area (ontology) and data programming. In the second part of the article, we propose to take another step towards automating the implementation of IS business logic: to automate the formation of training sets for ML-models using the technology of ontology-based generating of labeling functions.

2   Machine Learning Models in MSIS Architecture

2.1   ML for Universal Implementation the Business Logic

Universal implementation of business logic that does not require the involvement of developers (programmers or model designers) every time a new application function appears is one of the most urgent issues of implementing MSIS. The existing approaches to solving this problem (Domain-Driven Design – DDD [1], Model Driven Architecture – MDA [2]) are based on the idea of creating a good model of the subject area, which fully and accurately reflects the business logic of the created IS. But they solve the problem only partially - shifting, in essence, the problem of formalizing logic from programmers to model designers. This allows you to reuse the obtained formalized knowledge for solving various problems (as in the case of DDD) or for implementing business logic within various architectural platforms (as in the case of MDA). However, in both cases, the creation of the model requires the high involvement of IS developers.

A promising approach to the ultimate solution of the problem is the rejection of attempts at the deterministic design of business logic in favour of its statistical interpretation. In this case, the program code is considered as a black box approximating the reaction to a certain set of input data expressed in the output set. The reference standard for determining the correct reaction is a domain model, which in this case is an arbitrary generated (but large enough) set of facts available for machine interpretation. It is not required to explicitly determine the business logic of the system within the model, it should be reflected implicitly, through a set of facts contained in the model. If you take this approach, it becomes possible to use machine learning, in particular, artificial neural networks (ANN), which are often called the "universal approximator," to implement the business logic [3].

Despite the problems and limitations of ML that are actively discussed today, related to reproducibility, interpretability, p-hacking, etc. (see for example [4]), the idea of using a "universal algorithm" for solving problems remains very attractive. In favour of the prospects of this approach, some arguments can be given. The complexity of modern problems increasingly alienates their solutions from "mechanics" and brings them closer to "art", where ML demonstrates the best capabilities of computer automation. On the other hand, in a broad sense, any program code is an approximation, since it can work only on "correct" data (from a predefined domain) and produce a result of limited accuracy. With the complication of software systems, machine learning and software engineering are gradually moving closer to the degree of difficulty in explaining the internal logic of the systems built on their basis. Thus, the actual fundamental difference today is only in the accuracy of the approximation. However, this gap is rapidly shrinking: in particular, the results of a successful solution of problems in an exact mathematical formulation with use of ANN have already appeared [5]. Modern breakthrough successes are mainly associated with the use of deep learning (DL).

In turn, the accuracy of ANN approximation depends on the quality of its training if we leave out of scope the question of choice of network architecture, which today is still "alchemy" [6]. The formation of high-quality labelled data sets used for training the DL model has so far been recognized as the main limitation to the widespread use of machine learning [7]. If for widespread tasks, such as speech or visual images recognition, there are well-verified, usually crowdsourced, sets of labelled data, then for specific tasks, in particular those related to regional management, such data does not exist, while obtaining them is a very hard and time-consuming task requiring the involvement of experienced experts.

2.2 Weak Supervision/Data Programming Approach

The weak supervision [8] is promising for solving the problem of creation a training set of a sufficiently large volume for training DL models. Approaches in this area involve training of models with using of labelled sets with poor labelling quality. Such sets may be partially labelled and/or assigned labels may not accurately characterize samples and/or contradict each other. Among the existing weak supervision approaches, active learning [9] and semi-supervised learning [10, 11] can be distinguished. Active learning involves labelling by experts only certain samples, for example, those that are very likely to belong to several classes. Semi-supervised learning, in turn, does not involve the using of experts. Labelling in that case is performed by various comparisons of the unlabelled and labelled parts using generative [12, 13] or graph models [14, 15], low-density separation methods [16, 17] and disagreement-based methods [10, 18].

A relatively new approach to weak supervision is data programming (DP) [19]. The authors of this approach propose the use of so-called labelling functions (LF) for automatic labelling samples of a set. Labelling functions are defined by the domain expert and represent heuristic rules for label assignment based on the structure and content of samples. Thus, the training set is created programmatically, and not by manual labelling. In this case, LFs can be formed by various experts and can be reused for labelling of newly emerging data sets. Thus, LF allows you to freely accumulate the collective knowledge of experts. In this case, the negative effect of possible incorrectness and contradictions is leveled due to a statistical truth assessment of the labels.

In addition to expert heuristics, LFs during the label assignments can access to third-party resources (ontologies, thesauruses, etc.), as well as use existing trained models. This allows you to integrate different types of sources for weak supervision within a single labelling process. Of course, labels obtained as a result of applying LFs can be contradictory or overlap each other. Therefore, further on this noisy set, a generative model is trained, which ultimately allows you to evaluate the truth of the assigned labels (get a noise-aware set). The final training set with weighted labels is used to train the discriminative model (for example, a neural network).

The authors of this approach developed the Snorkel software framework that allows one to describe labelling functions in Python language to train the generative model based on the results of their application. The model allows to assess accuracy of each LFs and obtain weighted labelled set for training the target (discriminative) model, which can be used furthermore to solve applied problems.

In the context of MSIS, DP has a number of important advantages:

- The possibility of accumulating the knowledge of many experts allows us to solve the problem of variability and heterogeneity of domain knowledge. At the same time, within the LFs logic of arbitrary nature can be encoded - heuristics, formal logical rules obtained from third-party knowledge bases, low-quality results of manual marking, etc.
- Programming LFs is a simpler task than programming complex business logic. This opens up opportunities for quick adaptation of business logic to new or modified tasks.
- Within the approach, formal mathematical methods have been developed to assess the quality of the labelling, which in practice cannot be performed in case of manual labelling.
- Automation of the labelling process allows you to quickly label large amounts of data, while changing the data set does not require manual re-labelling - it is enough to just re-run the previously created LFs. It is also an answer to the challenges associated with the variability of data and applied functions of MSIS.

2.3 Data-Programming Based Model-Centric Architecture

The use of DP in the framework of the MSIS significantly changes the "model landscape" of the system (Fig. 1). In aggregate, the discriminant and generative ML-models, the set of labelling functions and the training samples formed with their help characterize (with different details, in different notations and with different target orientation) the problem is solved, that is, they are different representations of the task model. At the same time, it is possible to separate the perspectives of the subject area and tasks in the model landscape and to abandon a priori modelling of all possible tasks (for example, in the form of algorithms and software modules for their solution) in favour of the formation of their models on-demand based on formalized knowledge stored in the MSIS information bases. It should be noted that the knowledge base can be formed from arbitrary sources (provided that a sufficient level of reliability and accuracy is observed) - existing ontologies, expert knowledge, knowledge automatically extracted from big data or natural language texts. This dramatically expands the possibilities of increasing the volume of IS knowledge bases and allows applying the concept of knowledge lakes within the architecture [20]. Subject knowledge (model) can be collecting not only purposefully, as part of the process of developing a particular IS with specific functions (which is typical for DDD and MDA approaches and a priori reduces the potential for reuse of the corresponding models), but also independently of the development process. This expands the scope of the domain model and creates the prerequisites for the model reuse and to solve "future" tasks that were not formulated at the development stage on its base. The corresponding architecture can be called a "model-centric".

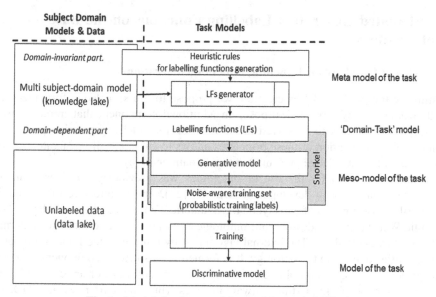

Fig. 1. Models landscape of the model-centric MSDIS

The use of weak-supervised learning based on data programming in MSIS, in addition to solving the problems of heterogeneity and variability, provides a compromise between the "statistical" and "cognitive" approaches to the implementation and use of artificial intelligence in applied systems [21]. This compromise is ensured by labelling functions (and their more general presentation proposed in this paper) which link the domain model with rich explanatory capabilities and the ML-model, which effectively simulates cause-effect relationships within simulated objects and processes, but does not give ideas about their internal structure and nature.

Such architecture allows making a significant movement towards the implementation of "programming by everybody at any time" principle of the modelling-as-programming concept [22]. In this case, applied logic is based on the domain model, which plays the role of a deep model, reflecting the implicit representations of the developer and user about the task (intrinsic model). At the same time, the developer and user do not need specific programming skills or the use of highly specialized tools for modelling. In the proposed architecture, programming in the technical sense moves from the design plane of a subject model, as in MDA and DDD, to the plane of defining some general laws of the subject area in the form of labelling functions. This eliminates the time-consuming and costly process of explicitly defining complex business logic in a conceptual model or directly in program code. At the same time, the formation of numerous labelling functions that assign labels to the source data is a key problem in the framework of this approach, since, on the one hand, this process is quite time-consuming (taking into account the need to form multiple initial markups of large volumes of data) and, in general, heuristic, and on the other hand, the remaining steps of weak supervising are performed automatically in the Snorkel framework.

3 Automated Generation Labelling Functions on the Base of Ontology

3.1 Using of Ontology for Labelling Function Generation

To simplify the process of LFs creation, we propose to use knowledge formalized in the domain ontology. For this purpose, an additional component that implements a meta-model of the task to be solved in the form of a set of LF generation principles is introduced. Application of these principles allows to automatically generate a set of LFs based on the knowledge presented in the domain ontology.

A similar scenario for the use of ontologies was previously considered in the Ontology-driven software development (ODSD) [23]. The architecture of the application in this case consists of two layers: the Semantic Web layer and Internal layer. The Semantic Web layer includes domain ontologies and program interfaces for external services to access to them. The internal layer partially represents the logic of processing the entities defined in the ontology. It is formed from software components that are either generated based on ontologies of Semantic web level [24], or are created based on the reuse of code from existing software libraries. Thus, in the framework of ODSD, the architecture of application and its general principles of information processing are determined by ontologies.

This state of affairs makes this conception similar to the MDA. However, unlike MDA, ODSD involves, in addition to generating program code based on a conceptual model, also its "execution" during the runtime of the program. Such an opportunity is provided by describing ontologies with Ontology Web Language (OWL), based on descriptive logic. In this case, the ontology can be considered as a set of logical statements (OWL-axioms). That allows to use logical reasoners to verify ontology consistency, as well as perform logical inference of new statements about the domain. Thus, it becomes possible to define the business logic of the application in a declarative style within the ontology. However, in practice, this required the determination of a large number of logical statements in the ontology that would allow the machine to receive non-trivial conclusions on it. As a result, it was difficult to create and maintain such "executable" ontologies, since this required, in addition to knowledge of the modeled domain, special methods of using OWL.

Another problem that hampered the widespread use of the ODSD approach was the relatively low performance and high memory consumption of logical reasoners in case of large number of complex axioms specified in the ontology. Thus, even if we successfully created a rather complex ontology that fully enough represents the domain logic, the performing of logical inference on it directly in the runtime of the application could take unacceptable time.

All this limits the possibility of the practical use of ontologies as "executable" models that implement a significant part of the business logic of the application. However, ontologies are well suited as declarative descriptions of the domain, providing the possibility of a formal definition of the semantics of concepts and automatic verification of its logical consistency. This feature of formal ontologies is supposed to be used within the framework of the proposed approach for the LF generation.

One of the main target characteristics of the formed set of LFs is the proportion of samples of the initial set labelled by them. The high label coverage guarantees the participation of a larger number of samples in the subsequent training of the discriminative model and thereby potentially increases the efficiency of using the initial data set. The use of ontology in the LF generation creates the prerequisites for satisfying this requirement by taking into account the entire variety of accumulated collective expert knowledge about the domain in the generated set of LFs that reflect its various aspects.

In addition to the set of concepts of the domain, ontology also defines their relations. That makes possible to take into account during labelling process the context of the concept's representation in the processing samples. For example, during labelling samples for training a model for recognizing patterns in photo images, you can take into account the presence and location of objects that correspond to related concepts. In addition, the use of OWL, which has a logical basis and existing logical reasoners, allows you to dynamically define lists of concepts for which certain generation principles are applicable. For example, in the case of LF generation based on the fact that there is some relation representation in a sample, it is possible to use a logical inference to obtain a set of ontology concepts between which this relationship exists directly or logically follows, and apply this principle to them. It also allows expanding the set of obtained LFs after replenishing the ontology with new concepts and/or defining new relation between them.

3.2 The Technology of LFs Generation

The work of the LF consists in analyzing the sample passed to it as an argument and the subsequent formation of a certain label. In the case of using the ontology for LF generation, the analysis of the sample is carried out by comparing it with some labelling pattern (LP), formed on the basis of some ontology fragment. This pattern can be represented in various form (character string, regular expression, etc.). It is included in the function as a result of its generation. The labelling sample can also be preprocessed in order to identify elements for comparison with LP. Along with this, the function also needs to define a mechanism for label formation (labelling rules, LR). The structure of label in this case depends on the requirements of the training algorithm of the discriminative model, which in turn depends on the problem solved using the trained model. The general LF generation technology scheme is presented in Fig. 2.

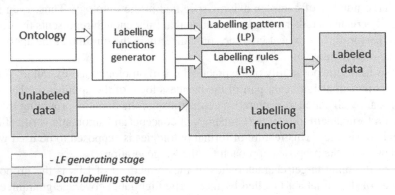

Fig. 2. General scheme of the LF generation technology

LPs can be formed both on the basis of general ontology elements that are invariant to the domain, and using its domain-dependent properties and content. Depending on this, the degree of universality (the possibility of reuse for various subject areas) of the LF generation functions (LF-generators, LFG) varies. However, obviously, increasing the universality of the generator leads to a decrease in the ability to reflect the complex domain logic in the generated LFs.

So, the most common elements of OWL ontology, allowing to obtain universal, domain-independent LFGs, include:

- Class - defines a certain set of objects of the domain, similar to each other. Classes can be in the relations of inheritance, equivalence and disjointness.
- Individual (Instance) - indicates a specific object of the domain corresponding to a certain class.
- Object property - a binary relation between individuals.
- Datatype property - the relation between an individual and a literal value of some type.
- Annotation - this property can accompany any of the listed elements. It is used to define human readable description or simply the name of an ontology element.

The considered structural elements are provided by the web ontology language (OWL) itself. Therefore, they are usually present in most of OWL ontologies. For this reason, these elements can be used to define the general principles generation. For example, you can define in LFG the generation principle, which forms LFs for labelling text fragments based on various values of a certain annotation property of ontology instances. An example of another general principle can be the formation of LFs that can detect in text sentences the name of the object properties which are defined between ontology classes or individuals, and depending on this, assign a label.

When defining the generation principles, one can also take into account the specifics of the concrete ontology, which expands the possibilities of reflecting the domain logic in the LFs. For example, if the domain ontology uses as a basis any top-level ontology (DOLCE [25], Basic Formal Ontology (BFO) [26], General Formal Ontology (GFO) [27], etc.), then its abstract concepts are usually used as parents of the concepts of domain ontology. So it becomes possible to use the facts of the existence of these taxonomic relations during LF generation.

Another feature of the ontology, which can be used to increase the possibilities of representing applied logic in LFs, is the use of the content ontology design pattern (CODP) during its development [pat]. CODP are small ontological fragments that are solutions to common problems of ontological modeling (for example the representation of an object participating in a certain event, the functions of the object, part and whole etc.). The use of CODP in the development of ontologies allows to rely on their elements and relationships to determine more specific principles for LF generation. For example, the use of the "Object-Role" CODP in the ontology to represent a set of functions (Role) performed by a certain object allows one to define corresponding syntactic patterns - "X is used as Y", "The function of X is Y" etc. The latter can be used to form LFs that will take into account presence inside the analyzed fragments of defined text fragments and, depending on this, assign a label. Note that such orientation on the specifics of concrete ontologies during definition of the generation principles limits their universality and complicates their reuse in relation to other ontologies. However, at the same time, this allows one to set more complex generation principles, which allow to create LFs capable of performing a more complex analysis of labelling samples.

The decision of assigning a label to the sample is made as a result of its comparison with some LP. The logic of the matching is represented by labelling rules and depends on the given LP, its formation principles (they may imply some data preprocessing or logical inference on the ontology), and task of training of discriminative model. Different types of tasks may require labels of different formats and different principles for identifying an ontology fragment and comparing it with the labelling sample.

3.3 Technology Implementation Example

As an example, consider the generation of LFs for labelling text fragments to create a training set for a model aimed at solving the named entity recognition problem (NER). A named entity is a word or phrase denoting an object that can be categorized. Examples of named entities are the names of people, organizations and locations. Solution of NER problem implies identification and classification named entities in the text.

The initial unlabeled set in that case is a set of sentences from natural language texts that could potentially contain named entities. The result of applying the LF to some sentence containing a named entity will be the formation and assigning of a label in the form - (left border of the entity, right border of the entity, category of entity):

```
Sentence: Yandex launches carsharing service
Label: [0, 6, ORGANISATION]
```

As an example, we consider the application of the general principle for generation LFs based on ontology classes and their individuals. In accordance with this principle, for each class, a function will be generated that implements the following labelling rule: If the sentence contains an individual of class A, then the sentence is assigned a label that includes the boundaries of the found name and the category corresponding to the name of class A. A simple Python implementation of this principle using the Snorkel framework is as follows:

```
def make_instances_lookup_lf(class_name, label,
ontology):
    instances_names = get_instances_names(class_name,
                        ontology)
    cls_name = class_name.replace("_", " ")
    abbreviated_class_name = "".join(w[0].upper() for w in
cls_name.split())
    return LabelingFunction(
      name=f"ontoclass_{abbreviated_class_name}",
      f=instances_lookup,
      resources=dict(label=label, instances_names=
      instances_names),
    ) if len(instances_names) > 0 else None

def instances_lookup(x, label, instances_names):
    entities = [entity for entity in instances_names if
            entity in x.text]
    if entities:
        left_border, right_border =
                    get_entity_borders(x, entities[0])
        return left_border, right_border, label
    else:
        return 0, 0, -1
```

The make_instances_lookup_lf () function returns a marking function that performs sentence analysis (variable - x) using instance names (variable - instance_names) with a label (variable - label) corresponding to the ontology class. To do this, the get_instance_names (class_name, ontology) function is called. It extracts the necessary fragment of the ontology—a list of instance names of the specified class. The generalized process of matching this fragment with the sentence and label formation is defined in the instances_lookup (x, label, instance_names) function. This simple example illustrates only the principle of generation itself, leaving out of the scope the details of the analysis of the ontology to extract its fragment, as well as the procedure for determining the boundaries of an entity in a sentence.

Using such principles of generation allows you to automatically generate a set of LFs using the domain ontology. Moreover, if the ontology will be replenished with new concepts a new set of modified LFs to take changes into account can be regenerated with minimal labor. We also note that as a result of the generation, the ontology fragment is represented directly inside the LF. It is more preferable from the point of view of performance, than the requesting and analysis of ontology at each call of LF during labelling a large data set.

The operability and efficiency of considered principle was tested in the experiment on training of the language model and its subsequent application to solve the problem of extracting named entities from specialized Russian-language texts of the subject field "Economic activity in the Arctic". The ontology of the Arctic activity was used as an ontology[1]. Classes and instances of this ontology represent various types of industrial and research activities in the Arctic, as well as objects associated with it.

For each instance of the classes of this ontology, according to the principle considered, a LF was generated that allows you to determine the boundaries of the sentence fragment corresponding to the name of the instance and form a label that includes a category equal to the class name of this instance. Using the obtained set of LFs, the labelling of sentences of about 300 texts which could potentially contain concepts represented in the ontology as class instances was carried out. As a result, a training set containing about 700 labelled sentences was formed.

As a language model for training, a multilingual model from the python-library SPAcY was used. This model in its initial state is trained on the texts of Wikipedia articles and is focused on searching in the texts of entities related to the following types: organization, person, and location. After training the model on the formed set, its quality was checked. For this, on the basis of several test texts that were not used at the training stage, a validation set similar in structure to the training sample was created. It represents the reference result of named entity recognition. Next, the model was used to process test texts and the result was compared with the validation set for precision and recall. The following results were obtained:

- initial model: precision = 0.12, recall = 0.04
- trained model: precision = 0.97, recall = 0.42

The obtained results indicate a positive training outcome. For its improvement, it is necessary to increase the size of the training set. This will require the use of more texts for labelling and/or the use of a greater number of LFs, providing better coverage with labels of a set. However, these requirements, if there are appropriate LFGs and ontologies, are only a technical problem that does not require the involvement of domain experts to train the model. This is especially important when developing MSIS components based on the use of machine learning, as it allows to reduce the cost of training a set of models focused on solving problems in areas to which MSIS is oriented. At the same time, the possibility of reusing existing LFGs for different ontologies makes it possible to accelerate the retraining of models and thereby increase the adaptability of the MSIS for solving problems in other domains.

---

[1] https://github.com/palandlom/ontology-of-integrated-knowledge-space/blob/master/src/pol tes.owl.

4   Conclusion

Information support of the development of complex territorial systems requires the creation of large-scale ISs that can work effectively in conditions of heterogeneity and variability of the functional requirements for the system. The urge to satisfy these requirements naturally leads to the evolution and variability of the individual components of the system. A key problem in the development of the MSIS is the provision of quick adaptation of the system to changes in functional requirements (the emergence of new business functions). A promising approach to solving this problem is the use of machine learning to implement the business logic of the system. Despite the well-known limitations of ML, modern ML models, in particular, deep ANNs, show good results in solving an increasingly wide range of problems. This allows us to hope that machine learning can occupy more significant positions in IS architectures - not only as a means of solving particular tasks of data analysis, but also to implement system functionality in a broad sense.

The most significant factor restraining the use of deep learning in new applied problems is the lack of high-quality sets of labelled data suitable for training the ML model. A new promising approach to solving this problem is the data programming methodology, which is one of the implementations of the weak supervising providing automatic labelling of data sets using simple software constructs - labelling functions. At the same time, some key features of the data programming approach make it a good answer to the problems of heterogeneity, large scale and variability, typical for MSIS: the simplicity of creating LFs and the possibility of programming arbitrary (heterogeneous) logic within their framework; the ability to quickly automatically generate noise-aware training sets; the ability to reuse LFs for marking up new data.

Within the DP, actual programming is reduced to the creation of relatively simple labelling functions, which eliminates the need for highly qualified programmers to develop IS's functionality and to a large extent ensure one of the key principles of M2P - "programming without programming". In this paper, we propose one more step in this direction - the technology of automatic LFs generation based on domain knowledge formalized in the form of an ontology. With this approach, the subject expert is completely freed from programming (even simple LFs) and works with ontology, and not with program code. The use of common, subject-independent elements of ontologies in the automatic generation of LFs to a large extent provides a solution to the problem of heterogeneity of MSIS. The experiments performed demonstrated the principal operability and effectiveness of the proposed technology.

Thus, at present, technological prerequisites have been created for the effective use of machine learning to implement the business logic of information systems. The use of the DP approach and the proposed technology for the automated generation of LFs based on ontologies significantly expand these prospects. However, the limitations of this approach remain:

- To train the ML model, a large amount of training data is required.
- ML is only suitable for tasks that can be restated as a problem of pattern recognition. Theoretically, any task can be interpreted in this way, but there is a problem with the size of the training sample.

- Creating an ML-model is a rather lengthy process, even taking into account the automation of a number of key stages.
- The complexity of implementing the technology of automatic LFs generation when using subject-dependent ontology elements approaches the complexity of their manual defining. This limits the possibility of applying the technology to define complex subject-specific logic of the IS.

In modern conditions, seems to be productive to combine the indirect determining the business logic in the framework of ML-models through data programming and the deterministic (direct) determination of business logic within programming appropriate components of the IS in the classical sense. Similarly, when using DP in the development of MSIS, it seems reasonable to combine automatic and manual methods of forming labelling functions to allow a compromise between the complexity of creating an ML model and the depth of presentation of business logic within its framework.

The direction of further work on the use of ML for the implementation of the business logic of the MSIS on the base of the proposed approach is to assess the effectiveness of the technology for generating LFs when using subject-dependent elements of the ontology to implement more complex applied logic. Also, an important issue to study is the opportunities and limitations of reusing LFs generated using various ontology elements within various subject areas.

Acknowledgement. The study was partially funded by RFBR, project number 20-07-00754.

References

1. Evans, E.: Domain-Driven Design Reference: Definitions and Pattern Summaries. Dog Ear Publishing, LLC (2014)
2. Model Driven Architecture (MDA)| Object Management Group. https://www.omg.org/mda/
3. Gorban, A.N.: Generalized approximation theorem and computational capabilities of neural networks. Sib. Zh. Vychisl. Mat. **1**, 11–24 (1998)
4. Stewart, M.: The Limitations of Machine Learning. https://towardsdatascience.com/the-limitations-of-machine-learning-a00e0c3040c6
5. Lample, G., Charton, F.: Deep Learning for Symbolic Mathematics (2019)
6. Rahimi, A., Recht, B.: Reflections on Random Kitchen Sinks. http://benjamin-recht.github.io/2017/12/05/kitchen-sinks/ (2020)
7. Ratner, A., Varma, P., Hancock, B., Ré, C.: Weak Supervision: A New Programming Paradigm for Machine Learning. http://ai.stanford.edu/blog/weak-supervision/ (2019)
8. Zhou, Z.-H.: A Brief Introduction to Weakly Supervised Learning. Oxford University Press (2018)
9. Settles, B.: Active Learning Literature Survey. University of Wisconsin–Madison (2009)
10. Zhou, Z.-H., Li, M.: Semi-supervised learning by disagreement. Knowl. Inf. Syst. **24**, 415–439 (2010). https://doi.org/10.1007/s10115-009-0209-z
11. Zhu, X.: Semi-supervised learning literature survey. Comput. Sci. **2** (2008). (University of Wisconsin-Madison)
12. Fujino, A., Ueda, N., Saito, K.: A Hybrid Generative/Discriminative Approach to Semi-Supervised Classifier Design (2005)

13. Miller, D.J., Uyar, H.S.: A mixture of experts classifier with learning based on both labelled and unlabelled data. In: Advances in Neural Information Processing Systems 9 - Proceedings of the 1996 Conference, NIPS 1996, pp. 571–577. Neural information processing systems foundation (1997)
14. Zhou, D., Bousquet, O., Lal, T., Weston, J., Olkopf, B.: Learning with local and global consistency. Adv. Neural Inf. Process. Syst. **16**, 16 (2004)
15. Zhu, X., Ghahramani, Z., Lafferty, J.: Semi-Supervised Learning Using Gaussian Fields and Harmonic Functions (2003)
16. Joachims, T.: Transductive Inference for Text Classification Using Support Vector Machines. ICML. (2001)
17. Li, Y.-F., Tsang, I., Kwok, J., Zhou, Z.-H.: Convex and scalable weakly labeled SVMs. J. Mach. Learn. Res. **14** (2013)
18. Zhou, Z.-H., Li, M.: Tri-training: exploiting unlabeled data using three classifiers. IEEE Trans. Knowl. Data Eng. **17**, 1529–1541 (2005). https://doi.org/10.1109/TKDE.2005.186
19. Ratner, A., Bach, S., Ehrenberg, H., Fries, J., Wu, S., Ré, C.: Snorkel: rapid training data creation with weak supervision. VLDB J. **29** (2019). https://doi.org/10.1007/s00778-019-00552-1
20. Beheshti, A., Benatallah, B., Nouri, R., Tabebordbar, A.: CoreKG: a knowledge lake service. Proc. VLDB Endow. **11**, 1942–1945 (2018). https://doi.org/10.14778/3229863.3236230
21. Katz, Y.: Noam Chomsky on Where Artificial Intelligence Went Wrong. https://www.the atlantic.com/technology/archive/2012/11/noam-chomsky-on-where-artificial-intelligence-went-wrong/261637/
22. Thalheim, B., Jaakkola, H.: Models as Programs: The Envisioned and Principal Key to True Fifth Generation Programming, vol. 20 (2019)
23. Knublauch, H.: Ontology-Driven Software Development in the Context of the Semantic Web: An Example Scenario with Protégé/OWL. Presented at the (2004)
24. Steinmetz, C., Schroeder, G., Roque, A., Pereira, C., Wagner, C., Saalmann, P., Hellingrath, B.: Ontology-driven IoT code generation for FIWARE (2017)
25. Borgo, S., Masolo, C.: Ontological foundations of dolce. In: Poli, R., Healy, M., Kameas, A. (eds.) Theory and Applications of Ontology: Computer Applications, pp. 279–295. Springer, Netherlands, Dordrecht (2010)
26. Arp, R., Smith, B., Spear, A.: Introduction to Basic Formal Ontology I: Continuants. Presented at the August 24 (2015)
27. Herre, H., Heller, B., Burek, P., Hoehndorf, R., Loebe, F., Michalek, H.: General Formal Ontology (GFO) - A Foundational Ontology Integrating Objects and Processes [Version 1.0]. (2006)

Conceptual Model Reuse for Problem Solving in Subject Domains

Nikolay A. Skvortsov(✉)

Institute of Informatics Problems of Federal Research Center
"Computer Science and Control" of Russian Academy of Sciences, Moscow, Russia

Abstract. The paper is dedicated to reusing domain models from one research problem being solved in the domain community to another. The accustomed approach to research including immediate integration of existing data resources and services for problem-solving is not efficient. Domain modeling can be applied to solve this issue. It allows reusing results of previous research in a domain community which include data resources, method implementations, and results of their integration. An approach to domain specification reuse is demonstrated in examples of solving astronomical problems. The experience in domain specification reuse shows the fast saturation of specifications during solving different problems in a domain within a community.

Keywords: Research community · Conceptual modeling of research domains · Ontology · Conceptual schema · Domain specification reuse

1 Introduction

A popular approach to research problem solving is the data-driven one. It begins with selecting data sources relevant to the problem. Problems for research are often stated only keeping in mind what data are available and what can be done with them. Researchers access data sources using related formats, interfaces, and protocols and integrate them. After that, they program a solution to the problem using integrated data and available services and libraries. The results are represented in one of the known formats and stored. The implemented methods and obtained data are mostly used in isolated research groups. They also can be integrated into another research problem-solving.

Such an approach is still alive and used by many researchers. For instance, it is clear from most of the research problems solved using Python language so popular in the wide research community. There are some advantages of the described approach. It can be useful for research from scratch, for script languages and widely used method libraries, and manipulating original data sources.

The research was carried out using the infrastructure of shared research facilities CKP "Informatics" of FRC CSC RAS [1], supported by the Russian Foundation for Basic Research (grants 19-07-01198, 18-29-22096, 18-07-01434).

© Springer Nature Switzerland AG 2021
A. Dahanayake et al. (Eds.): M2P 2020, CCIS 1401, pp. 191–211, 2021.
https://doi.org/10.1007/978-3-030-72696-6_10

However, the disadvantages of the data-driven approach may be very serious. Implementations are tied to data sources and require programming over them again and again for other research groups, new research problems being solved, or changed data sources. Reusability and automation of data processing are complicated since source data, methods, and research results remain heterogeneous for the research community. So the approach doesn't provide scalability by sources and research problems and is weakly reused. Finally, it is not convenient and sufficient for research data infrastructures to maintain, share, and reuse data.

The problem of research data and result reuse has been solved for many years using many different approaches, methods, and technologies. Software reuse practices use modularity, type substitution, method libraries, software components, patterns, search by metadata, knowledge-based approaches [13, 22, 34]. Methods of specification refinement for critical software development [12, 27] are considered as a formal ground for verifiable specification reuse until implementation. Refinement relation guarantees that substitution of refined specification with refining one does not affect the user.

Collections of research workflows include problem-solving process specifications for shared in communities, using calls of services, library methods, and templates [15, 17]. Communities use semantic approaches to the digital publication of all kinds of resources including data, software tools, mathematical models, and others [6]. Researchers make searchable containers of data, metadata, software, and other resources for data sharing and reuse [32]. Digital repositories collect and share data for wide domain communities. Today efforts are intensified to develop collaborative research data infrastructures [3, 4, 10]. Domain and interdisciplinary communities make findable and accessible data resources, services, storage and computing capacities supporting full research lifecycle. Meanwhile, the challenges of FAIR data principles [24, 33] inherited from data reuse practices guide manipulating data in a way making them findable, accessible, interoperable, and as a result reusable. For this purpose, data should be identifiable, accompanied by rich metadata and provenance information, comply with known data models and domain standards.

According to the FAIR data principles data management in research infrastructures should strive for a human- and machine-readable description of data and services. Machine-readability means machine-actionability as well. Due to that, FAIR data are considered to be achievable in the long term. That could become possible using semantic approaches. For this purpose, metadata should be used in a formal way allowing reasoning over domain knowledge. It implies the maintenance of formal domain-specific knowledge in research communities that will reuse data.

Domain specifications such as shared ontologies and standardized conceptual schemas have been developed and maintained in almost any research domain for many years. They have great potential for data interoperability and reuse. To make data FAIR, not only data themselves but other domain resources once developed or integrated should be available for reuse in research with minimal efforts. They may include data models, domain knowledge and constraints, data structure, methods, integration results, and others. A comprehensive approach to the development of formal domain specifications was described in [30]. In [29], a research lifecycle was proposed to provide interoperability and reuse of data.

The paper is dedicated to the reuse of domain specifications for effective research problem-solving in domain communities. Research groups and communities can collect domain specifications, reuse them for solving domain problems. The paper demonstrates applying previously developed domain specifications for solving a problem in the same domain and extending domain specifications. The purpose is to see which kinds of data could be reused, developed, and published during problem-solving in the domain. Some of the described decisions are implemented, others dont imply immediate implementation but are discussed as important principles.

The rest of the paper is structured as follows. In Sect. 2 important statements about domain models including ontologies and conceptual schemas with structural and behavior specifications as a base for FAIR data management are presented. Section 3 describes in detail different aspects and stages of domain model reuse in communities. As an example, reusing research results in astronomical problem solving is demonstrated. Section 4 briefly describes the necessity of publication of research problem-solving results to make them reusable in domain communities. In the end, conclusions from the experience of problem-solving using domain model specifications are proposed.

2   Domain Specifications in the Middle of Research Communities

Conceptual modeling is a semantic grounding of definitions with domain concepts shared by specialists of the domain. Semantic approaches to domain modeling can help for managing data FAIRly by communities working in those domains. Domain modeling in research infrastructures includes formal (allowing reasoning) ontologies to maintain domain knowledge and constraints, and conceptual schemas for issues of domain information representation.

Ontologies and conceptual schemas are often combined and considered at the same level of heterogeneity, ontologies are considered as a kind of data representation schemas. However, the problems of matching concepts of entities and homogeneous representation of data about objects have their specificities [20,31]. Ontologies are the basis of meaning compliance and also can be useful in the search for relevant data and definition of their semantics in the domain, but data ontologically relevant to the specified requirements still can be represented in different data models, use different structures and types defined by conceptual schemas.

2.1   Ontological Modeling of Research Domains

Ontologies contain concepts as a category of knowledge, not data presentation. Semantic approaches introduce ontological commitments to formally defined concept interpretations for all participants of a community. Concepts are defined by relations between them and constraints to limit their consistent interpretations. We use ontologies for describing the meaning of described objects in the domain. It makes possible the search for the relevant resources among the available ones. Concepts can refer to the meaning of data itself, data schema elements, behavior definitions like methods, and other entities. For this purpose, any specifications can be semantically annotated to determine their meaning in certain domains. It is preferable not to limit formal annotations by naming ontological concepts but to use subconcept in terms of ontologies expressing the meaning of annotated entities in an ontological modeling language. Semantic annotations are the metadata that may formally define data semantics in several domains or subdomains simultaneously using expressions.

A module structure of domain ontologies is important for dividing knowledge into domains and subdomains. Different domains may be agreed upon, maintained by different communities, and become standards for them. Upper ontologies like BWW, BFO, DOLCE are optionally used to be a glue for common hierarchy and relations of concepts. Domain ontology modules are related to some research objects. Specific subdomain ontology modules are maintained by different small subcommunities with special interests. More specific domain modules use concepts of generalized ones. Different modules can have mutually defined concepts. Most common domain modules, for instance, ontologies of processes and measurements and their quality, are shared and used among almost all communities in wide disciplines. Some special-purpose modules, for example, data provenance ontology PROV-O [16], should be used by all communities to provide FAIR principles. Application or task ontology modules are not intended for extending a domain ontology. They contain concepts defining the special interests of researchers but too specific to distinguish them among other objects in the domain.

For example, during problem-solving [30] in the domain of binary and multiple stellar systems, the following ontologies were gathered (see Fig. 1). Common ontology modules describe measurements, dependencies, and experiments as domains related not only to astronomy but to any data-intensive domain. The first one includes measurement- and quality-related concepts for observed characteristics of research objects. Dependencies define calculations, events, functions, laws, hypotheses as a basis for ontological specifications of object behavior. Research experiment ontology describes concepts related to the scientific method. Special purpose ontologies are provenance ontology for define standard non-functional metadata for describing data and other resources. Data model ontology is used to describe elements of data models, search, and integrate them. The domain model of stellar astronomy includes modules defining concepts related to different astronomical object types, their astrophysical parameters, observation methods (like photometry), and observable parameters. The specialized domains are defined for binary or multiple stellar systems and systems with known orbital parameters.

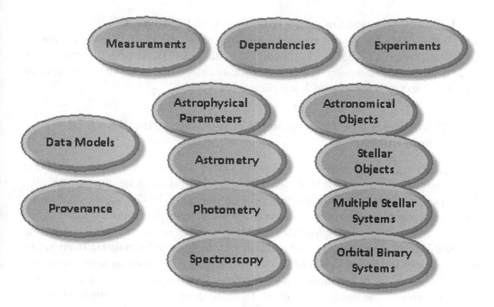

Fig. 1. Ontological modules of the stellar astronomy domain.

Problem-specific concepts may be defined too. For example, the High Multiplicity Stellar Systems are specializations of Multiple Stellar System. But it may be considered as redundant for including in their specifications as shared domain specifications.

The ontologies are defined using OWL [18] providing a formal model for ontologies, shared in domain communities, and used for defining the semantics of data and resources concerning the domain knowledge.

2.2 Conceptual Schemas for Domain Modeling

The Object Management Group (OMG) standardized the Meta-Object Framework [8] providing the levels of modeling. It defines the level of data that is represented in a particular model. The level of models defines schemas for data representation. The meta-model level defines data models like relational, object-based, graph ones, and different modeling languages for them. Different meta-models may be specified in terms of the unified self-defining meta-meta-model. It is useful for the integration of data models [19].

Conceptual schemas are based on underlying data models defined by modeling languages for describing the structure and behavior of information objects in the domain. Notions in conceptual modeling were summarized in [25]. Entity types, the main notion of conceptual modeling, are dedicated to specifying data structure, classify objects, and describe the behavior of domain objects. Behavioral specifications include domain events defined by preconditions and postconditions.

The Entity-Relationship model (ER) family and the data definition language of SQL standards focus on structural descriptions of a domain. Business Process Modeling Notation (BPMN) [2] specifies domains as dependences of events. The Unified Modeling Language (UML) graphic notation together with a constraint language like OCL focuses on both dimensions.

2.3   Development of Conceptual Models and Using Them in Communities

In [21], a requirement-driven methodology was proposed for problem-solving using decomposition of goal tree formulated in natural language and formalizing these specifications as operations in a process language. In [30], a semantic-based and requirement-driven approach to conceptual schema development draws upon ontological modeling. It begins with building a requirement model decomposing the problem into subrequirements. Then ontologies are formalized from terms and sentences in the requirement model. The ontology is used to generate a conceptual schema for the domain. Specifications of conceptual schemas are annotated in terms of the domain ontology. Requirements are operationalized, so the schema is complimented with method definitions. Semantic rules for value transformation, entity resolution criteria, and other ad-hoc specifications are defined in the research domain.

Communities of domain researchers develop their domain models. They can use them for the semantic search for resources using ontologies and integration of them mapping their schemas into the conceptual schemas of the domain. They acquire domain-specific data collections and methods and maintain registries of specifications and resources. Inference from semantic annotations of resources allows classifying them in terms of ontologies. Researchers in communities can collaborate using previous research results.

Further problem-solving in the community can reuse existing specifications and should be used to enhance the domain model for new requirements. Any activities in a community are performed with the commitment to the domain models. Querying ontologies with problem requirements over specifications registries is used to retrieve identifiers of relevant resources (data sources, schema elements, method implementations, services, workflows, and so on). The result of previously performed resource integration also is accessible from registries and can be reused. Research problems are naturally stated and solved over integrated resources reusing data, methods, resource integration results shared in communities. Shared conceptual schemas are preferably used for information representation.

In [30], the example of the domain model was developed during solving the problem of finding high multiplicity stellar systems. Decomposed requirements included matching stellar components, identification of visually observable in photometry pairs of stars, and then matching close pairs that observed by other means besides photometry (see Fig. 2). Further decomposition reveals methods of matching different entities by their parameters and inherent behavior. Ontologies of the subdomains mentioned above were developed since the problem

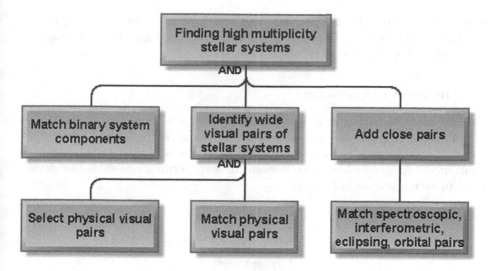

Fig. 2. The requirement model of the problem of finding high multiplicity stellar systems.

referred to different types of stellar objects, their observational and astrophysical parameters, observation methods, and other details. The conceptual schema was designed from the ontology knowledge, criteria for entity resolution were specified. The workflow for the problem-solving was generated from the requirement model. Generally, each observation type is a special knowledge domain with its own observed parameters and features of the studied objects. Data on pairs of different observational types are stored in different data resources with their own structure. Data resources were mapped to the domain model including some photometrical catalogs of single stars (HD, HIP, and others), visual binary stars (WDS, CCDM, TDSC), and different types of close binary stars (GCVS, SB9, ORB6, INT4). Once mapped they may be accessed in a unified structure of the domain model using virtual or materialized view approaches.

These specifications remain searchable and accessible using the ontology and semantic annotations. In the current research, the developed domain model is reused for solving another astronomical problem.

3 The Reuse of Different Specifications

Research problem-solving can draw on the experience of the domain community. Domain specifications and published results of other research can be retrieved from the community registries and reused. So researchers comply with the community requirements, avoid multiple integration and problem-solving on different stages of research, and increase research efficiency. The problem-solving includes requirement analysis, the conceptualization of the problem, relevant data resource selection and integration, method selection and implementation, data processing to solve the problem, and representation and publishing of the results [29]. There are different reusable data and metadata for each stage of problem-solving that can be retrieved or created.

3.1 Reuse of Requirements

On the stage of requirement model development and decomposition, textual requirements of previously solved research problems can be found by text relevance. It makes it possible to reuse branches of requirement model trees. Requirement model fragments having no relevant reused specifications should be developed in such a way as in [30].

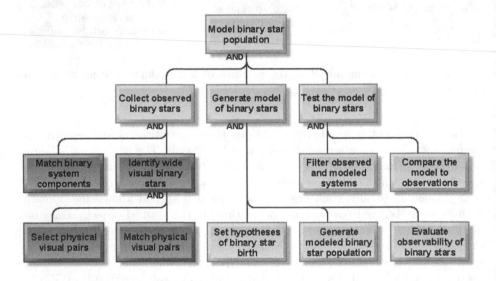

Fig. 3. The requirement model of the problem of modeling a population of binary stars (reused stages are highlighted).

As an example, a fragment of the requirement tree (see Fig. 3) for the astronomical problem of modeling a population of binary stars in the Galaxy is analyzed [23]. Components (stellar objects considered as single) and pairs of components in multiple stellar systems can be observed visually using photometry. There are several catalogs of visual binary stars in which data on different binaries may be duplicated. Pairs located close optically but at different distances from the observer are removed from consideration, only physical pairs are considered. Only visual binary stars are considered in the model yet. The Galaxy model of generated binary stars should give distributions of some parameters similar to the distributions of observed parameters of real-world binary stars.

To model the Galaxy of binary stellar systems consisting of pairs of stellar components, it is necessary to collect data on components and physical pairs of stars from catalogs, generate data of modeled binary star Galaxy population, and then test the quality of the model comparing the model to the collected observational data.

The requirements of collecting and identifying observed binary systems may be reused from the previously solved problem. It includes matching components as single objects and selecting physical pairs. These reused requirements have already been decomposed so that visual pairs are also matched and identified to deduplicate data from different catalogs.

After collecting observed binary stars, models may be generated and tested. There were no relevant problems solved before, so these requirements should be decomposed and implemented.

Further decomposition (not shown in Fig. 3) of the requirement of the binary star birth hypothesis generation allows making a set of sub-hypotheses: a distribution of mass ratios with different pairing functions, a distribution of binaries by semi-major axes of orbits, a distribution of component separation, and a distribution of eccentricity. These requirements will be operationalized for modeling. Different hypotheses of several star birth parameters are combined, a set of models is generated.

The observability of generated stars from the Earth is evaluated. Finally, distributions of observable characteristics of populations are calculated and compared to observed ones. So the most similar model of binary stars can be chosen.

Reused requirements may be applied in different ways. It is possible to use their decompositions. Their links to ontologies, conceptual schemas, methods, and workflows generated from them can be reused too. Even the results of previously solved and reused requirements are accessible for reuse. All these opportunities for reuse of requirement model fragment should be verified for correctness in the following stages of problem-solving.

3.2 Knowledge Reuse

Researchers detect domain concepts, their relations, and constraints in the problem statement and the requirement model. It is necessary to detect concepts existing in the domain ontology. Knowledge of related concepts can be reused in solving problems. Knowledge from descriptions in the requirement model must be checked for compliance with the domain ontology. Additional restrictions may mean that a subconcept of the domain ontology concept should be defined. Contradictions may mean that some irrelevant concepts of the domain ontology have been selected. The main notion of semantic interoperability and reuse on the ontological level is subconcept relation (subsumption, generalization/specialization). Ontological models with different expressive power supporting automatic reasoning may be used to check relations between concepts [14].

Knowledge retrieved from the requirements but not relevant to existing domain concepts is represented as an application ontology. The concepts of the application ontology may become candidates for the domain ontology extension. Application ontologies or extensions of domain ontologies must match the domain ontology. Participating in the domain community means the commitment to the interpretations of its concepts.

Managing non-functional requirements to resources as metadata in terms of some special ontologies allows taking into account data provenance, the validity in time and space, licensing, and so on.

Table 1. Reused domain concepts and conceptual schema entity types (not reused generated concepts are marked in bold)

Ontology module	General concepts defined in the module	Entity types
Astronomical Objects, Stellar Objects	Astronomical Object, Observational Type, Compound Object, Component, Stellar Object, Star, Stellar System	Component
Astrometry	Coordinate, Coordinate System, Equatorial Coordinate System, Right Ascension, Declination, Precession, Parallax, Distance, Proper Motion, **Galactic Coordinate System, Galactic Latitude, Galactic Longitude**	Coordinate
Astrophysical Parameters	**Star Age, Star Mass**	
Multiple Stellar Systems	Multiple Stellar System, Pair, Primary Component, Secondary Component, Visual Pair, Physical Visual Pair, **Mass Ratio, Projected Separation, Binary Star Birth Function**	Pair, System
Photometry	Photometric System, Passband, Frequency, Magnitude, Epoch	
Orbital Parameters	Relational Position, Position Angle, Angular Separation, Orbital Movement, Period, Semi-Major Axis, Eccentricity	RelPosition, Orbit

The domain concepts are widely reused in the problem being solved (see Table 1). There are astrometric, photometrical concepts, stellar system concepts for describing them in the domain via components and pairs with some parameters. The domain ontology is extended with the concepts of star birth hypotheses, concepts of galactic coordinates, dependencies between equatorial and galactic coordinates, some binary star parameter concepts like the mass ratio and the projected separation of pairs not considered earlier.

The following example of concept definitions is represented in the Manchester syntax of OWL [18]. It is useful for expression-like specifications in terms of ontologies. The same expressions can be used for semantic annotations and queries to the resource registry. In the example, ontological concepts *Pair* and *VisualPair* are defined. Specifications are mostly reused from the domain ontology. New relations to additional concepts *MassRatio* an *Separation* that enhance existing knowledge are marked in bold. A fragment of the superconcept has specifications of relations to concepts *Parallax* an *ProperMotion* that will be necessary later. Specifications of new domain concepts for parameters mass and age related to any astronomical object are omitted but necessary too.

Example 1. Domain ontology concepts.

```
StellarObject subclassOf (
  AstronomicalObject ...
  and (parallax max 1 Parallax)
  and (properMotion max 1 ProperMotion) ...)
Pair subClassOf (
  CompoundObject
  and StellarObject
  and (isPairOf only StellarSystem)
  and (hasComponent max 2 Component))
  and (hasPrimaryComponent max 1 Component)
  and (hasSecondaryComponent max 1 Component)
  and (hasObservationType only ObservationalType)
  and (hasSeparation max 1 Separation)
  and (hasMassRatio max 1 MassRatio)
  and (hasOrbit max 1 Orbit))
VisualPair subClassof (
  Pair
  and (hasRelationalPosition only RelationalPosition)
  and (hasObservationalType value Visual))
```

The binary star birth function concept is introduced, which is a subconcept of the hypothesis concept from the research experiment ontology module. A set of hypotheses included in the binary star birth function is described using existing concepts. The hypotheses include the distribution of mass ratios with different pairing functions, the distribution of binaries by semi-major axes of orbits, the distribution of component separation, and the distribution of eccentricity. A combination of these distributions in the Galaxy model should form stars with observational parameter distributions similar to ones of observed visible binary stars.

All these hypotheses are expressible in terms of existing concepts as their subconcepts using OWL. For example, the hypothesis of the distribution of pairs by eccentricity implies a dependency of the number of pairs on their eccentricity. It can be expressed with the semantic annotation as follows.

Example 2. Semantic annotation.

```
subClassOf (
  Hypothesis
  and (isCorrelationOf some (Eccentricity))
  and (isCorrelationOf some (
    Quantity
    and (hasElement only (Pair)))))
```

Semantic annotations in terms of formal domain ontologies are a good basis for publishing, classifying, and semantic search for resources to be reused. Ontology reuse provides opportunities for reuse in further stages. The domain concepts are used to form the conceptual schema entity type specifications or to search for existing entity types relevant to the problem. It allows finding ontologically relevant data resources, conceptual schema elements for reuse.

3.3 Conceptual Schema Reuse

There is a useful tendency in research communities to use or even standardize common conceptual schemas or interfaces for data representation and exchange in their domains. For example, schemas are reconciled in the most common subdomains like astrometry and photometry in astronomy [7,9]. Smaller communities with specific interests can make their own specifications to use together with more common standard schemas. Conceptual schemas and even schemas of previously solved problems may be reused for further problem-solving in communities.

Conceptual schemas refer to domain ontologies with semantic annotations. Relevant conceptual schema elements can be found for the problem-solving requirements referring to the same ontologies. For this purpose, the requirements should be annotated by subconcepts of the annotations of reused schemas.

Then conceptual specifications of the problem are developed in terms of the domain schemas. To reuse the domain schemas properly the problem specifications should refine them.

The conceptual schema of the domain with the entity types (see Table 1, col. 3) is reused for the problem of the binary star Galaxy modeling. The following example is an implementation of the conceptual schema entity type in the relational model. Table *Pair* defines foreign keys to *StellarSystem*, *Component*, *Coordinate*. Orbital movement is defined in *Orbit*, relational positions of components in pairs are defined in *RelPosition*. *ObsType* implements the ability to define multiple values of observational types of a pair. The attributes of the same names are defined in the table. There are several new parameters necessary for the problem to be solved. Two of them, *massRatio* and *separation*, are derived from new relations in the ontology, the others, *massSum* and *age* are derived from new relations in superconcepts. Some reused attribute of the *Pair* table like *parallax*, *properMotion*, *epoch* derived from superconcepts of the Pair concept too.

Example 3. Conceptual schema entity type.
```
CREATE TABLE Pair(
    pair_id NUMBER(10) PRIMARY KEY,
    pair_of NUMBER(10),
    coordinate NUMBER(10),
    epoch TIMESTAMP,
    parallax FLOAT,
    properMotion FLOAT,
    primaryComponent NUMBER(10),
    secondaryComponent NUMBER(10),
    obsType NUMBER(10),
    age FLOAT,
    massSum FLOAT,
```

```
massRatio FLOAT,
separation FLOAT,
relPosition NUMBER(10),
orbit NUMBER(10),
is_physical BOOLEAN,
FOREIGN KEY(pair_of) REFERENCES StellarSystem(system_id),
FOREIGN KEY(coordinate) REFERENCES Coordinate(coordinate_id),
FOREIGN KEY(primaryComponent)
   REFERENCES Component(component_id),
FOREIGN KEY(secondaryComponent)
   REFERENCES Component(component_id),
FOREIGN KEY (obsType)
   REFERENCES Pair_ObsType(pair_obstype_id)),
FOREIGN KEY (relPosition)
   REFERENCES RelPosition(relposition_id),
FOREIGN KEY (orbit) REFERENCES Orbit(orbit_id);
```

The conceptual schema is also extended with an entity type definition for a binary star birth hypothesis generated from the ontology. The enhancement of the schema with new attributes and entity types may be a subject for the development of the domain model in the community or using subtyping in the problem specifications.

3.4 Data Model Specification Reuse

Speaking about heterogeneous data resources, data models which they use should be mentioned. There is a set of data models used in certain domain communities. For example in astronomy, the fixed-length string format is mostly used for resources with different data structures. Meanwhile, there are more complex data formats like FITS [5], VOTable [11], ObsCore [26] which encapsulate data and rich astronomical metadata. All these meta-models should be supported in the astronomical community, have mapping rules into a chosen canonical data model used in the community. Extensions of the canonical model are created that represent rules for mapping of the data model elements to the canonical one. Unification of data models [19] is required for the possibility of homogeneous work with many schemas and correct transformation of data and metadata between them.

Results of data model unification should be reused to transform specifications of all resources that use the same data model to homogeneous representation in the canonical model. Once mapped, a data model with mapping rules may be found and reused for multiple resources with different schemas.

3.5   Data Resource Reuse

If some data resources were used in the domain, they had probably been integrated using domain specifications. It means that resource schemas and extents are described and annotated in terms of the domain ontologies and provenance ontology, and mapped to the conceptual schemas of the domain. The results of these activities are published in the registry and accessible for further research.

Registered data resources can be reused. Expressions produced from the requirements of the problem being solved are subconcepts of the domain ontology. These expressions are used as queries to the registry to find relevant data resources. Schemas of ontologically relevant resources have already been mapped to the conceptual schema of the domain, so the resources can be reused in problem-solving without additional integration. If schemas of resources were not integrated into domain specifications, they should be mapped to the conceptual schema of the domain. Ontological relevance can be useful for it to find relevant schema elements such as entity types, attributes, associations, methods, classes. Correct mapping of resource schemas should refine domain specifications. Method reuse is described separately below.

Schema mapping includes resolving conflicts between domain entity representation in resources and their representation of requirements accepted in the research community. Resource entity type reducts are allocated that refine corresponding reducts of entity types in the domain schema or the specifications of the problem. From entity type reducts of different resources, compositions can be formed to implement an entity type of the domain. It should be verified that the compositions of reducts refine the domain specifications. Then data from the resources may be reused.

Since resources relevant to the problem being solved are found and integrated, they may be reused on the level of conceptual schemas. Both specifications of the problem reusing the domain schema and specifications of reused resources refine the domain schema. But to become implementations reused in the problem, resource specifications themselves should refine the problem specifications. So additional schema mapping and programming may be required.

Observational data on visual binary stars have been reused for solving the problem of the binary star Galaxy model. Table structures of several catalogs of visual binaries (WDS, CCDM, TDSC) have already been mapped to the domain specifications, described in terms of the domain ontology. Their schemas are related to the type *Pair*. They have semantic annotations relating them to the concepts of visual binaries and their observational parameters. Those specifications are stored in the registry. To find relevant catalogs in the registry it is sufficient to query it for the semantic annotation of the entity type *Pair*, or the semantic annotation of the problem requirement of identifying visual binaries. Returned global identifiers will contain references to the mentioned catalogs. They do not need to be integrated one more time. The information about the domain schema fragments (reducts) covered by the catalogs is reused from the registry.

If previous results of matching visual binaries stars were published in the registry, they can be retrieved as a data resource too. It is possible to understand the relevance between that resource and the original catalogs of visual binaries using the provenance information about the retrieved resource. The provenance metadata provided during publication contains information, which data catalogs were used to generate the data, and which methods were used for it. The results of matching could be reused instead of original catalogs and methods of matching.

One more catalog that should be integrated into the domain model is the Gaia release which contains information about parallaxes that is not covered by other catalogs.

3.6   Entity Resolution Criterion Reuse

The next stage of data integration and reuse is object matching and correct composition of different objects from data of multiple resources. Entity resolution and data fusion tasks should be performed.

Generally speaking, entity resolution criteria should not depend on specific data resources. Criteria for identification of objects of specific entity type could be determined from the domain knowledge using values of their attributes and relations to other objects. If the criteria are not included in the conceptual schema, they may be implemented once, included in the domain specifications of the community, and reused later in any research. Entity resolution for problem-specific types or subtypes of the domain entity types can be performed separately reusing domain entity resolution criteria. Data fusion rules are usually problem-specific.

During solving previous research problems, the system of entity resolution criteria for multiple stellar system matching [28, 30] has already been developed. It includes criteria of component matching and visual pair matching which can be reused in the current research.

3.7   Method Reuse

The conceptual schema of the problem being solved contain method specifications operationalized from the requirement model or activity concepts of ontologies. Some of them reuse the methods of the domain schema. Method implementations can be related to specific data resources, or they can exist as separate resources, such as services and libraries. The selection of method implementations starts with a search in the registry. Requirements specifications as queries can express both the semantics of activities performed by methods and concepts of their input and output parameters in terms of the domain ontology. The reuse of ontologically relevant behavior specifications is based on the principle of substitution with verification of preconditions and postconditions of methods and invariants of entity types. Implementations should refine the requirements. Methods in requirements not having a reusable implementation must be implemented, or found outside the registry and integrated.

The requirement model of the problem being solved reuses some leaf requirements. Corresponding methods of the domain conceptual schema operationalized from requirements and their implementations registered in collections can be reused. So the following methods are reused: matching binary system components (matchComponents), selecting physical visual pairs (selectPhysical), and matching physical visual pairs (matchPairs).

Methods specifications generated for other leaf requirements are setting hypotheses of binary star birth (setHypothesis), generating modeled binary star population (generatePopulation), evaluating observability of binary stars (calcObsParams), filtering observed and modeled systems (filterBinaries), and comparing distributions of observational parameters for the model and the observational data (testModel). The workflow is developed from reused and implemented methods to resolve the problem.

Separate hypotheses decomposed from the requirements are have been operationalized too. For instance, the specification of the eccentricity distribution hypothesis shown earlier as a subconcept of dependency was naturally used to generate a method with parameters of the eccentricity and the number of pairs having similar eccentricity.

3.8   Process Reuse

Specifications of processes (or workflows) can be considered to be methods as a whole, and they consist of some activities which are method calls. So both processes as a whole and any of their fragments as well as individual activities can be considered as methods to be reused. To ensure that they are reused correctly, it is verified that the specifications of the reused methods or process fragments are refinements of the specifications of the domain and or the problem requirements.

Different types of requirements are processed similarly in different research domains. In particular, the subdomain of research experiments with modeling research objects and testing hypotheses on them represents a typical part of research in various domains. Such domains may be specified using specialized ontology and design patterns for application to particular domains. So, domain specifications of research experiments may be reused in solving different problems.

On one hand, objects with defined observational parameters are collected, stored, and processed in terms of that schema. Parameters of pairs are used such as equatorial coordinates, magnitudes of pair, and components in different passbands, eclipsing. On the other hand, modeled parameters of pairs, initial binary birth parameters such as component masses, mass sum, mass ratio, component separation, orbital parameters, Galactic coordinates, pair orientation. They are generated with hypothetical distributions. Using domain knowledge defined in the conceptual schema, observational parameters are calculated from modeled ones and stored in terms of the conceptual schema.

Since the same schema is reused to represent observed parameters and modeled ones, their distributions can be compared using statistical methods implemented in the experimenting subdomain.

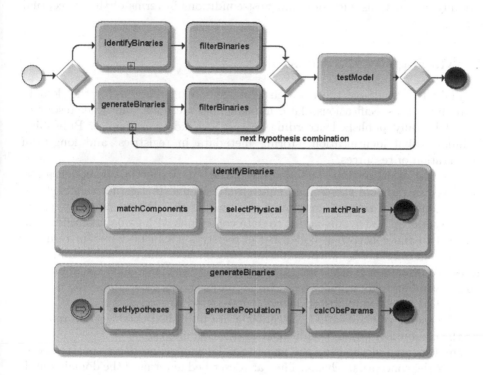

Fig. 4. The workflow for binary star galaxy modeling.

The requirement model of the binary star Galaxy modeling problem has been implemented in BPMN [2] as a workflow calling operations generated for requirements (see Fig. 4). Further decomposition into a subtree helps in the development of operation implementations.

On one hand, the identifyBinaries operation calls the subprocess that matches components of multiple stellar systems from catalogs (matchComponents), selects physical pairs (selectPhysical), and matches them (matchPairs) to resolve and deduplicate entities. These steps can be reused from the research performed earlier in the community. On the other hand, the generateBinaries operation calls the subprocess that generates hypotheses of binary system birth function (setHypotheses), generates a model of the Galaxy of binary stars (generatePopulation), and evaluates possible observational parameters for modeled entities from generated fundamental star birth and positional parameters (calcObsParams). Both observed and modeled data are filtered with similar conditions (filterBinaries) to make clean and complete samples, and these samples are compared by different parameter distributions (testModel). The results of testing for different combinations of hypotheses are stored. The workflow uses methods defined in the developed conceptual schema shared in the domain. To represent, store, transfer data between the operations, process them, and represent research results, the entity types of the conceptual model are used. Requirements are specified formally as functions with pre- and post-conditions in terms of the conceptual schema.

4 Making Results Reusable

To make the results of the research problem-solving reusable for the domain community, its specifications, data, implemented methods, and other resources should be duly published according to the FAIR data principles. Publishing includes global identification, storing metadata in registries, and long-term preservation of resources.

The best of the generated populations of the binary star Galaxy model can be preserved in terms of the domain conceptual schema. It uses native structures of the conceptual schema annotated in terms of the domain ontology, so its entity types can be trivially added to data collections with global identifiers and mapped to the conceptual model in the registry. It can be found in terms of the domain ontology by participants and machines of the research community, accessed and reused in any other research. The results of matching visual binaries from several astronomical catalogs can be published as a new data resource too if they had not been published before.

The results of Gaia catalog integration are published making Gaia reusable for the community without additional integration efforts.

Implemented methods can be preserved. They have interfaces constrained in terms of the conceptual schema. They are described in terms of the domain ontology as subconcepts of dependencies, their pre- and post-conditions are defined by semantic annotations to make them searchable by inputs and outputs. Hypotheses, their implementations, testing methods, proved hypotheses as new laws can be published in the community to be reused in research.

The workflow can be published with detailed descriptions of its elements and their inputs, outputs, and their pattern types in terms of the domain ontology. So the workflow itself, and any fragments relevant to further research can be reusable.

New knowledge may be proposed to the community for the domain model enhancements procedure. New knowledge of the solved problem can be related to the domain model and be accessible for analysis of the community.

5 Conclusion

The experience of problem-solving within and among some research groups working in astronomy suggests the need to define well the research domain specifications and shows the advantages of their reuse with minimal extension for solving various research problems in this domain. Ontologies and schemas of specialized subdomains have been created and reused as unified structures for mapping data sources to them and for solving research problems in terms of the same unified data presentations. Conceptual models of research domains are fastly saturated during solving different problems in the domain. Communities manage the development and commitment of their domain models.

Conceptual models can be widely reused to formulate and solve new research problems. Registered resources including data and methods can be found by semantic annotations in terms of domain ontologies and reused in terms of conceptual schemas of domains. Research problems are solved in homogeneous terms accepted in the community.

Results of solving research problems are naturally provided to be reusable. They may include gathered, reformatted, selected, modeled, derived data, metadata including semantic annotations and provenance, mapped data resources with integration results, implemented methods, programs, workflows, research software, mathematical models, new domain specifications, new preservation data resources, and others. All these resources may be shared with the community in some policies.

References

1. Regulations of CKP "Informatics". http://www.frccsc.ru/ckp
2. Business Process Model and Notation (BPMN) Version 2.0.2. OMG (2013). https://www.omg.org/spec/BPMN/2.0.2/PDF
3. European Open Science Cloud. https://www.eosc-portal.cu/
4. The EUDAT Collaborative Data Infrastructure. https://www.eudat.eu/
5. FITS: Flexible Image Transport Specification. http://fits.gsfc.nasa.gov/
6. Bournea, P., et al., (eds.): Improving Future Research Communication and e-Scholarship. The Future of Research Communications and e-Scholarship (2011). https://www.force11.org/
7. IVOA Photometry Data Model. Version 1.0. IVOA (2013). http://www.ivoa.net/documents/PHOTDM/
8. OMG Meta Object Facility (MOF) Core Specification. Version 2.5.1. OMG (2019). https://www.omg.org/spec/MOF/2.5.1/PDF
9. Space-Time Coordinate Metadata for the Virtual Observatory Version 1.33. IVOA (2011). http://www.ivoa.net/documents/latest/STC.html
10. Strasbourg Astronomical Data Center (CDS). http://cdsportal.u-strasbg.fr/
11. VOTable Format Definition Version 1.4. IVOA Recommendation. IVOA (2019). http://www.ivoa.net/documents/VOTable/
12. Abrial, J.-R.: The B-Book: Assigning Programs to Meanings. Cambridge University Press, Cambridge (1996)
13. Ambrosio, A.P.: Introducing semantics in conceptual schema reuse. In: Proceedings of the Third International Conference on Information and Knowledge Management, pp. 50–56 (1994)
14. Baader, F., Horrocks, I., Lutz, C., Sattler, U.: Introduction to Description Logic. Cambridge University Press, Cambridge (2017)
15. Belhajjame, K., et al.: Workflow-centric research objects: a first class citizen in the scholarly discourse. In: ESWC 2012 Future of Scholarly Communication in the Semantic Web (SePublica 2012), vol. 903, pp. 1–12. CEUR-WS (2012)
16. Belhajjame, K., et al.: PROV-O: The PROV Ontology. W3C Recommendation, World Wide Web Consortium W3C (2013). https://www.w3.org/TR/prov-o

17. Goble, C.A., De Roure, D.C.: myExperiment: social networking for workflow-using e-scientists. In: WORKS 2007: Workflows in Support of Large-Scale Science, pp. 1–2 (2007). https://doi.org/10.1145/1273360.1273361
18. Horridge, M., et al.: The Manchester OWL syntax. In: OWL: Experiences and Directions (OWLED), vol. 216. CEUR-WS. http://ceur-ws.org/Vol-216/submission_9.pdf
19. Kalinichenko, L.A., Stupnikov, S.A.: Heterogeneous information model unification as a pre-requisite to resource schema mapping. In: D'Atri, A., Saccá, D. (eds.) Information Systems: People, Organizations, Institutions, and Technologies, pp. 373–380. Springer, Heidelberg (2009). https://doi.org/10.1007/978-3-7908-2148-2_43
20. Kogalovsky, M.R., Kalinichenko, L.A.: Conceptual and ontological modeling in information systems. Program. Comput. Softw. 35(5), 241–256 (2009). https://doi.org/10.1134/S0361768809050016. MAIK Nauka/Interperiodica, Moscow. Pleiades Publishing Inc.
21. Lapouchnian, A., Yu, Y., Mylopoulos, J.: Requirements-driven design and configuration management of business processes. In: Alonso, G., Dadam, P., Rosemann, M. (eds.) BPM 2007. LNCS, vol. 4714, pp. 246–261. Springer, Heidelberg (2007). https://doi.org/10.1007/978-3-540-75183-0_18
22. Liskov, B., Wing, J.: A behavioral notion of subtyping. ACM Trans. Program. Lang. Syst. (TOPLAS) 16(6), 1811–1841 (1994)
23. Malkov, O., et al.: Evaluation of binary star formation models using well-observed visual binaries. In: Manolopoulos, Y., Stupnikov, S. (eds.) DAMDID/RCDL 2018. CCIS, vol. 1003, pp. 91–107. Springer, Cham (2019). https://doi.org/10.1007/978-3-030-23584-0_6
24. Mons, B., et al.: Cloudy, increasingly FAIR; revisiting the FAIR data guiding principles for the European open science cloud. Inf. Serv. Use 37(1), 49–56 (2017). https://doi.org/10.3233/ISU-170824
25. Olive, A.: Conceptual Modeling of Information Systems. Springer, Heidelberg (2007). https://doi.org/10.1007/978-3-540-39390-0
26. Louys, M., et al.: Observation Data Model Core Components and Its Implementation in the Table Access Protocol. Version 1.1. IVOA Recommendation. IVOA (2017). http://www.ivoa.net/documents/ObsCore/
27. Saleem, A.: Specification Reuse Using Data Refinement in Dafny. National University of Ireland Maynooth (2013)
28. Skvortsov, N.A., Kalinichenko, L.A., Karchevsky, A.V., Kovaleva, D.A., Malkov, O.Y.: Matching and verification of multiple stellar systems in the identification list of binaries. In: Kalinichenko, L., Manolopoulos, Y., Malkov, O., Skvortsov, N., Stupnikov, S., Sukhomlin, V. (eds.) DAMDID/RCDL 2017. CCIS, vol. 822, pp. 102–112. Springer, Cham (2018). https://doi.org/10.1007/978-3-319-96553-6_8
29. Skvortsov, N.A.: Meaningful data interoperability and reuse among heterogeneous scientific communities. In: Kalinichenko, L., Manolopoulos, Y., Stupnikov, S., Skvortsov, N., Sukhomlin, V. (eds.) Selected Papers of the XX International Conference on Data Analytics and Management in Data Intensive Domains (DAMDID/RCDL 2018), vol. 2277, pp. 14–15. CEUR (2018). http://ceur-ws.org/Vol-2277/paper05.pdf
30. Skvortsov, N.A., Stupnikov, S.A.: Formalizing requirement specifications for problem solving in a research domain. In: Welzer, T., et al. (eds.) ADBIS 2019. CCIS, vol. 1064, pp. 266–279. Springer, Cham (2019). https://doi.org/10.1007/978-3-030-30278-8_29

31. Skvortsov, N.A.: Specificity of ontology mapping approaches. SCMAI Trans. Artif. Intell. Issues **2**, 83–95 (2010)
32. Wittenburg, P.: From persistent identifiers to digital objects to make data science more efficient. Data Intell. **1**(1), 6–21 (2019). https://doi.org/10.1162/dint_a_00004
33. Wilkinson, M.D., et al.: The FAIR guiding principles for scientific data management and stewardship. Sci. Data **3** (2016). Article number: 160018. https://doi.org/10.1038/sdata.2016.18
34. Wohed, P.: Conceptual patterns for reuse in information systems analysis. In: Wangler, B., Bergman, L. (eds.) CAiSE 2000. LNCS, vol. 1789, pp. 157–175. Springer, Heidelberg (2000). https://doi.org/10.1007/3-540-45140-4_12

Applying Model-Driven Approach for Data Model Unification

Sergey Stupnikov$^{(\boxtimes)}$

Institute of Informatics Problems, Federal Research Center "Computer Science and Control" of
the Russian Academy of Sciences, Vavilova Street 44-2, 119333 Moscow, Russia
sstupnikov@ipiran.ru

Abstract. A lot of scientific data sources currently are concentrated within data infrastructures supporting the whole cycle of data processing and management. Heterogeneous data are represented using various data models from the relational model to various NoSQL models. That is why data integration issues within data infrastructures become more and more important. This paper is devoted to the implementation of data model unification techniques considered as a formal basis for data interoperability, integration, and reuse within data infrastructures. The implementation applies a model-driven engineering approach, namely, formal methods allowing us to define data model syntax and semantic transformations of one data model to the other. To emphasize the advantages of the model-driven approach MDE-based implementation is compared with previous implementation utilizing metacompilation and term rewriting techniques.

Keywords: Model-driven engineering · Data model unification · Data integration

1 Introduction

A general way to manage scientific data sources currently is to concentrate them within data infrastructures like EUDAT[1] that are intended to support the whole cycle of data management and processing from harvesting and curation to storage and analysis. Data are intended to be used for problem solving in various subject domains like astronomy, biology, medicine, physics, material science, etc. To effectively manage and reuse scientific data, Force11 academic community proposed in 2014 a set of scientific data management principles called FAIR. According to these principles, scientific data should be Findable (data have sufficient metadata with unique and persistent identifiers), Accessible (metadata and data are understandable to humans and machines and placed in a shared repository), Interoperable (data or tools from different sources can operate and integrate; metadata use a formal and shared knowledge representation language) and Reusable (data and collections are clearly licensed and provide provenance information) [1].

---

[1] https://eudat.eu/.

© Springer Nature Switzerland AG 2021
A. Dahanayake et al. (Eds.): M2P 2020, CCIS 1401, pp. 212–232, 2021.
https://doi.org/10.1007/978-3-030-72696-6_11

A huge problem for data infrastructures is that data are quite heterogeneous. Data are represented using various data models[2]: relational model, object models, graph and array-based models, RDF framework for representing information in the Web, ontological models like OWL, models for representation of semi-structured data like XML, JSON, other NoSQL models, and others. The data definition and data manipulation (query) languages constituting the data models differ a lot. So data integration issues within data infrastructures become more and more important. Integration makes data much findable, accessible, interoperable and reusable than heterogeneous data stored in non-cooperating sources.

The most well-known kinds of data integration systems are *data warehouses* and *subject mediators* [2] performing *materialized* and *virtual* data integration respectively. Both kinds of systems requires a *unifying data model* intended to serve as a common language for heterogeneous source data models. For instance, a novel interoperability architecture [4] proposed as a reference implementation of FAIR considers RDF [5] as the unifying data model.

Subject mediators apply unifying data model to describe global data schema and user queries. Queries are transformed from unifying data model into the source data models and passed to the data sources via wrappers. Query answers are transformed from the source data models back to the unifying data model, merged and passed to the user. *Data lakes* seem like promising area to apply virtual data integration techniques [3]. Data warehouses usually apply Extract-Transform-Load (ETL) approach: data are extracted from the heterogeneous sources, transformed into the unifying warehouse data model, and then loaded into a warehouse.

Source data models have to be *unified* which means to be mapped into the unifying data model preserving their semantics. Only after source data model mappings into the canonical model are constructed, verified, and implemented it is possible to transform arbitrary source schemas into the unifying model and apply schema matching and integration techniques. So source data model unification is a *pre-requisite* for source schema integration [26]. Note that this paper addresses only data model mapping issues and not schema integration issues.

Data model unification techniques considered as a formal basis for data interoperability, integration, and reuse within data infrastructures were extensively studied [6]. This particular paper is devoted to implementation of data model unification techniques based on the *Model-driven engineering* approach [7]. MDE-based formal methods allowing us to define data model syntax and semantic transformations of one data model to the other are considered. To emphasize the advantages of the model-driven approach the MDE-based implementation is compared with the other (previous) implementation utilizing metacompilation and term rewriting techniques.

The rest part of the paper is structured as follows. Section 2 overviews the general principles of data model unification. Section 3 illustrates the stages of data model unification and their implementation issues applying the model-driven approach.

---

[2] In the frame of this work the term *data model* means a combination of a data definition language (DDL) and a data manipulation language (DML). So a data model is a language intended to describe some concrete database schemas and queries.

Advantages introduced by the MDE approach are distinguished. Section 4 overviews related work. Conclusions summarize the results of the work.

2 Data Model Unification Principles

A data infrastructure concentrates data sources that are represented using various data models. These data models and their data manipulation languages should be unified in the frame of some canonical data model C.

The main principle of the canonical model design for a data infrastructure is the *extensibility* of the canonical model kernel (that is fixed) in a heterogeneous environment [6] to cover features of source data models. A specific source data model R of the environment is said to be *unified* if it is mapped into the canonical model C. This means the creation of such extension E of the canonical model kernel $Kernel_C$ (note that the extension can be empty) and such mapping M of a source model into extended canonical one that the source model *refines* the extended canonical one. Model refinement of C by R means that for any admissible specification (schema) S represented in R its image $M(S)$ in C under the mapping M is refined by the specification S (Fig. 1). Horizontal arrows show the direction of refinement: schema S *refines $M(S)$*, or, in other words, S is a refinement of $M(S)$.

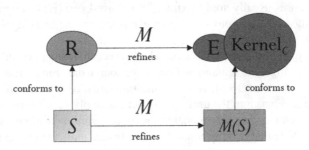

Fig. 1. A source data model unification

Note that the construction of data model mappings is a complicated task. One can construct quite different and even incorrect mappings for the same pair of data models. We would like to apply only *refining* mappings of data models that preserve operations and information of a source model after mapping it into the canonical one. Such preservation should be formally proven and it means that the mapping is constructed correctly.

The canonical model for the data infrastructure is combined as the union of extensions, created for all source models applied within the infrastructure.

Three groups of formal languages and methods are required to support data model unification. The first one is a kernel of the canonical data model. The second group includes formal methods allowing us to define a data model syntax and semantic transformations of one model to the other. The third group includes methods intended for the data model's semantics formalization and support of verification of refinement reached by the mapping.

Data unification techniques [6, 8–10, 14] apply the SYNTHESIS language [11] as *a kernel of the canonical data model*. The SYNTHESIS language, as an object-oriented data model including features like abstract data types, classes and metaclasses, functions and processes, logical formulae facilities. Frames that are basic specification constructs of the language serve also for the representation of semistructured data (see Sect. 4 of [11] for further details). Wide range of constructions like metaclasses, metaframes, assertions, and generic data types are used for the extension of the canonical model kernel. Note that the SYNTHESIS language is not the only option to serve as a kernel of the canonical data model. Other popular data models like RDF or SQL can be considered as a kernel within the same data unification techniques.

For the *data model's semantics formalization and verification of the refinement,* the AMN (Abstract Machine Notation) language [12] was used. AMN is based on the first-order predicate logic and Zermelo-Frenkel set theory. AMN specifications combine state space definitions (variables) and behavior definitions (operations). Refinement of AMN specifications is formalized as a set of refinement proof obligations that are theorems of first-order logic. These theorems are generated automatically and should be proven with the help of automatic and interactive theorem prover like Atelier B [13]. Details and examples on the application of formal verification methods for data model unification are out of the scope of this paper and can be found in [6, 9, 10].

Two approaches for the *formal description of model syntax and transformations* were developed and prototyped. The first approach [8, 9] was based on the metacompilation languages SDF (Syntax Definition Formalism) and ASF (Algebraic Specification Formalism). A tool support called Meta-Environment [15] and based on full context-free grammars and term rewriting techniques is provided for these languages. The implementation revealed several deficiencies of the SDF-ASF approach that are discussed further. To overcome the deficiencies, other approach based on the Model-Driven Engineering (MDE) [7] was proposed and implemented.

3   Implementation of Data Model Unification Using Model-Driven Approach

Unification of a source data model R with the canonical model C that is, in fact, construction of a verifiable mapping of R into C, includes the following stages:

- syntax formalization for the models R and C;
- integration of abstract syntaxes of the models R and C;
- creation of a required extension E of the canonical model C;
- construction of a transformation of the model R into C combined with E;
- semantics formalization for the models R and C;
- verification of refinement of the extended canonical model by model R.

All these stages were implemented applying both SDF-ASF and MDE approaches mentioned in the previous section. Comparison of the approaches w.r.t. several basic criteria is overviewed in Table 1. Every criterion is clarified and illustrated by examples in a respective subsection of this section below.

Table 1. Comparison of SDF-ASF and MDE approaches for implementation of data model unification: an overview

Criterion	SDF-ASF	MDE
Concrete syntax definition	Syntax definition formalism, context-free grammars	Defined using EMFText or XText frameworks integrated with Eclipse Modeling Framework (EMF), is bound with predefined abstract syntax
Abstract syntax definition	A template is automatically extracted from concrete syntax by a specific tool, should be completed manually by an expert	Defined independently on any concrete syntax using MOF-compliant Ecore M3-model
Integration of abstract syntaxes	The specific tool is applied to establish similarities of data model elements	Similarities can be established manually in Ecore2Ecore editor or using third-party model matching EMF tools
Construction of transformations	Algebraic specification formalism, term rewriting techniques	Model transformation languages like ATL or QVT
Transformation template generation	Specific Java implementation	Template generator itself is implemented using ATL

Unification of Web Ontology Language (OWL) [16] as a source data model with the SYNTHESIS language [11] as the canonical data model is considered below as an example to illustrate MDE implementation of data unification techniques. Deficiencies of the SDF-ASF approach and advantages of the MDE approach are distinguished at the end of each subsection corresponding to a stage of the data model unification.

3.1 Data Model Syntax Formalization

Abstract syntax formalization is developed based on some normative document for a data model. For instance, a normative document for the OWL is W3C Recommendation [16]. OWL syntax is defined in [16] using a sort of Backus-Naur form, a couple of rules for the OWL object property is shown below:

```
ObjectPropertyAxiom :=
   InverseObjectProperties | ObjectPropertyDomain | ObjectPropertyRange |
      SymmetricObjectProperty | TransitiveObjectProperty
ObjectPropertyDomain := 'ObjectPropertyDomain'
   '(' ObjectPropertyExpression  ClassExpression ')'
```

According to the MDE approach, a data model abstract syntax is defined by applying *Ecore*[3] metametamodel. It is an implementation of OMG's Essential Meta-Object Facility [18] used in Eclipse Modeling Framework [17]. Comparing with concrete syntax, abstract syntax omits any syntactic sugar.

A subset of OWL abstract syntax[4] represented in Ecore model editor is shown in Table 2. Ecore allows defining metamodels via entities like classes (*EClass*), attributes (*EAttribute*), references (*EReference*) and data types (*EDataType*). For instance, in Table 1 the *OWLObjectProperty* class is defined in the *OWL* package. The class is intended to represent object properties of the OWL language. *OWLObjectProperty* is a subclass of *RDFSProperty* and has several references like *domain, range, superProperty* and *inverseProperty*. Specific kinds of object properties like *TransitiveProperty* are defined as subclasses of *OWLObjectProperty*.

Table 2. OWL abstract syntax in Ecore model editor

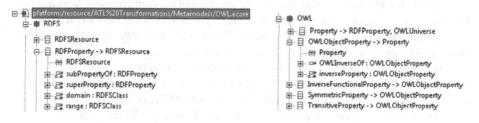

Ecore models can be serialized in XMI format for further reuse, for instance, right column of Table 2 is represented in XMI as follows (only a subset of specification is provided to save space):

```
<?xml version="1.0" encoding="ISO-8859-1"?>
<xmi:XMI xmi:version="2.0"
    xmlns:ecore="http://www.eclipse.org/emf/Ecore">
<ecore:EPackage name="OWL">
  <eClassifiers xsi:type="ecore:EClass" name="OWLObjectProperty"
    eSuperTypes="/1/Property">
    <eStructuralFeatures xsi:type="ecore:EReference" name="OWLInverseOf"
        eType="/1/OWLObjectProperty"/>
  </eClassifiers>
  <eClassifiers xsi:type="ecore:EClass" name="TransitiveProperty"
    eSuperTypes="/1/OWLObjectProperty"/>
</ecore:EPackage>
</xmi:XMI>
```

---

[3] Ecore API. URL: https://download.eclipse.org/modeling/emf/emf/javadoc/2.9.0/org/eclipse/emf/ecore/package-summary.html#details.

[4] https://github.com/sstupnikov/ModelTransformation/blob/master/OWL2Synthesis/metamodel/OWL.ecore.

Concrete syntax of data models is formalized using frameworks like EMFText [19]. The aim of the concrete syntax is to bind syntactic sugar with the abstract syntax. A concrete syntax rule for the OWL[5] object property looks as follows:

```
SYNTAXDEF owl
FOR <http://org.emftext/owl.ecore> <owl.genmodel>
RULES{
OWLObjectProperty ::= "ObjectProperty:" iri[IRI] (
   | "Domain:" domain ("," domain)*
   | "Range:" range ("," range)*
   | "SubObjectPropertyOf:" subPropertyOf (","subPropertyOf)*
   | "ObjectInverseOf:" OWLInverseOf
  )*;
}
```

The rule determines the general syntactic structure of the element using *terminal symbols* embraced by quotes (like *"ObjectProperty:"*), *nonterminal symbols* corresponding to attributes and associations of the concept (like *domain* or *subPropertyOf*); grammar constructions denoting multiplicity (*), and choice (|).

The overall structure of a data model syntax formalization process is shown in Fig. 2. Both concrete and abstract syntaxes for a data model are developed based on some normative documents. Textual syntax definition tool like EMFText automatically generates an editor and a grammar parser for a data model. So every schema of the data model that conforms to concrete syntax can be parsed and automatically transformed to Ecore abstract syntax model. Syntax of the canonical data model is formalized in a similar way[6], so details are omitted here. It should be only noted that the normative document for the SYNTHESIS language is [11].

One can compare the MDE approach for a data model syntax formalization with the SDF-ASF approach [9]. Data model syntax is represented using SDF that is a version of extended Backus–Naur form. The approach has shortcomings raised by the lack of abstract syntax representation.

SDF language provides facilities for the definition of concrete syntax grammars only gluing syntactic structures with syntactic sugar like keywords or auxiliary symbols. ASF data model transformations in their turn operate SDF grammars thus significantly depend on concrete syntax. Note that data models can provide several concrete syntax representations (formats), for instance, OWL can be represented using XML or functional-style syntax. So for every pair of a source model concrete grammar and a canonical model concrete grammar an individual transformation have to be developed.

To summarize the subsection, the following advantages of the MDE approach for data model SYntax Formalization (SYF) are distinguished.

---

[5] https://github.com/sstupnikov/ModelTransformation/blob/master/OWL2Synthesis/metamodel/owl.cs.

[6] https://github.com/sstupnikov/ModelTransformation/tree/master/Synthesis/metamodel/.

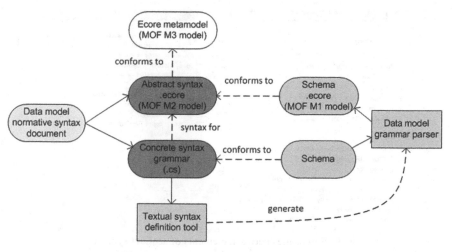

Fig. 2. A data model syntax formalization

Advantage SYF1. Abstract syntaxes of data models (either source or canonical or semantical) are defined as MOF M2[7] models conforming to the same MOF M3 model (Ecore) and making them compliant with the whole MOF architecture. The abstract syntax can be easily serialized in XML.

Advantage SYF2. For a data model definitions of abstract syntax and concrete syntax are separated. The abstract syntax can be bound with any kind of concrete syntax. Concrete syntax editors and parsers are generated automatically based on concrete syntax grammars.

Advantage SYF3. A data model abstract syntax defined once can be further applied in various transformations either as input or as output model.

3.2   Integration of the Abstract Syntaxes of a Source and the Canonical Model

The integration of the abstract syntaxes aims to identify the relevant elements of a source and the canonical model. These pairs of relevant elements (similarities) are intended to serve as the initial point of construction of a transformation of the source model into the canonical model.

Figure 3 illustrates several similarities between the OWL (left-hand part of the figure) and the SYNTHESIS (right-hand part of the figure) data models elements. For instance, OWL object property (*OWLObjectProperty*) corresponds to the attribute of an abstract data type (*AttributeDef*).

---

[7] OMG MOF [18] is designed as a four-layered architecture. M3 is a layer for meta-meta models like Ecore intended to build metamodels of layer M2. These metamodels are actually languages or data models like UML, SQL, or OWL. M2-models describe elements of the layer M1 which are schemas defined using M2-layer languages. The last M0-layer is used to describe real-world objects.

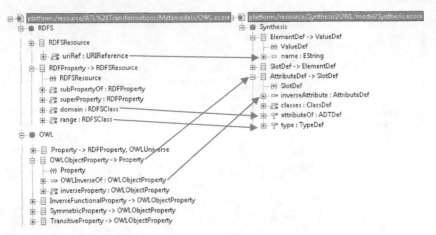

Fig. 3. Similarities between elements of abstract syntaxes

Inverse property reference (*OWLInverseOf*) of the object property corresponds to the inverse attribute reference of *AttributeDef* (*inverseAttribute*).

Similarities can be established manually by an expert using tools like *Ecore2Ecore* editor that is a part of Eclipse EMF Core libraries[8] or with the help of more advanced model matching tools like AtlanMod Model Weaver[9].

Final list of similarities can be represented using different formats, for instance, in the *ecore2ecore* format, and serialized in XML:

```
<?xml version="1.0" encoding="UTF-8"?>
<ecore2ecore:Ecore2EcoreMappingRoot xmi:version="2.0"
xmlns:ecore2ecore="http://www.eclipse.org/emf/2004/Ecore2Ecore">
<nested>
  <inputs href="OWL.ecore#/1/OWLObjectProperty"/>
  <outputs href="Synthesis.ecore#//AttributeDef"/>
</nested>
<nested>
  <inputs href="OWL.ecore#/0/RDFProperty/range"/>
  <outputs href="Synthesis.ecore#//AttributeDef/type"/>
</nested>
<inputs href="OWL.ecore#/"/>
<outputs href="Synthesis.ecore#/"/>
</ecore2ecore:Ecore2EcoreMappingRoot>
```

This XML file contains similarities between input *OWL.ecore* model and output *Synthesis.ecore* model like *OWLObjectProperty* to *AttributeDef* or *RDFProperty.range* to *AttributeDef.type*.

---

[8] Eclipse Modeling Framework. URL: https://www.eclipse.org/modeling/emf/.
[9] http://www.inf.ufpr.br/didonet/amw/.

MDE approach for the integration of the abstract syntaxes can be compared with the SDF-ASF approach [9]. According to the SDF-ASF approach, an abstract syntax template has to be extracted from the concrete syntax definition first. This template should be then refined by an expert using an abstract syntax editor. After that relevant elements of a source and the canonical model have to be identified using specific tools. Obviously, the MDE approach procedure is much simpler due to the separation of abstract and concrete syntaxes considered in the previous subsection.

To summarize the subsection, the following advantage of the MDE approach for Integration of the Abstract Syntaxes (IAS) is distinguished.

Advantage IAS1. Various existing schema matching methods can be implemented using MDE frameworks and applied for the integration of the abstract syntaxes of a source and the canonical model. A list of similarities between elements of abstract syntaxes is represented itself as a MOF M1 model and can be serialized in XML.

3.3 Creation of an Extension of the Canonical Model

Unification of the OWL with the SYNTHESIS data model requires a number of extensions. For instance, specific constructions are required to represent in the SYNTHESIS various kinds of object properties like transitive, symmetric, reflexive, etc. [16]. Such object properties are represented using *association metaclasses* [11], for instance, reflexive properties are represented using the following metaclass:

```
{ Reflexive; in: association, metaclass;
instance_section: {
  domain: type; range: type;
  reflexivity: { in:nvariant;
  {{ all x,y (is_in([x,y], this) -> is_in([y,x], this)) }}
} } }
```

Reflexive association metaclass above is defined using the SYNTHESIS language, for more details see [11], subsection *7.4 Association metaclasses.*

Association metaclass is a collection of associations that are sets of associated pairs of objects. The metaclass *Reflexive* includes invariant *reflexivity* stating reflexivity of the association. Semantics of the metaclass id defined as follows. Let x, y be objects. If x is associated with y according to the association a then y is also associated with x according to a. Every association declared as an instance of the *Reflexive* metaclass is reflexive. In the metaclass specification above *this* refers to the current association instance, *is_in* denotes set membership predicate, *[x, y]* denotes a pair of associated objects. The invariant specification is defined with a first-order logic formula: *all* denotes universal quantifier, - > denotes implication.

Association metaclasses like *Reflexive* serve themselves as extensions of the canonical model intended to represent specific object properties. Note that no syntactic extension of the canonical model kernel is required, just a specific data structure and axiom are defined. So this kind of extension can be represented as MOF M1 model conforming canonical MOF M2 model (to be precise, *Synthesis.ecore*[10] that is partially illustrated in the previous subsection). To illustrate an extreme case of syntactic extension we consider association metaclass syntactic construction as an extension of the canonical model below.

Canonical model extensions are treated as data models themselves, so their abstract and concrete syntaxes are defined in the same way as in Subsect. 3.1. Association metaclass abstract syntax is shown on the right-hand part of Fig. 4. It is considered as an extension of the abstract syntax of the canonical model kernel. Similarities between a source model and an extension are established in the same way as illustrated in the previous subsection. Similarities between OWL elements and association metaclass extension elements are also shown in Fig. 4. OWL object property corresponds to association metaclass. *Domain* and *range* of object property correspond to *domain* and *range* of association metaclass respectively. Inverse property reference (*OWLInverseOf*) of the object property corresponds to the inverse association (*inverse*) of the association metaclass.

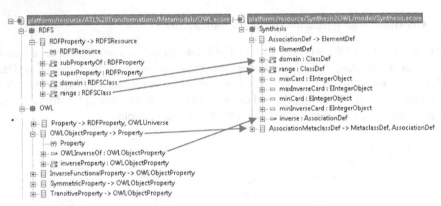

Fig. 4. Association metaclass abstract syntax and it's matching with the canonical model abstract syntax

The abstract syntax of an extension is bound with concrete syntax via concrete grammar rules, a rule for association metaclass is shown below:

```
AssociationMetaclassDef ::=
"{" name[] ";" ("inverse" ":" inverse[] ";")?
  ("association_type" ":" "{" "{" minCard[DECIMAL_INTEGER_LITERAL] ","
      maxCard[DECIMAL_INTEGER_LITERAL] "}"  ","
   "{" minInverseCard[DECIMAL_INTEGER_LITERAL] ","
      maxInverseCard[DECIMAL_INTEGER_LITERAL] "}" "}" ";" )?
  ("domain" ":" domain[] ("," domain[])*  ";")?
  ("range" ":" range[] ("," range[])* ";" )?
"}";
```

---

[10] https://github.com/sstupnikov/ModelTransformation/blob/master/Synthesis/metamodel/Synthesis.ecore.

The rule is considered as an extension of the concrete syntax grammar of the canonical model kernel[11]. A detailed explanation of association metaclass elements and their semantics can be found in [11], subsection *7.4 Association metaclasses*.

To summarize the subsection, the following advantages of the MDE approach for the Extension of the Canonical model (EC) are distinguished.

Advantage EC1. The abstract syntax for a syntactic extension of the canonical model is defined as an extension of the canonical MOF M2 model. The concrete syntax of the syntactic extension is defined as an extension of the canonical model concrete syntax.

Advantage EC2. An extension of the canonical model that utilizes syntactic and semantic features of the canonical model kernel (specific data structures like types and classes, dependencies, axioms, etc.) is defined as the MOF M1 model conforming canonical MOF M2 model.

Advantage EC3. An extension is matched with a source model using conventional schema matching tools developed using MDE frameworks.

3.4 Construction of a Transformation of a Source Model into the Extended Canonical Model

Data model transformations are defined using the ATLAS Transformation Language (ATL) [20]. The language is intended for the declarative specification of transformations, but provides for imperative features also. ATL transformation programs are composed of rules that define how source model elements are matched and navigated to create and initialize the elements of the target models. Note that ATL is not the only way to express model transformations. For instance, the QVT family of languages [25] is standardized by the OMG so it can be also applied for the data model unification.

For ATL transformations their *templates* can be generated automatically [21] based on of similarities between a source and the canonical model elements illustrated in Subsect. 3.2. An example of the transformation rule template[12] generated for the OWL object property is shown on the left-hand part of Table 3. Similarities shown in Subsects. 3.2 and 3.3 are used to generate the rule.

According to similarities, for any OWL object property *op* (typed as *OWLObjectProperty*) the rule creates a SYNTHESIS attribute *at* (typed as *AttributeDef*) and an association metaclass *am* (typed as *AssociationMetaclassDef*). Elements like *name*, *attributeOf*, and *type* of *AttributeDef* and *name* of *AssociationMetaclassDef* are initialized according to the respective similarities in the declarative target pattern of the rule (*to* section). Elements like *inverseAttribute* of *AttributeDef* and *inverse, domain, range* of *AssociationMetaclassDef* are initialized in the imperative *do* section of the rule.

---

[11] https://github.com/sstupnikov/ModelTransformation/blob/master/Synthesis/metamodel/Synthesis.cs.

[12] https://github.com/sstupnikov/ModelTransformation/blob/master/OWL2Synthesis/transformation/OWL2SynthesisTemplate.atl.

Table 3. Model transformation template and complete transformation example

Transformation template	Complete transformation
| ```
module OWL2Synthesis;
create OUT: Synthesis from IN: OWL;

rule OWLObjectProperty {
from op: OWL!OWLObjectProperty to




at: Synthesis!AttributeDef(
 name <- op.uriRef->any(e | true).
   fragmentIdentifier.name,
 attributeOf <-
   op.domain->any(c | true),
 type <- op.range->any(c | true);
),

am:
 Synthesis!AssociationMetaclassDef(
 name <- op.uriRef->any(e | true).
   fragmentIdentifier.name)
do {
 at.inverseAttribute <- thisModule.
  resolveTemp(op.OWLInverseOf,'at');
 am.inverse <- thisModule.
  resolveTemp(op.OWLInverseOf, 'am');
 am.domain <- thisModule.
  resolveTemp(domain, 'class');
 am.range <- thisModule.
  resolveTemp(range, 'class');
} }
``` | ```
module OWL2Synthesis;
create OUT: Synthesis from IN: OWL;

rule OWLObjectProperty{
from op: OWL!OWLObjectProperty
using{
 domain: OWL!OWLClass = op.domain->
  any(c| c.oclIsKindOf(OWL!OWLClass));
 range: OWL!OWLClass = op.range->
  any(c | c.oclIsKindOf(OWL!OWLClass));
}
to
at: Synthesis!AttributeDef(
  name <- op.resourceName(),

   attributeOf <- domain,

  type <- range
),

am:
 Synthesis!AssociationMetaclassDef(
  name <- op.resourceName() +
   'Metaclass')
do{
 at.inverseAttribute <- thisModule.
  resolveTemp(op.OWLInverseOf,'at');
 am.inverse <- thisModule.
  resolveTemp(p.OWLInverseOf, 'am');
 am.domain <- thisModule.
  resolveTemp(domain, 'class');
 am.range <- thisModule.
  resolveTemp(range, 'class');
if (op.oclIsKindOf(
    OWL!ReflexiveProperty))
 am.superclasses <-
  assoc.superclasses->
  including(Synthesis!MetaclassDef.
   allInstances()->any(m |
    m.name = 'Reflexive'));
} }

helper context OWL!RDFSResource
def: resourceName(): String =
let r : OWL!LocalName =
 self.uriRef->any( e |
  e.oclIsKindOf(OWL!URIReference)).
  fragmentIdentifier
in if not r.oclIsUndefined()
then r.name else 'AResource' endif;
``` |

Some additional details on ATL transformation template construction[13] can be found in [21].

---

[13] https://github.com/sstupnikov/ModelUnifier.ATL/blob/master/transformations/TTC.atl.

Anyway, a model transformation has to be completed (extended, modified) by an expert. An example of modified transformation[14] is shown on the right-hand part of Table 3. Similar pieces of template and complete transformation code are aligned. The following modifications are distinguished:

- auxiliary variables *domain, range* referring some input elements are defined in the *using* section of the rule to remove redundancy and make the code more readable;
- transformation of a URI reference into element name is separated as a *helper* function *resourceName*;
- if *op* object property is reflexive then *am* association metaclass is set to be a subclass of *Reflexive* association metaclass defined in the previous subsection.

MDE approach for the construction of model transformations can be compared with the SDF-ASF approach. Data model transformations are defined in the ASF language as modules which are sets of functions. A function defines a transformation of a syntactic element of a source model into a syntactic element of the canonical model as a term rewriting.

Functions operate concrete syntax terms, so recursive function calls are mixed with the syntactic sugar symbols (including spaces, tabulations, and newlines) in term expressions. A transformation function is usually defined as a set of term rewritings rather than one to take into account various options of the input term structure. Debugging complicated transformations consisting of many functions can be very tricky.

To summarize the subsection, the following advantages of the MDE approach for the Construction of data model Transformations (CT) are distinguished.

Advantage CT1. Transformations are independent of a data model concrete syntax. This makes the transformation program code clearer. Also, various input and output formats for the data model specifications can be applied without modification of a transformation.

Advantage CT2. Model transformation techniques are intended to be applied in a *declarative way*. Transformation rules define (1) for which kinds of source elements target elements must be generated and (2) the way the generated target elements have to be initialized. No nested term rewriting is required. Declarative style makes it easier to extend transformations. Nevertheless, imperative statements are allowed within a specific section of a transformation rule, so a potential way to define a transformation is quite flexible.

3.5 Data Model Semantics Formalization

Formalization of data model semantics means construction of transformations of source and canonical data model specifications into the AMN-specifications. For the AMN specification language, the respective abstract syntax model[15] conforming the *Ecore*

---

[14] https://github.com/sstupnikov/ModelTransformation/blob/master/OWL2Synthesis/transformation/OWL2Synthesis.atl.

[15] https://github.com/sstupnikov/ModelTransformation/blob/master/Synthesis2AMN/Metamodels/AMN.ecore.

metamodel is provided. This allows to define the required transformation[16] using the ATL, details can be found in [22]. Examples of semantic AMN-specifications for the OWL and the SYNTHESIS can be found in [6]. In this section, we just illustrate the semantic transformation of the SYNTHESIS into the AMN with the rule that defines semantics for the association metaclasses (to save space, the rule is simplified):

```
module Sunthesis2AMN;
create OUT : AMN from IN : Synthesis;

rule AssociationMetaclass{
from cls: Synthesis!AssociationMetaclassDef
using{
    type: Synthesis!ADTDef = cls.instanceType;
    ref: AMN!Refinement = thisModule.resolveTemp(cls.instanceType, 'ref');
}
to
    invRef: AMN!Conjunction(
        predicate <- thisModule.AssociationMetaclassVarTyping(cls),
        predicate <- thisModule.AssociationMetaclassVarEquality(cls) )
do{
    ref.abstractVariables <- cls.name;
    ref.initialization <- thisModule.AssociationMetaclassVarInit(cls);
    for(sup in cls.superclasses)
        thisModule.PutMachineToIncludesClause(type, sup.instanceType);
    for(d in cls.domain)
        thisModule.PutMachineToIncludesClause(type, d.instanceType);
    for(r in cls.range)
        thisModule.PutMachineToIncludesClause(type, r.instanceType);
} }
```

The rule defines semantics for an association metaclass referred to as *cls* in the *from* section of the rule. Semantics is concentrated in an AMN construct called *refinement* (*AMN!Refinement*) that is referred to as *ref* in the *using* section. The metaclass is represented by an *abstract variable* with the same name that is added to *ref* in the *do* section of the rule. A first-order logic formula that defines properties of association metaclass (like reflexivity) is constructed with the help of *AssociationMetaclassVarTyping* and *AssociationMetaclassVarEquality* rules and is referred to as *invRef* in the *to* section of the rule. Initialization of the variable is constructed with the help of *AssociationMetaclassVarInit* rule in the *do* section. The rule *PutMachineToIncludesClause* is applied to bind *ref* with refinements that represent domain, range, and superclasses of the *cls* association metaclass.

---

[16] https://github.com/sstupnikov/ModelTransformation/blob/master/Synthesis2AMN/Transformations/Synthesis2AMN.atl.

Semantic transformation of the canonical model kernel into the AMN was constructed in [22]. As far as association metaclasses are considered as a syntactic extension of the kernel (see Subsect. 3.3) then *AssociationMetaclass* rule is just a respective extension of the kernel semantic transformation.

To summarize the subsection, the following advantages of the MDE approach for a data model SEmantics Formalization (SEF) are distinguished.

Advantage SEF1. Semantic transformations of data models into the AMN are constructed using the same MDE framework (ATL) as transformations from source data models into the canonical data model in an extensible mixed declarative and imperative way.

Advantage SEF2. Semantic transformation of a canonical model kernel extension itself extends the semantic transformation of the canonical model kernel into the AMN.

3.6 Verification of Data Model Refinement

The final stage of a source data model unification is formal verification of the fact that the source data model *refines* the extended canonical model. Verification is performed via a set of the source data model patterns that are typical constructs of the data model (like *workflow patterns* [23] for process models) or via concrete schemas used for data integration. Verification is intended to ensure that data model transformation is constructed in a correct, semantic-preserving way.

Applying semantic ATL-transformations for any specification of the source and the canonical data model the AMN-specifications expressing their semantics are generated automatically. After that refinement of the canonical data model specification by a source model specification is reduced to the refinement of their semantic AMN-specifications. The refinement can be further verified with the help of the Atelier B theorem prover [13]. If a source data model mapping into the canonical one is constructed and implemented in a correct way then for every schema S of the source model it is possible to prove that S refines its image $M(S)$ in the canonical model. So the semantics of $M(S)$ is preserved by the mapping.

Data model refinement verification issues were already illustrated in previous works for the OWL unification [9], process models unification [14], array-based data model unification [24], graph data model unification [10] so we omit them here and just summarize advantages of MDE approach for data model Refinement Verification (RV).

Advantage RV1. All models and transformations developed using MDE frameworks during previous stages of unification are applied.

Advantage RV1.1. Concrete syntax editors are applied to define data model patterns and automatically produce MOF M1 *Ecore* models.

Advantage RV1.2. ATL transformations of source data models into the canonical data model are applied to generate canonical images of source data model patterns.

Advantage RV1.2. Semantic transformations are used to generate AMN specifications to be fed to the refinement theorem prover.

4 Related Work

Related works can be separated into three groups. The first group includes methods and tools for schema translation. The second group includes techniques for model transformation development. The third group concentrates on the verification of model transformations.

Schema Translation. Model Independent Data and Schema Translation (MIDST) approach [30] is intended to translate schemas from one data model to another in an "equivalent" way. Translations are expressed as Datalog rules. The main idea of MIDST is using a metamodel – a set of generic metaconstructs applied for the definition of data models that are instances of the metamodel. Every model is defined by its constructs and the metaconstructs they refer to. *Supermodel* is a data model containing constructions that correspond to all metaconstructions known to the system. Every data model is a specialization of the supermodel, so a schema expressed in any data model is a schema in the supermodel. Mapping of a schema expressed in one data model into the other is defined in terms of metaconstruction transformation. The arbitrary model translation is constructed automatically as a composition of basic translations that refer to single constructs. Basic translations are defined for several families of data models (entity-relationship, object-oriented, relational). A model can be accompanied by a set of propositions (invariants of the model) and the *model subsumption* concept is introduced. Model M_1 is subsumed by M_2 if and only if M_2 has at least the constructs of M_1 and, for those in M_1, it allows at least the same variants. The approach suites the structured models that can be expressed as a composition of metaconstructs. Significant preliminary work is required to define basic translations.

Model Independent Schema Management (MISM) approach [31] is an extension of MIDST offering schema manipulation operators including merge, difference, and a basic version of match, all implemented in a model-generic way. MIDST-RT platform [32] extends the MIDST approach further with runtime data transformation facilities. The main idea is starting with schema-level translation rules produced by MIDST generate views over source database for entities of the target schema. Such views serve as data transformations from source to target schema.

Comparing to MIDST the data model unification approach proposed in this paper is more general and semantically oriented. It is not limited to some families of structured models (for instance, data models can include functions and processes). Different data models can be chosen as the canonical model kernel. Arbitrary data model mappings not limited by compositions of basic transformations can be implemented using ATL. Using AMN for the definition of data model semantics allows proving the preservation of information and operations of the data model during mapping formally. However, in a limited environment of structured data models, the MIDST is more effective due to the significant reuse of basic translations. Data model unification also does not consider data transformation issues as MIDST-RT does.

Model Transformation Development. In [28] an approach for semi-automatic model transformation development is proposed. For a pair of a source and a target model, a *weaving model* capturing possible links between the source and the target model elements is created semi-automatically with manual modification. Then for every link, its similarity value is calculated using string similarity, dictionary of synonyms, and structural similarities based on internal properties of the model elements (types, cardinality, and the relationships between model elements). Links with the highest similarity value are selected and used to generate transformation rules. The approach seems well-applicable for schema transformations. But according to our experience data model (language) transformations are much harder to develop and the usefulness of schema matching methods is questionable due to semantical differences between data models.

In [36] a methodological and technical framework for the model-driven development of model transformations (MeTAGeM) is proposed. Development starts with a platform independent transformation (PIT) model that is a collection of relationships between the elements of source and target models specified by an expert. The PIT model is automatically transformed into a Platform Specific Transformation model for the Hybrid approach (PST-H) model. The PST-H model contains rules and operations for model transformation. After that, the PST-H model is automatically transformed into the ATL or RubyTL languages.

Comparing to [28] the approach for semi-automatic transformation generation illustrated in this paper [21] leaves abstract syntax matching for any third-party tools and concentrates on the generation of rules that are applicable for data model transformations. It also omits PST-H model applied in [36] for the sake of simplicity.

Verification of Model Transformations. A number of works apply different formal methods for verification of model transformations. In [29] formal specification, validation, and verification of model transformations is achieved using Abstract State Machines (ASM) supported by interactive and automatic theorem proving like model checkers. In [34] a formal calculus for operational QVT as provided implemented in the interactive theorem prover KIV allows proving properties of QVT transformations for arbitrary metamodels. In [35] a restricted set of ATL matched rules is converted into a transformation model conforming UML. Constraints of the transformation model to be verified are expressed using OCL. UML2Alloy tool is applied to translate the transformation model and OCL constraints into a specification for the Alloy model finder tool. In such way, any constraint reducible to Boolean satisfiability problem (SAT) can be verified.

In [33] a framework for model transformation verification is proposed. It is intended to support on the one hand a range of model transformation languages like QVT, ATL and graph-transformation languages and on the other hand a range of verification formalisms like AMN, Alloy, etc. A simple metamodel for modeling languages including entity type, primitive data type, data feature, structure, and constraint elements is proposed. Constraints are expressed using a subset of OCL. Formal semantics of the metamodel in first-order set theory is defined. Constraints are represented as axioms. A transformation specification metamodel is defined as well. Transformation mappings are defined using pre and postconditions that are OCL constraints. Several transformation verification properties are formalized and ways to apply different verification techniques are proposed. The approach has been implemented using the UML-RSDS language and toolset. Transformation specifications are defined by UML use cases and can be automatically translated to Z3 and AMN for semantic analysis.

Comparing to the approaches considered above the data model unification approach applies the AMN language for semantic representation of data models. It is not intended to prove arbitrary properties of model transformations using general-purpose provers but to apply specific interactive and automatic provers for verification of *data model refinement*. Verification is performed via a set of the source data model patterns that are typical constructs of the data model or via concrete schemas used for data integration.

It can be concluded that the data model unification approach combines MDE-based model transformation development techniques and verification of data model refinement to provide a formal basis for schema mapping and integration in heterogeneous data infrastructures.

5 Conclusions

Heterogeneous data concentrated within scientific data infrastructures have to be FAIR – Findable, Accessible, Interoperable and Reusable. A way to increase FAIRness of data is to integrate them within data integration systems like subject mediators and data warehouses. To overcome data model heterogeneity a specific approach called *data model unification* was proposed. The approach extensively utilizes methods and techniques for definition of data model syntax as well as mappings (transformations) of one data model to the other. Data model unification techniques were applied for a wide range of source data models like ontological models [9], process models [14], array-based models [24], graph models [10], some other kinds of NoSQL models [27]. Construction of respective semantic-preserving mapping were possible due to the hybrid semistructured and object-oriented facilities of the canonical model used as well as various constructions applied for the extensions [11]. This paper shows that Model-driven engineering can be applied for implementation of data model unification showing a number of important advantages.

Several ways to advance the data model unification approach can be distinguished. First, comprehensive schema and ontology matching methods and tools can be applied for establishing similarities between data model elements. This can give an initial confidence that a correct mapping can be constructed for an arbitrary source and canonical data models. Second, the approach should be applied using popular data models like SQL or RDF as the canonical models. And third, evaluation measures for the approach (like the amount of user input required) should be proposed and evaluated for some comprehensive use cases.

Acknowledgments. The research is financially supported by Russian Foundation for Basic Research, projects 18-07-01434, 18-29-22096.

References

1. Wilkinson, M.D., Dumontier, M., Aalbersberg, I.J., et al.: The FAIR guiding principles for scientific data management and stewardship. Sci. Data **3** (2016)

2. Briukhov, D.O., et al.: The middleware architecture of the subject mediators for problem solving over a set of integrated heterogeneous distributed information resources in the hybrid grid-infrastucture of virtual observatories. Informatics and Applications **2**(1), 2–34 (2008)
3. Hai, R., Quix, C., Zhou, C.: Query rewriting for heterogeneous data lakes. In: Benczúr, A., Thalheim, B., Horváth, T. (eds.) ADBIS 2018. LNCS, vol. 11019, pp. 35–49. Springer, Cham (2018). https://doi.org/10.1007/978-3-319-98398-1_3
4. Wilkinson, M.D., et al.: Interoperability and fairness through a novel combination of web technologies. Peer J Computer Science **3**, (2017)
5. Klyne, G., Carroll, J.J., McBride, B.: RDF 1.1 Concepts and Abstract Syntax. W3C Recommendation, 25 February 2014 (2014). https://www.w3.org/TR/2014/REC-rdf11-concepts-20140225/
6. Stupnikov, S., Kalinichenko, L.: Extensible unifying data model design for data integration in fair data infrastructures. In: Manolopoulos, Y., Stupnikov, S. (eds.) DAMDID/RCDL 2018. CCIS, vol. 1003, pp. 17–36. Springer, Cham (2019). https://doi.org/10.1007/978-3-030-235 84-0_2
7. da Silva, A.R.: Model-driven engineering a survey supported by the unified conceptual model. Comput. Lang. Syst. Struct. **43**, 139–155 (2015). https://doi.org/10.1016/j.cl.2015.06.001
8. Zakharov, V.N., Kalinichenko, L.A., Sokolov, I.A., Stupnikov, S.A.: Development of canonical information models for integrated information systems. Inf. Appl. **1**(2), 15–38 (2007)
9. Kalinichenko, L.A., Stupnikov, S.A.: Constructing of mappings of heterogeneous information models into the canonical models of integrated information systems. In: Advances in Databases and Information Systems: Proceedings of the 12th East-European Conference, pp. 106–122. Tampere University of Technology, Pori (2008)
10. Stupnikov, S.A.: Mapping of Graph Data Models into a Canonical Model for the Development of Data Intensive Systems. Systems of High Availability-Radiotechnika, Moscow (2014). 2:13-31p.
11. Kalinichenko, L.A., Stupnikov, S.A., Martynov, D.O.: SYNTHESIS: A Language for Canonical Information Modeling and Mediator Definition for Problem Solving in Heterogeneous Information Resource Environments. IPI RAN, Moscow (2007). 171p.
12. Abrial, J.-R.: The B-Book: Assigning Programs to Meanings. Cambridge University Press, Cambridge (1996)
13. Atelier, B.: The industrial tool to efficiently deploy the B Method. http://www.atelierb.eu/
14. Kalinichenko, L., Stupnikov, S., Zemtsov, N.: Extensible canonical process model synthesis applying formal interpretation. In: Eder, J., Haav, H.-M., Kalja, A., Penjam, J. (eds.) ADBIS 2005. LNCS, vol. 3631, pp. 183–198. Springer, Heidelberg (2005). https://doi.org/10.1007/11547686_14
15. van den Brand, M.G.J., et al.: The Asf + Sdf meta-environment: a component-based language development environment. In: Wilhelm, R. (ed.) CC 2001. LNCS, vol. 2027, pp. 365–370. Springer, Heidelberg (2001). https://doi.org/10.1007/3-540-45306-7_26
16. OWL 2 Web Ontology Language Structural Specification and Functional-Style Syntax (Second Edition). W3C Recommendation (2012). https://www.w3.org/TR/owl-syntax/
17. Steinberg, D., Budinsky, F., Paternostro, M., Merks, E.: EMF: Eclipse Modeling Framework, 2nd edn. Addison-Wesley Professional, Boston (2008)
18. OMG Meta Object Facility (MOF) Core Specification. Version 2.5.1 (2019). https://www.omg.org/spec/MOF/2.5.1/PDF
19. EMFText Concrete Syntax Mapper. https://github.com/DevBoost/EMFText
20. ATL - a model transformation technology. https://eclipse.org/atl/
21. Stupnikov, S.A., Kalinichenko, L.A.: Methods for semi-automatic construction of information models transformations. In: Proceedings of the 13th East-European Conference Advances in

Databases and Information Systems, Workshop Model – Driven Architecture: Foundations, Practices and Implications (MDA), pp. 432–440. Riga Technical University, Riga (2009)

22. Stupnikov, S.A.: A semantic transformation of the canonical information model into a formal specification language for the refinement verification. In: Proceedings of the 12th Russian Conference on Digital Libraries RCDL 2010, pp. 383–391. Kazan Federal University, Kazan (2010)

23. Russell, N., van der Aalst, W.M.P., ter Hofstede, A.H.M.: Workflow Patterns: The Definitive Guide. MIT Press, Cambridge (2016)

24. Stupnikov, S.A.: Unification of an array data model for the integration of heterogeneous information resources. In: Proceedings of the 14th Russian Conference on Digital Libraries RCDL 2012. CEUR Workshop Proceedings, vol. 934, pp. 42–52 (2012)

25. Meta Object Facility (MOF) 2.0 Query/View/Transformation Specification. Version 1.3. OMG Document Number: formal/2016-06-03 (2016). http://www.omg.org/spec/QVT/1.3

26. Kalinichenko, L.A., Stupnikov, S.A.: Heterogeneous information model unification as a prerequisite to resource schema mapping. In: D'Atri, A., Saccà, D. (eds) Information Systems: People, Organizations, Institutions, and Technologies, pp. 373–380. Physica-Verlag HD (2010). https://doi.org/10.1007/978-3-7908-2148-2_43

27. Skvortsov, N.A.: Mapping of NoSQL data models to object specifications. In: Proceedings of the 14th Russian Conference on Digital Libraries RCDL 2012, CEUR Workshop Proceedings, vol. 934, pp. 53–62 (2012)

28. Del Fabro, M.D., Valduriez, P.: Semi-automatic model integration using matching transformations and weaving models. In: Proceedings of the 2007 ACM symposium on Applied computing (SAC 2007). Association for Computing Machinery, New York, NY, USA, pp. 963–970 (2007). https://doi.org/10.1145/1244002.1244215

29. Di Ruscio, D.: Specification of Model Transformation and Weaving in Model Driven Engineering. Ph.D. Thesis in Computer Science, Dipartimento di Informatica Universit'a di L'Aquila (2007)

30. Atzeni, P., Cappellari, P., Torlone, R., et al.: Model-independent schema translation. VLDB J. **17**, 1347 (2008). https://doi.org/10.1007/s00778-008-0105-2

31. Atzeni P., Bellomarini L., Bugiotti F., Gianforme G.: MISM: A Platform for Model-Independent Solutions to Model Management Problems. In: Spaccapietra S., Delcambre L. (eds) Journal on Data Semantics XIV. Lecture Notes in Computer Science, vol 5880. Springer, Berlin, Heidelberg (2009). https://doi.org/10.1007/978-3-642-10562-3_5

32. Atzeni, P., Bellomarini, L., Bugiotti, F., Celli, F., Gianforme, G.: A runtime approach to model-generic translation of schema and data. Inf. Syst. **37**(3), 269–287 (2012). https://doi.org/10.1016/j.is.2011.11.003

33. Lano, K., Clark, T., Kolahdouz-Rahimi, S.: A framework for model transformation verification. Form Asp Comp **27**, 193–235 (2015). https://doi.org/10.1007/s00165-014-0313-z

34. Stenzel, K., Moebius, N., Reif, W.: Formal verification of QVT transformations for code generation. Softw. Syst. Model. **14**, 981–1002 (2015). https://doi.org/10.1007/s10270-013-0351-7

35. Büttner, F., Egea, M., Cabot, J., Gogolla, M.: Verification of ATL Transformations Using Transformation Models and Model Finders. In: Aoki, T., Taguchi, K. (eds.) ICFEM 2012. LNCS, vol. 7635, pp. 198–213. Springer, Heidelberg (2012). https://doi.org/10.1007/978-3-642-34281-3_16

36. Bollati, V.A., Vara, J.M., Jiménez, A., Marcos, E.: Applying MDE to the (semi-)automatic development of model transformations. Inf. Softw. Technol. **55**(4), 699–718 (2013). https://doi.org/10.1016/j.infsof.2012.11.004

Author Index

Printed in the United States
by Baker & Taylor Publisher Services